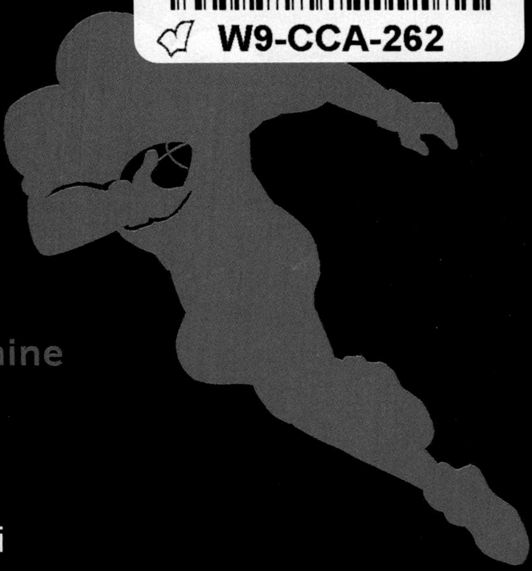

INTRODUCTION...

The idea was simple enough—create a handful of oversized one-shots expanding the already-acclaimed world of New Archie, featuring some of the characters and concepts that maybe hadn't gotten the spotlight yet.

As most diehard Archie fans know, the world of Archie and his friends isn't limited to the core five. There's super-genius Dilton, Josie and her band, the Pussycats, Sabrina the Teenage Witch and supermodel Katy Keene, to name a few. The Archie library of characters was a sprawling universe that could give Marvel and DC a run for their money. So when Archie's Publisher/CEO Jon Goldwater and President Mike Pellerito mentioned the idea, I was all for it. From a marketing perspective, it was akin to a pilot season. Throw a bunch of stuff against the wall and see what sticks. From a creative POV, I was hoping the stars would align.

When I first broached the subject of there being a one-shot starring THE ARCHIES, the Riverdale band comprised of Archie, Betty and Veronica, best pal Jughead and arch-frenemy, Reggie, I had the proverbial wind at my back. Paired with co-writer Matthew Rosenberg and artist Gisele Lagace, we'd created the sold-out ARCHIE MEETS RAMONES one-shot, which showed that maybe there was an audience for Archie and his pals in a band, and maybe the one-shot format could work again. But I think the best sales pitch I could muster for the book came over the phone with Jon, when I casually mentioned that a book like THE ARCHIES wasn't just about Archie and his pals. It was an all-star team.

"It could be our Avengers. Our Justice League."

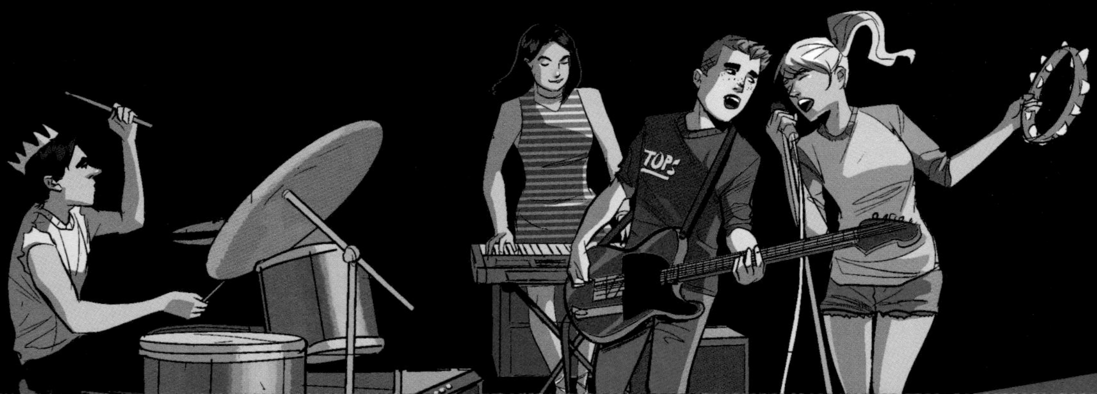
TOPS

Jon gave the thumbs up and Matt and I sat down and talked through what we wanted. While ARCHIE MEETS KISS and RAMONES were both fantastical tales featuring dimension-hopping, time-travel and magic, we knew we wanted this comic to happen in the current Archie story, to feel like a potent mix of physical comedy and the heartfelt coming-of-age that fans of the new series had come to expect, running parallel to the work of main ARCHIE writer Mark Waid. So, we lucked out when outgoing ARCHIE artist Joe Eisma signed up to provide art on the comic, giving the issue instant credibility. It felt like what happened in the one-shot not only counted, but could be read along with whatever was happening in the main book. The entire initiative was also helped a great deal by an all-star lineup of talent, that took existing Archie concepts and tweaked them enough to make them all the more compelling for a new reader.

Jughead as a werewolf? It's a real thing, and writer Frank Tieri and artist Michael Walsh present it in a chilling, unforgettable fashion. Big Moose as the star of his own comic? It might have happened before at some point, but not in the down-to-earth, engaging way it was presented by the likes of writers Sean Ryan, Ryan Cady, Gorf and artists like Cory Smith, Thomas Pitilli and Ryan Jampole. Moose took his star turn and made the best of it.

The end result is the collection you hold in your hands—six issues worth of great storytelling expanding the world of modern Archie, by some of the best talent in comics. How I got invited to this party I'll never know, but it's been a blast so far. Hope you enjoy the show.

Alex Segura
Co-Writer, THE ARCHIES

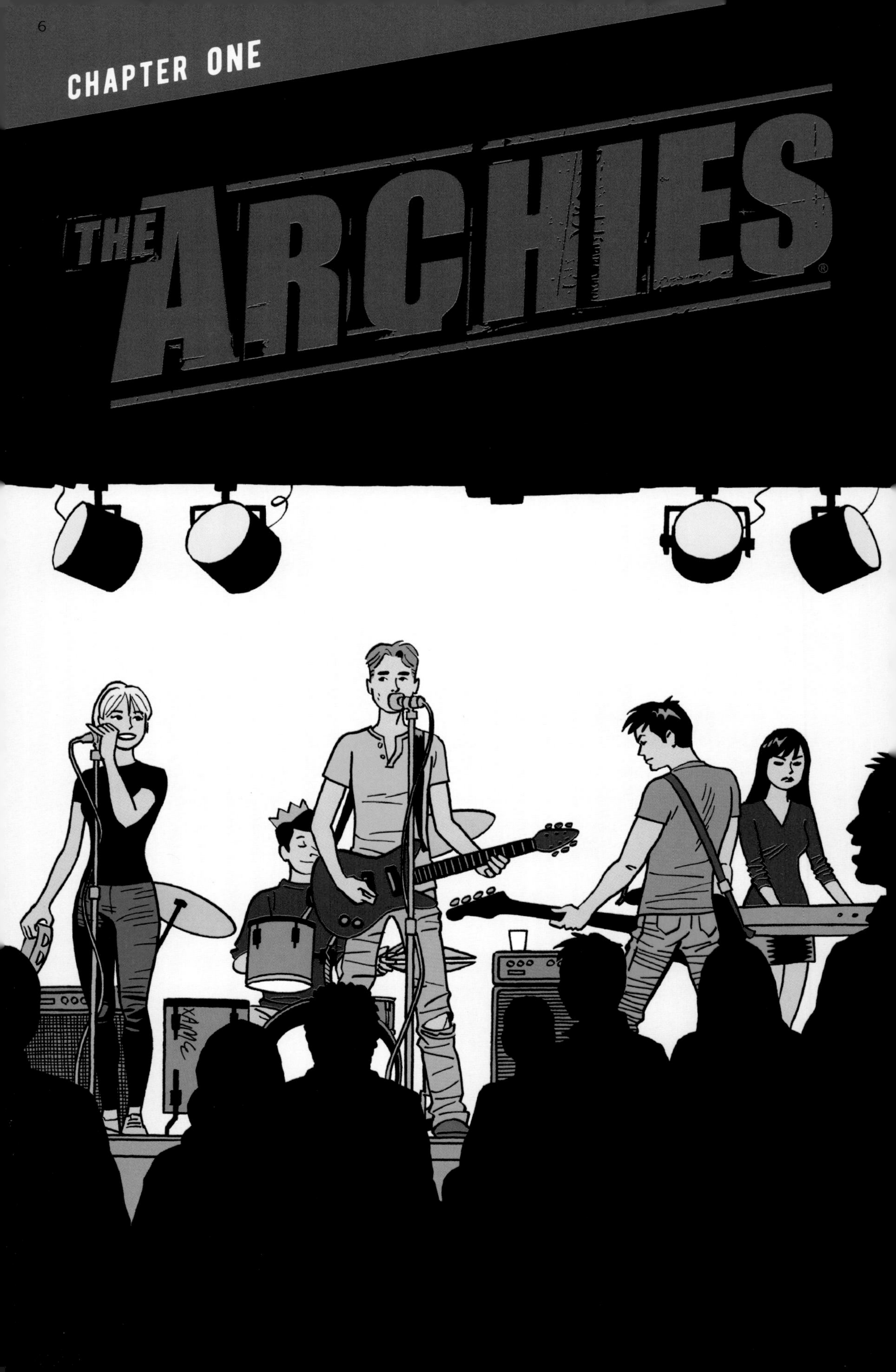
CHAPTER ONE
THE ARCHIES

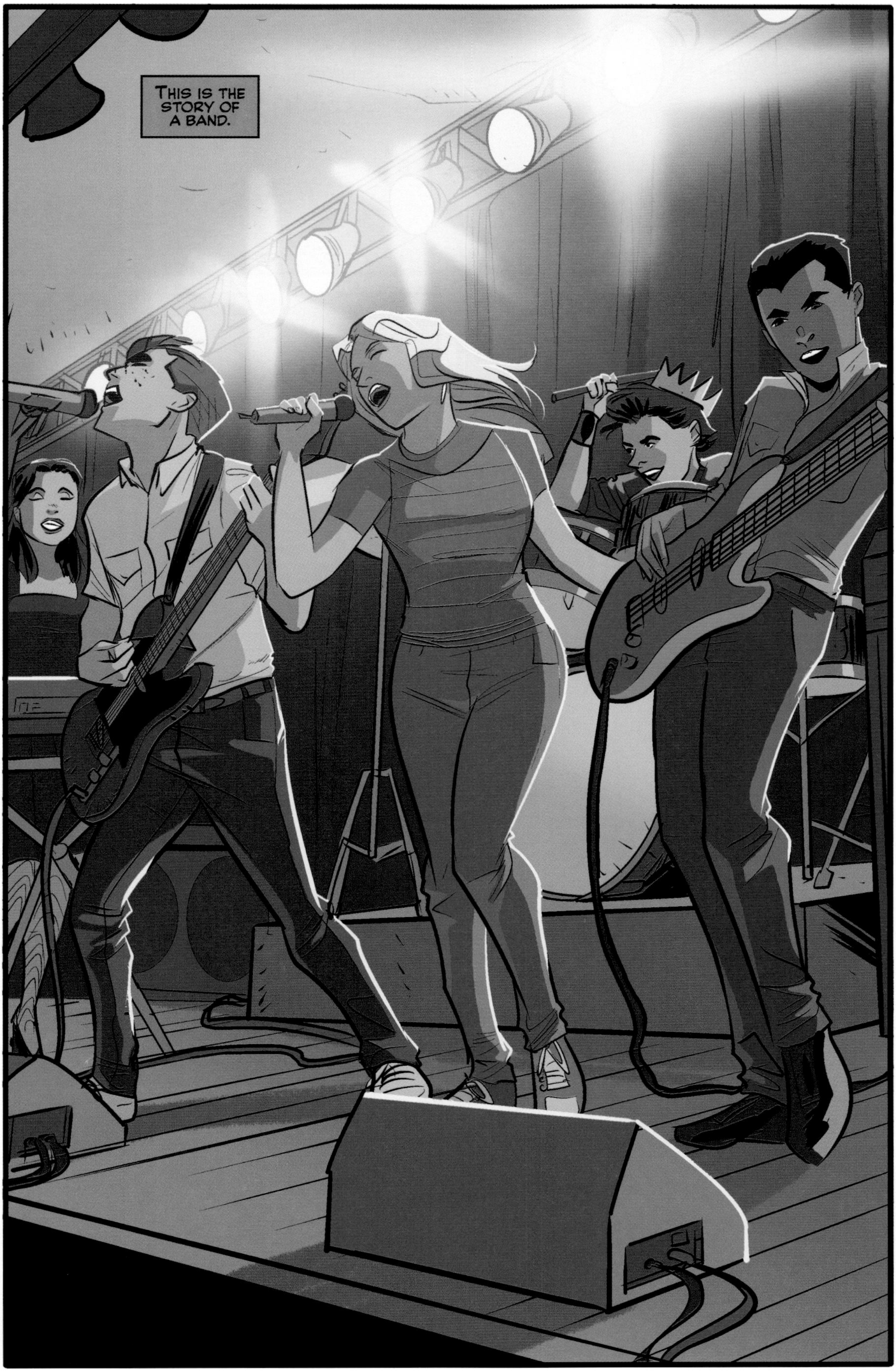
THIS IS THE STORY OF A BAND.

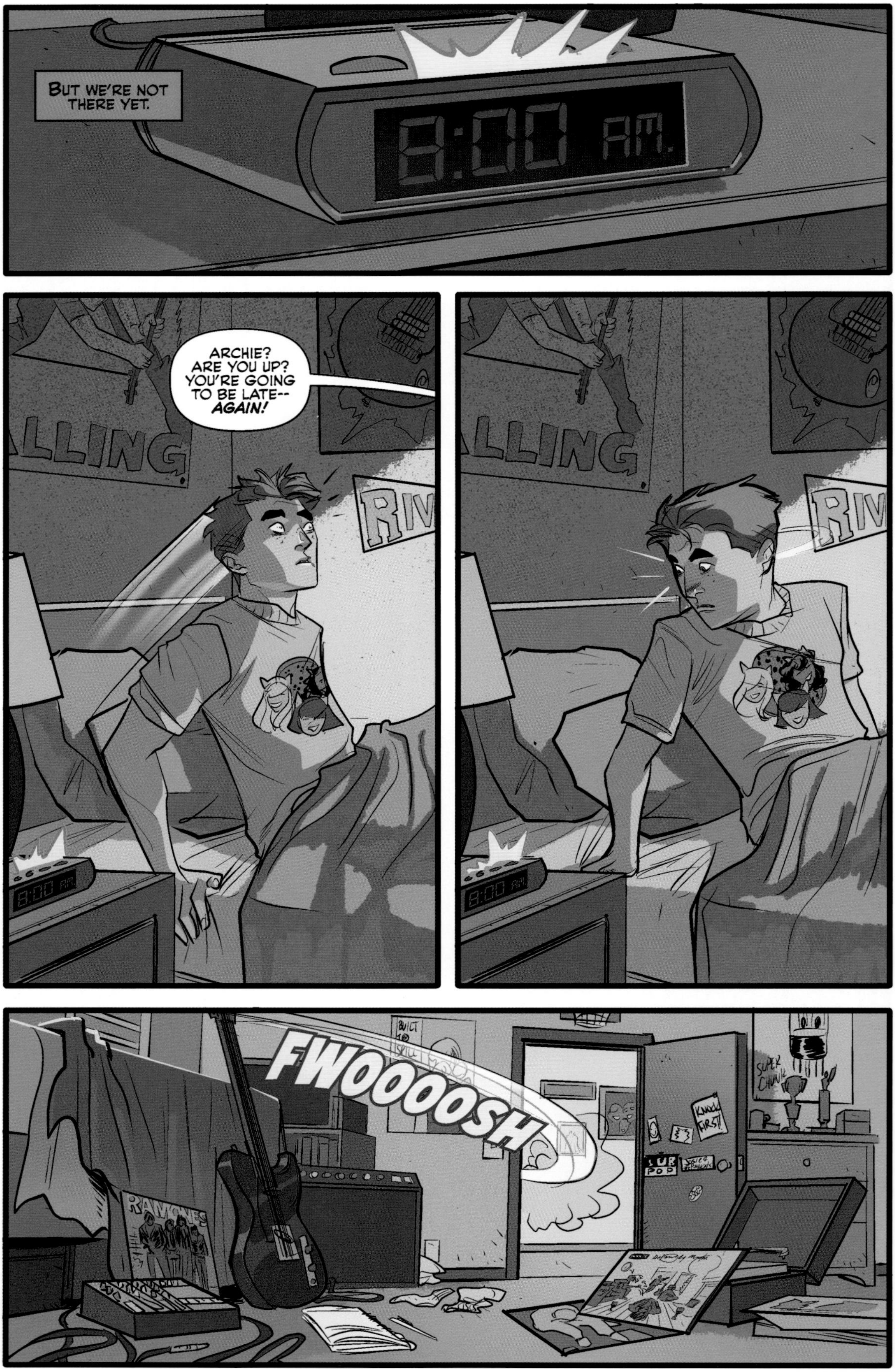
BUT WE'RE NOT THERE YET.
8:00 AM.
ARCHIE? ARE YOU UP? YOU'RE GOING TO BE LATE-- ***AGAIN!***
FWOOOOSH
RAMONES
KNOCK FIRST!
SUPER CHUNK

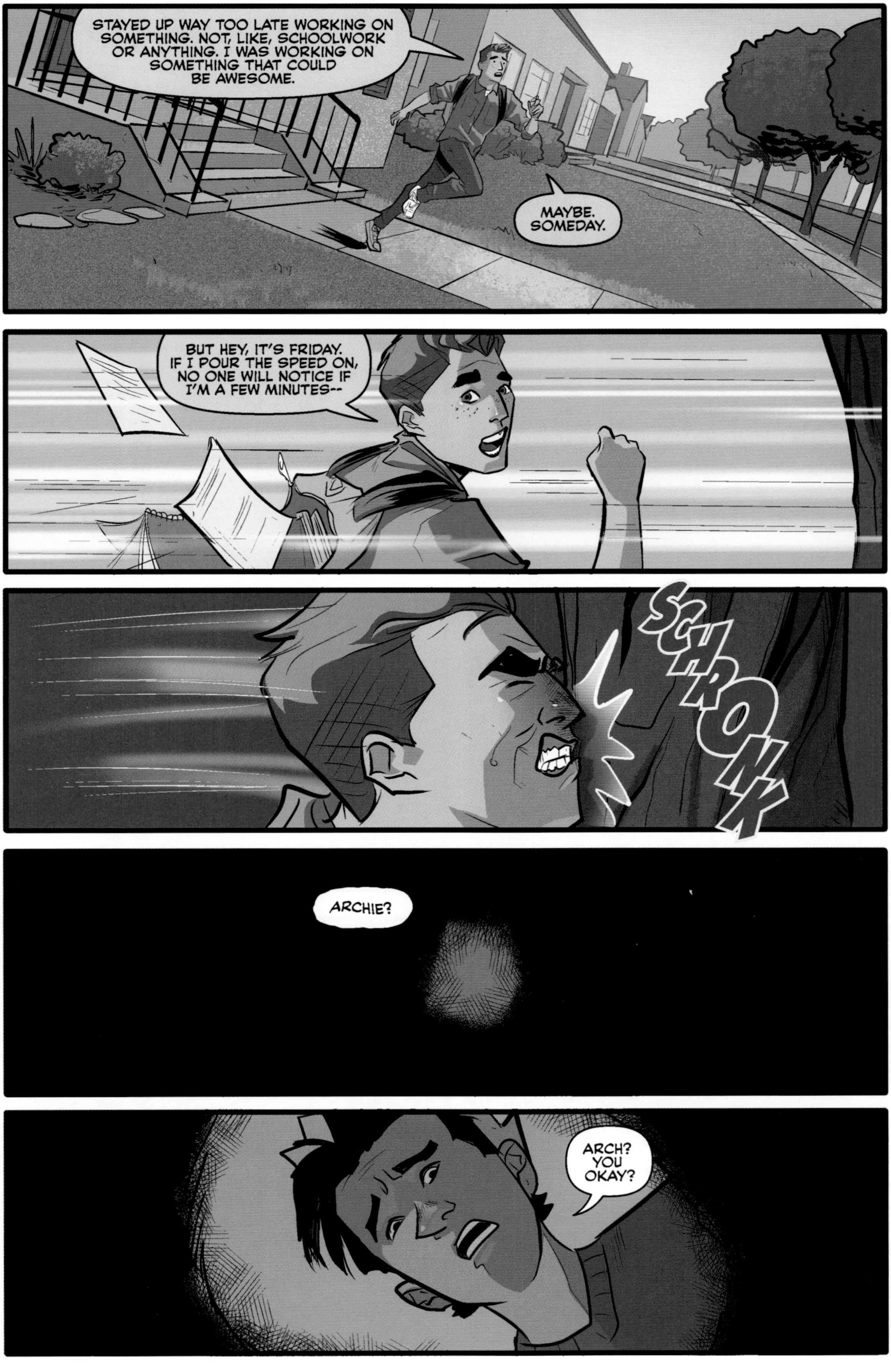
STAYED UP WAY TOO LATE WORKING ON SOMETHING. NOT, LIKE, SCHOOLWORK OR ANYTHING. I WAS WORKING ON SOMETHING THAT COULD BE AWESOME.
MAYBE. SOMEDAY.
BUT HEY, IT'S FRIDAY. IF I POUR THE SPEED ON, NO ONE WILL NOTICE IF I'M A FEW MINUTES--
SCHRONK
ARCHIE?
ARCH? YOU OKAY?

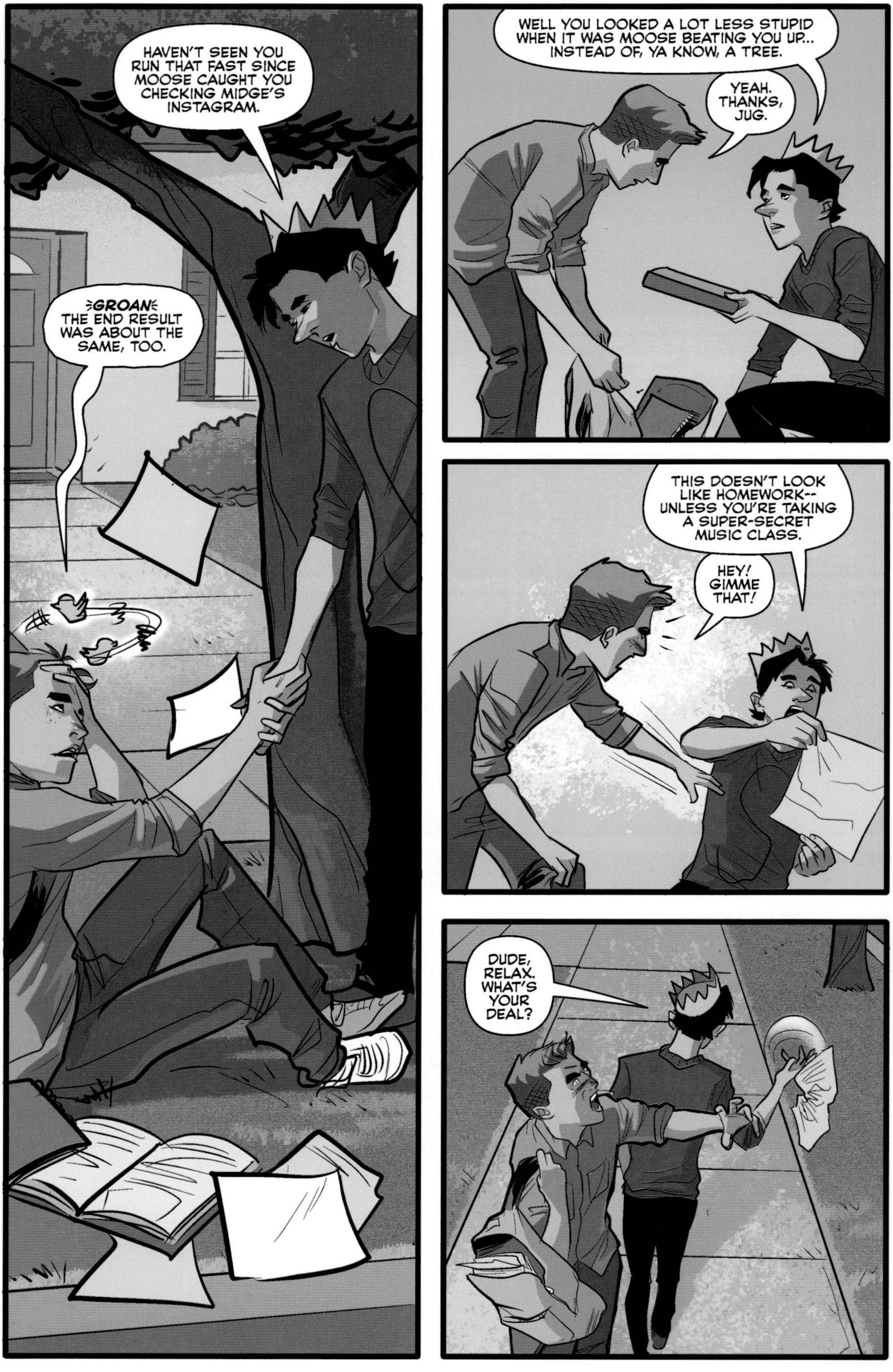
HAVEN'T SEEN YOU RUN THAT FAST SINCE MOOSE CAUGHT YOU CHECKING MIDGE'S INSTAGRAM.
GROAN
THE END RESULT WAS ABOUT THE SAME, TOO.
WELL YOU LOOKED A LOT LESS STUPID WHEN IT WAS MOOSE BEATING YOU UP... INSTEAD OF, YA KNOW, A TREE.
YEAH. THANKS, JUG.
THIS DOESN'T LOOK LIKE HOMEWORK-- UNLESS YOU'RE TAKING A SUPER-SECRET MUSIC CLASS.
HEY! GIMME THAT!
DUDE, RELAX. WHAT'S YOUR DEAL?

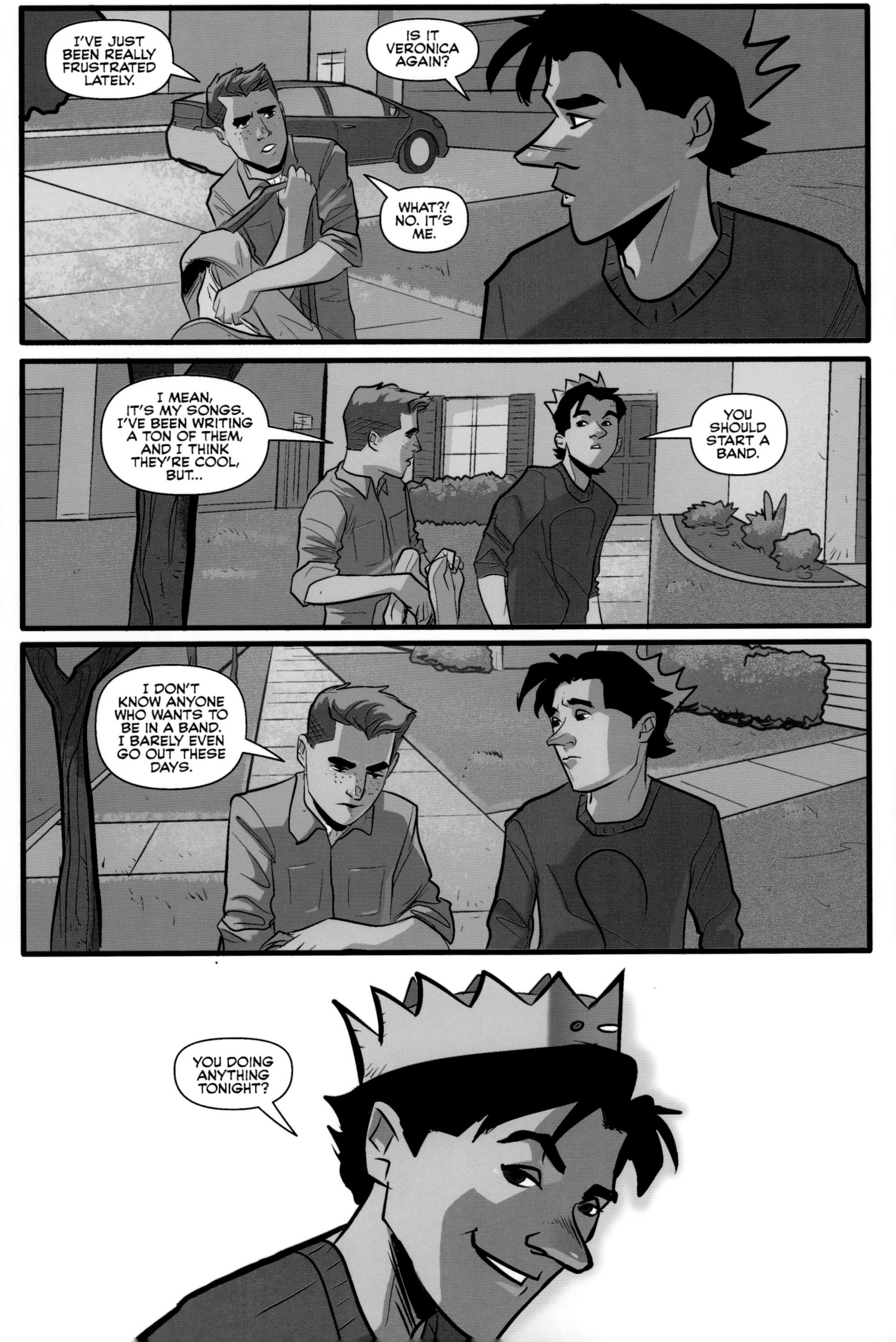
I'VE JUST BEEN REALLY FRUSTRATED LATELY.
IS IT VERONICA AGAIN?
WHAT?! NO. IT'S ME.
I MEAN, IT'S MY SONGS. I'VE BEEN WRITING A TON OF THEM, AND I THINK THEY'RE COOL, BUT...
YOU SHOULD START A BAND.
I DON'T KNOW ANYONE WHO WANTS TO BE IN A BAND. I BARELY EVEN GO OUT THESE DAYS.
YOU DOING ANYTHING TONIGHT?

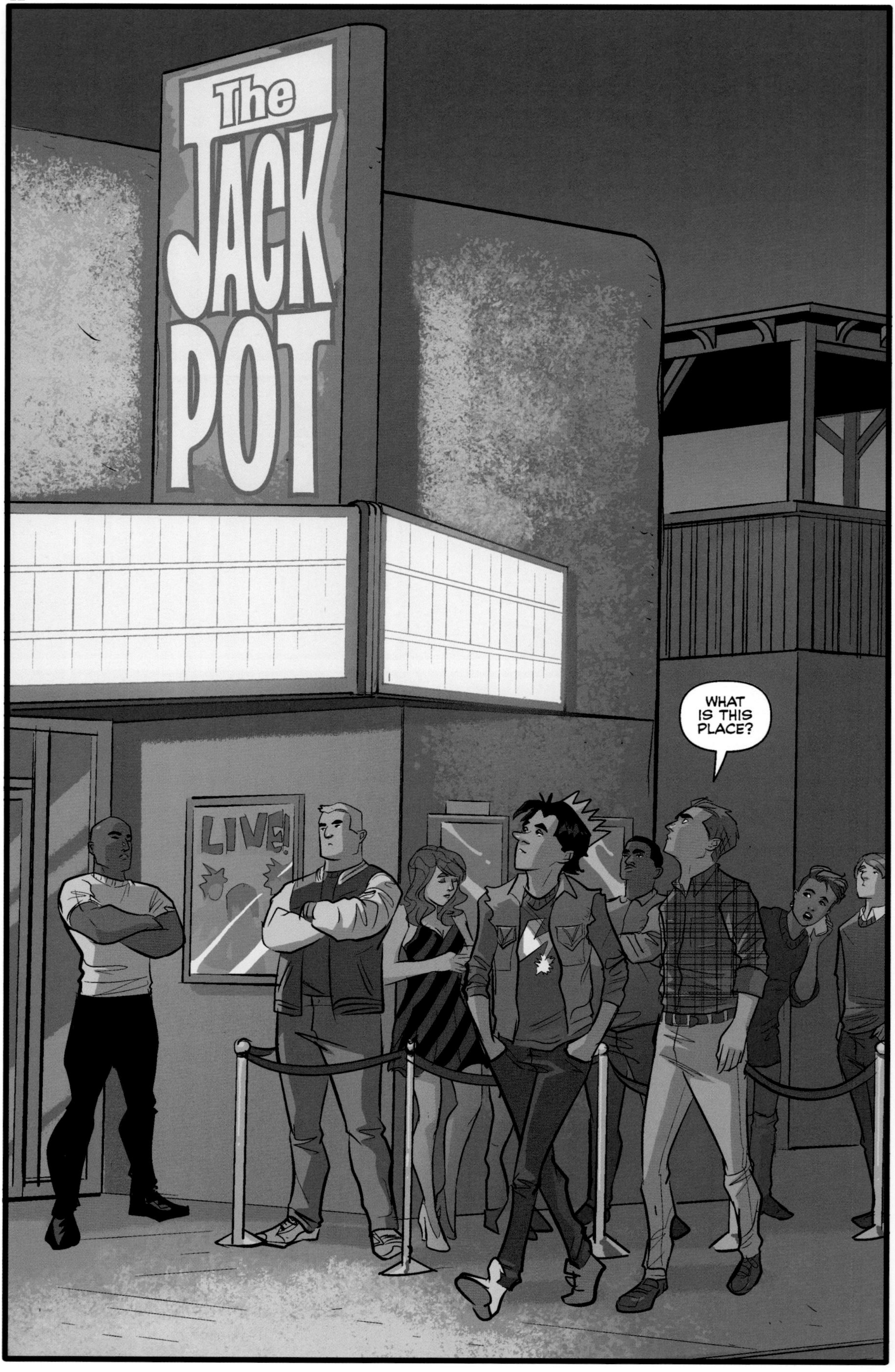
The JACK POT
LIVE!
WHAT IS THIS PLACE?

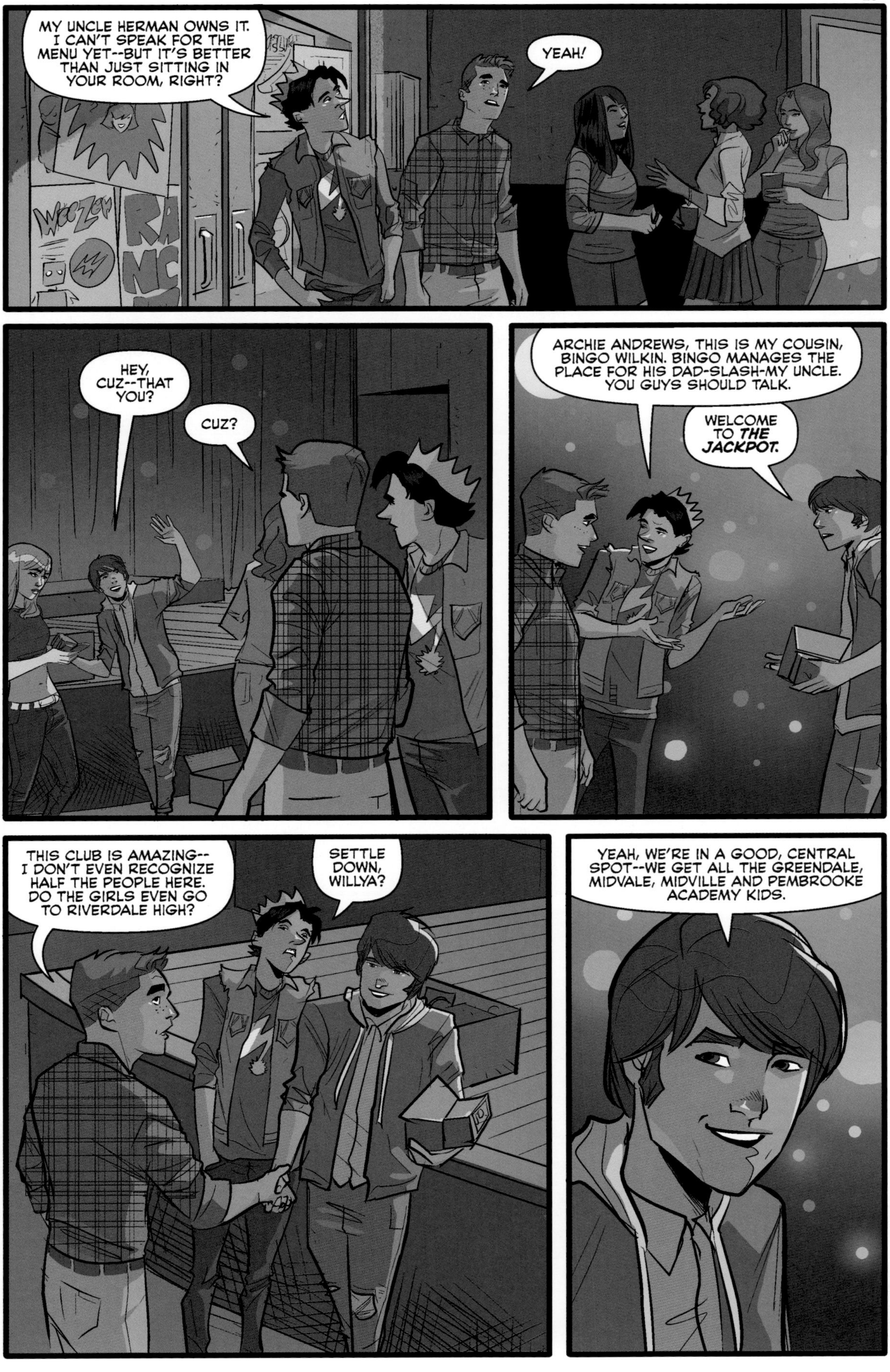
MY UNCLE HERMAN OWNS IT. I CAN'T SPEAK FOR THE MENU YET--BUT IT'S BETTER THAN JUST SITTING IN YOUR ROOM, RIGHT?
YEAH!
HEY, CUZ--THAT YOU?
CUZ?
ARCHIE ANDREWS, THIS IS MY COUSIN, BINGO WILKIN. BINGO MANAGES THE PLACE FOR HIS DAD-SLASH-MY UNCLE. YOU GUYS SHOULD TALK.
WELCOME TO *THE JACKPOT.*
THIS CLUB IS AMAZING--I DON'T EVEN RECOGNIZE HALF THE PEOPLE HERE. DO THE GIRLS EVEN GO TO RIVERDALE HIGH?
SETTLE DOWN, WILLYA?
YEAH, WE'RE IN A GOOD, CENTRAL SPOT--WE GET ALL THE GREENDALE, MIDVALE, MIDVILLE AND PEMBROOKE ACADEMY KIDS.

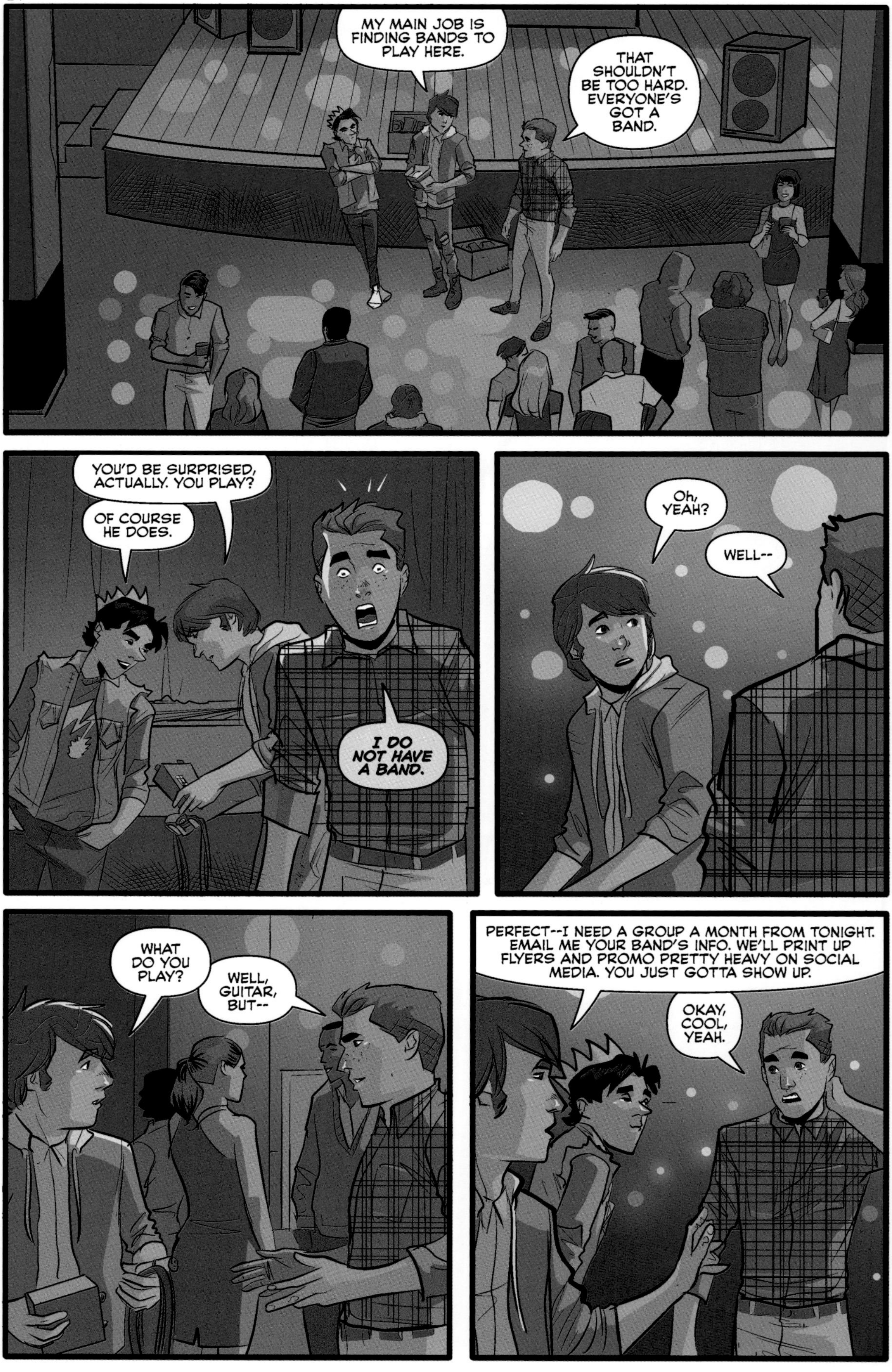
MY MAIN JOB IS FINDING BANDS TO PLAY HERE.
THAT SHOULDN'T BE TOO HARD. EVERYONE'S GOT A BAND.
YOU'D BE SURPRISED, ACTUALLY. YOU PLAY?
OF COURSE HE DOES.
I DO NOT HAVE A BAND.
Oh, YEAH?
WELL--
WHAT DO YOU PLAY?
WELL, GUITAR, BUT--
PERFECT--I NEED A GROUP A MONTH FROM TONIGHT. EMAIL ME YOUR BAND'S INFO. WE'LL PRINT UP FLYERS AND PROMO PRETTY HEAVY ON SOCIAL MEDIA. YOU JUST GOTTA SHOW UP.
OKAY, COOL, YEAH.

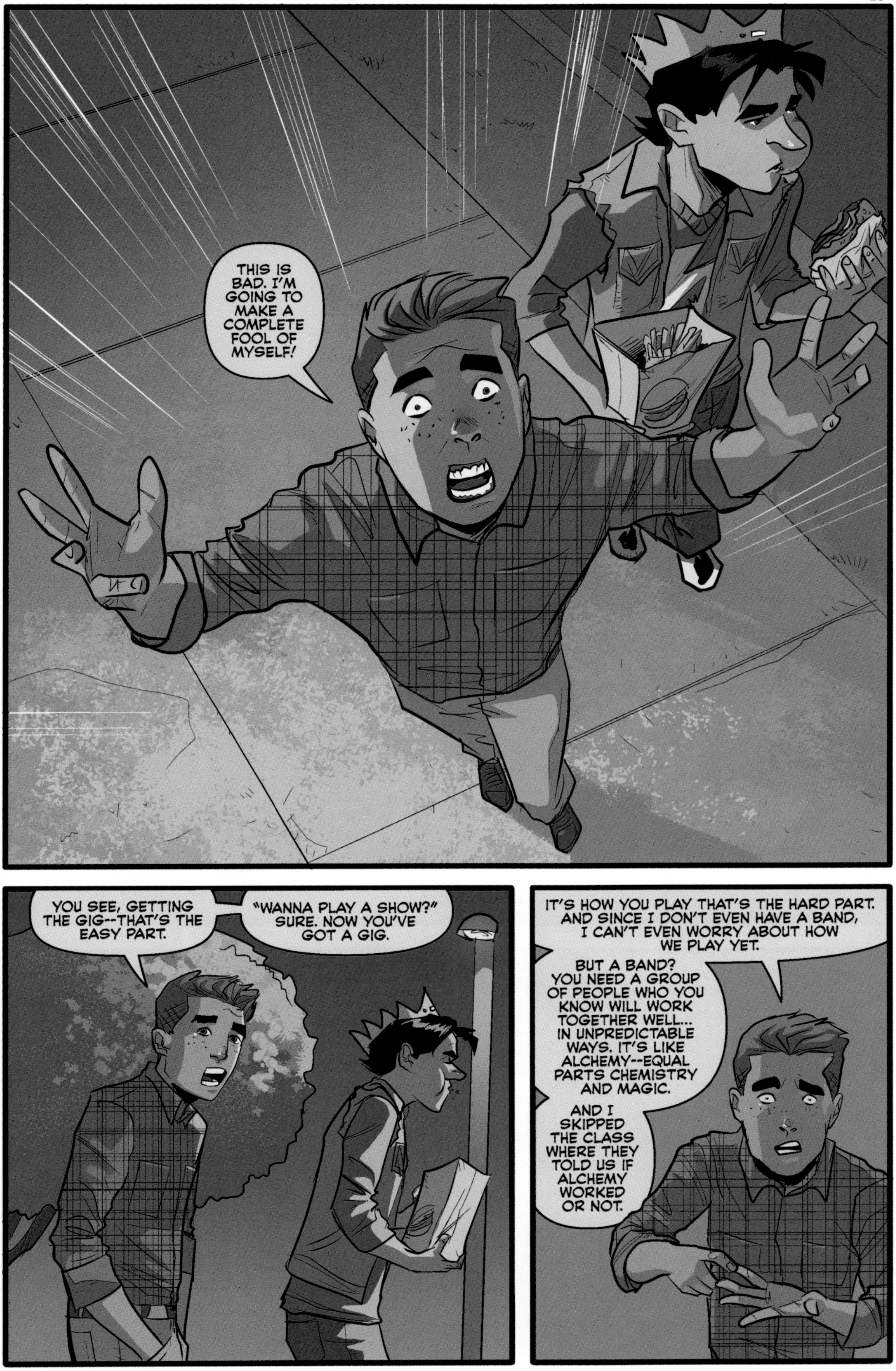
THIS IS BAD. I'M GOING TO MAKE A COMPLETE FOOL OF MYSELF!
YOU SEE, GETTING THE GIG--THAT'S THE EASY PART.
"WANNA PLAY A SHOW?" SURE. NOW YOU'VE GOT A GIG.
IT'S HOW YOU PLAY THAT'S THE HARD PART. AND SINCE I DON'T EVEN HAVE A BAND, I CAN'T EVEN WORRY ABOUT HOW WE PLAY YET.
BUT A BAND? YOU NEED A GROUP OF PEOPLE WHO YOU KNOW WILL WORK TOGETHER WELL... IN UNPREDICTABLE WAYS. IT'S LIKE ALCHEMY--EQUAL PARTS CHEMISTRY AND MAGIC.
AND I SKIPPED THE CLASS WHERE THEY TOLD US IF ALCHEMY WORKED OR NOT.

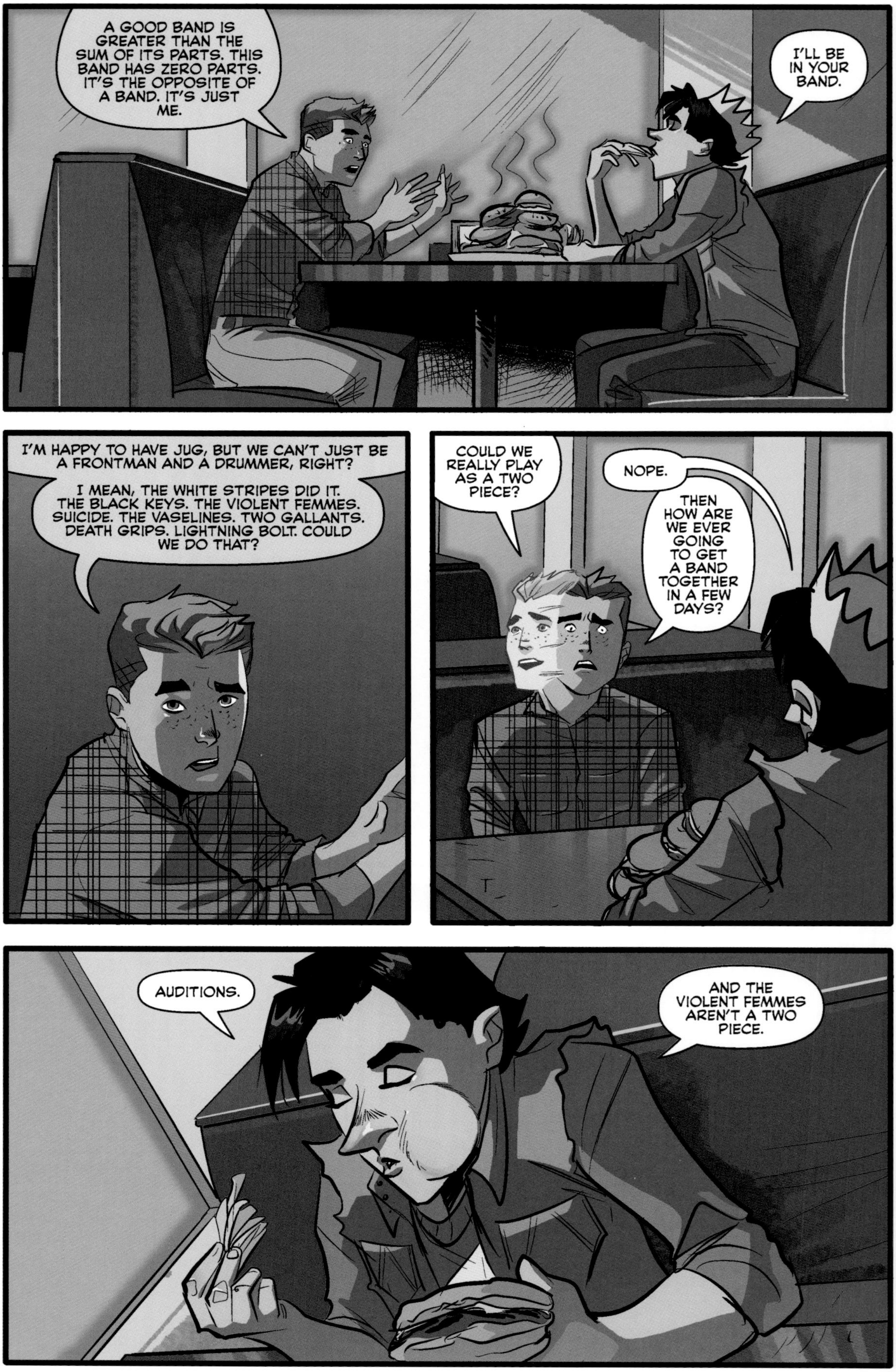
A GOOD BAND IS GREATER THAN THE SUM OF ITS PARTS. THIS BAND HAS ZERO PARTS. IT'S THE OPPOSITE OF A BAND. IT'S JUST ME.
I'LL BE IN YOUR BAND.
I'M HAPPY TO HAVE JUG, BUT WE CAN'T JUST BE A FRONTMAN AND A DRUMMER, RIGHT?
I MEAN, THE WHITE STRIPES DID IT. THE BLACK KEYS. THE VIOLENT FEMMES. SUICIDE. THE VASELINES. TWO GALLANTS. DEATH GRIPS. LIGHTNING BOLT. COULD WE DO THAT?
COULD WE REALLY PLAY AS A TWO PIECE?
NOPE.
THEN HOW ARE WE EVER GOING TO GET A BAND TOGETHER IN A FEW DAYS?
AUDITIONS.
AND THE VIOLENT FEMMES AREN'T A TWO PIECE.

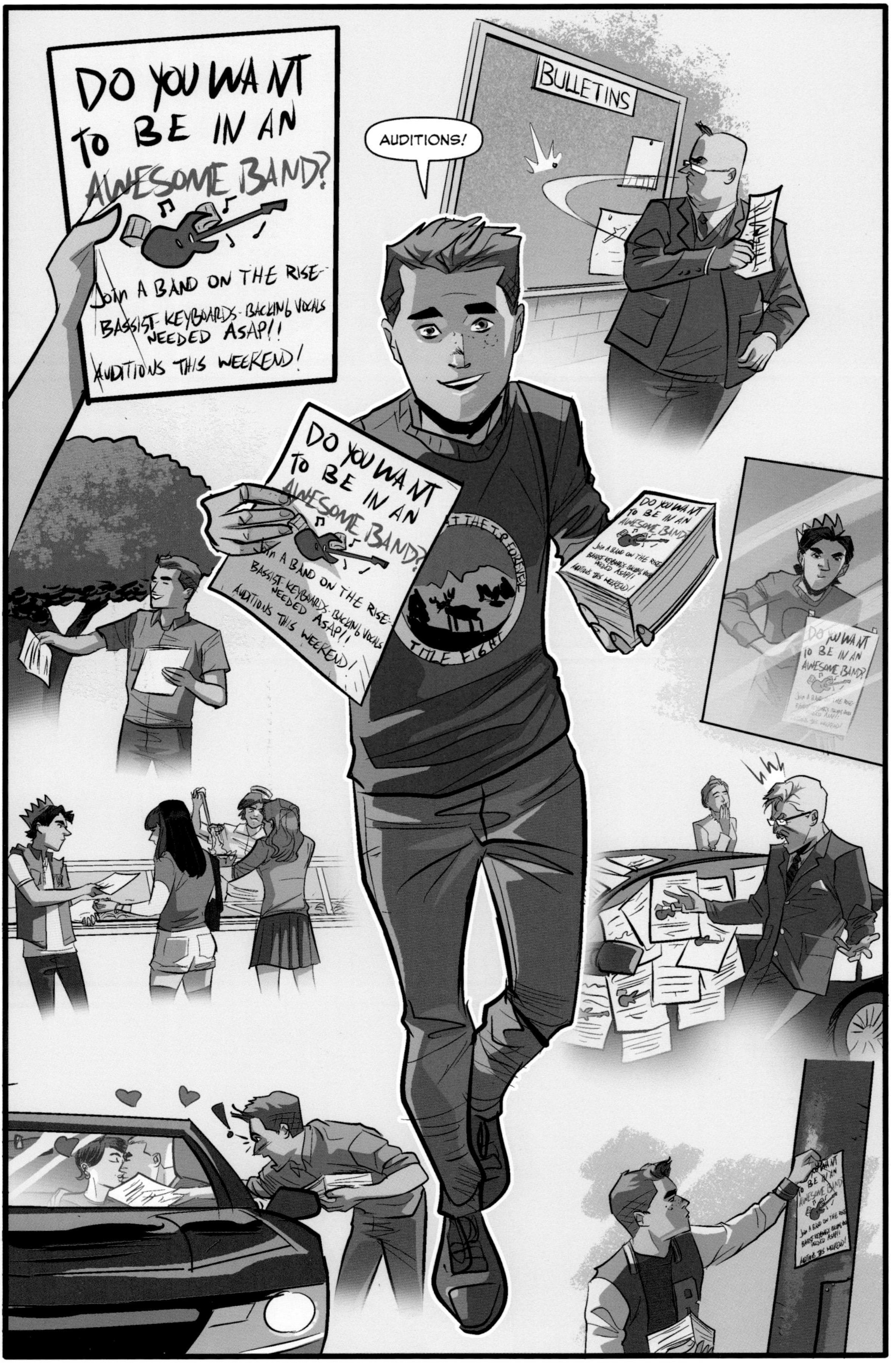
DO YOU WANT TO BE IN AN AWESOME BAND?
JOIN A BAND ON THE RISE-
BASSIST- KEYBOARDS- BACKING VOCALS NEEDED ASAP!!
AUDITIONS THIS WEEKEND!
BULLETINS
AUDITIONS!

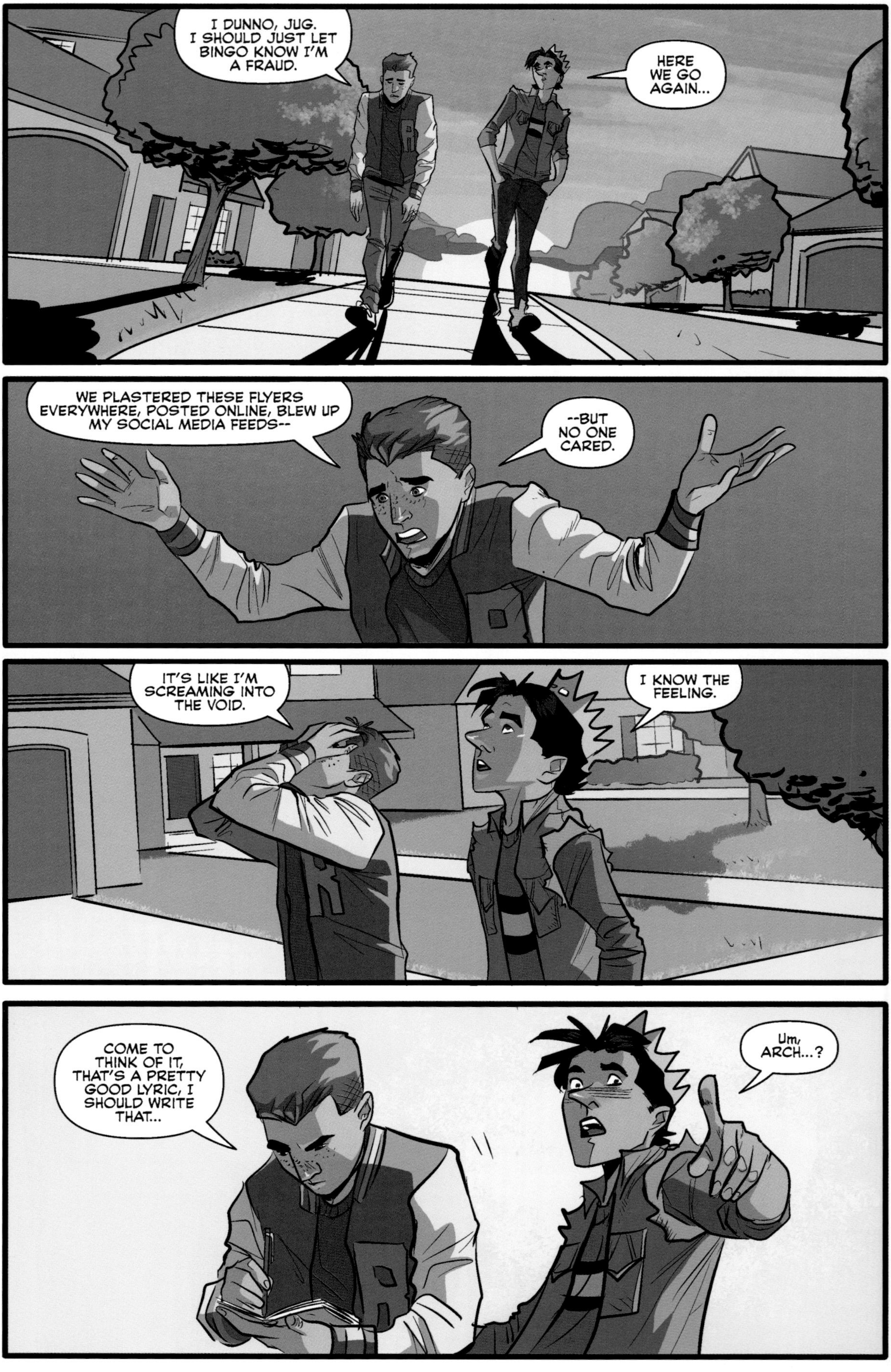
I DUNNO, JUG. I SHOULD JUST LET BINGO KNOW I'M A FRAUD.
HERE WE GO AGAIN...
WE PLASTERED THESE FLYERS EVERYWHERE, POSTED ONLINE, BLEW UP MY SOCIAL MEDIA FEEDS--
--BUT NO ONE CARED.
IT'S LIKE I'M SCREAMING INTO THE VOID.
I KNOW THE FEELING.
COME TO THINK OF IT, THAT'S A PRETTY GOOD LYRIC, I SHOULD WRITE THAT...
Um, ARCH...?

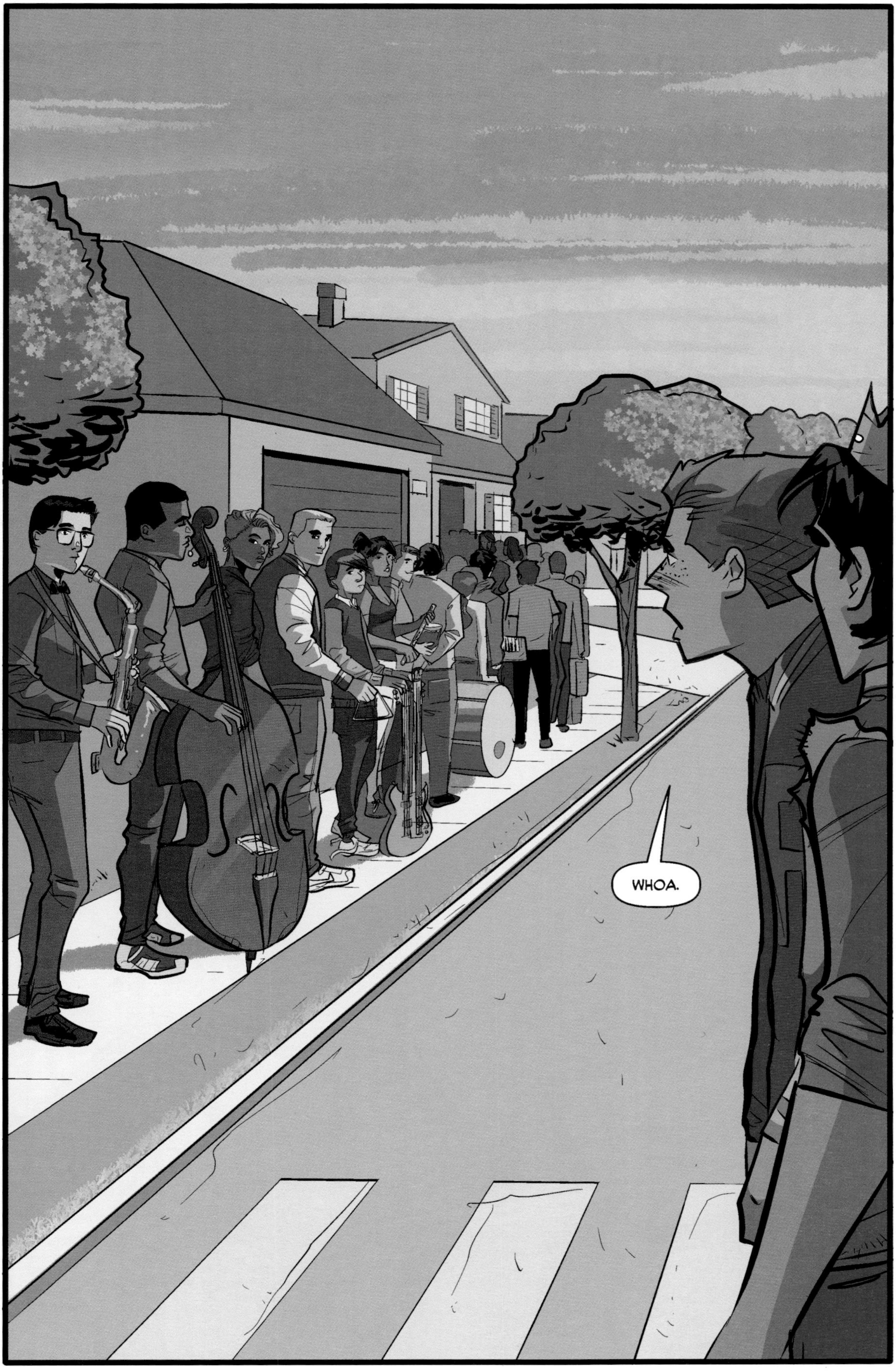
WHOA.

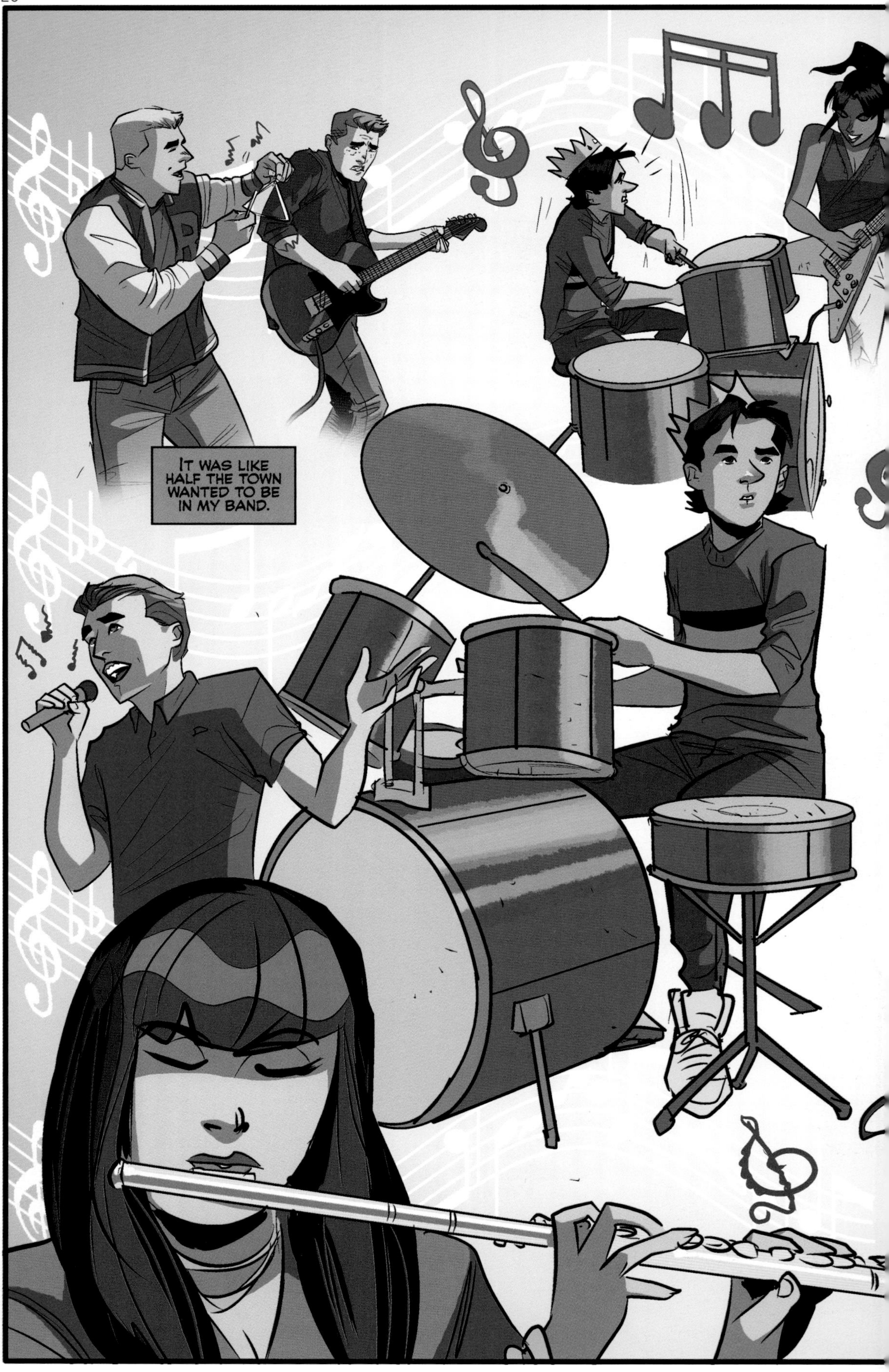
IT WAS LIKE HALF THE TOWN WANTED TO BE IN MY BAND.

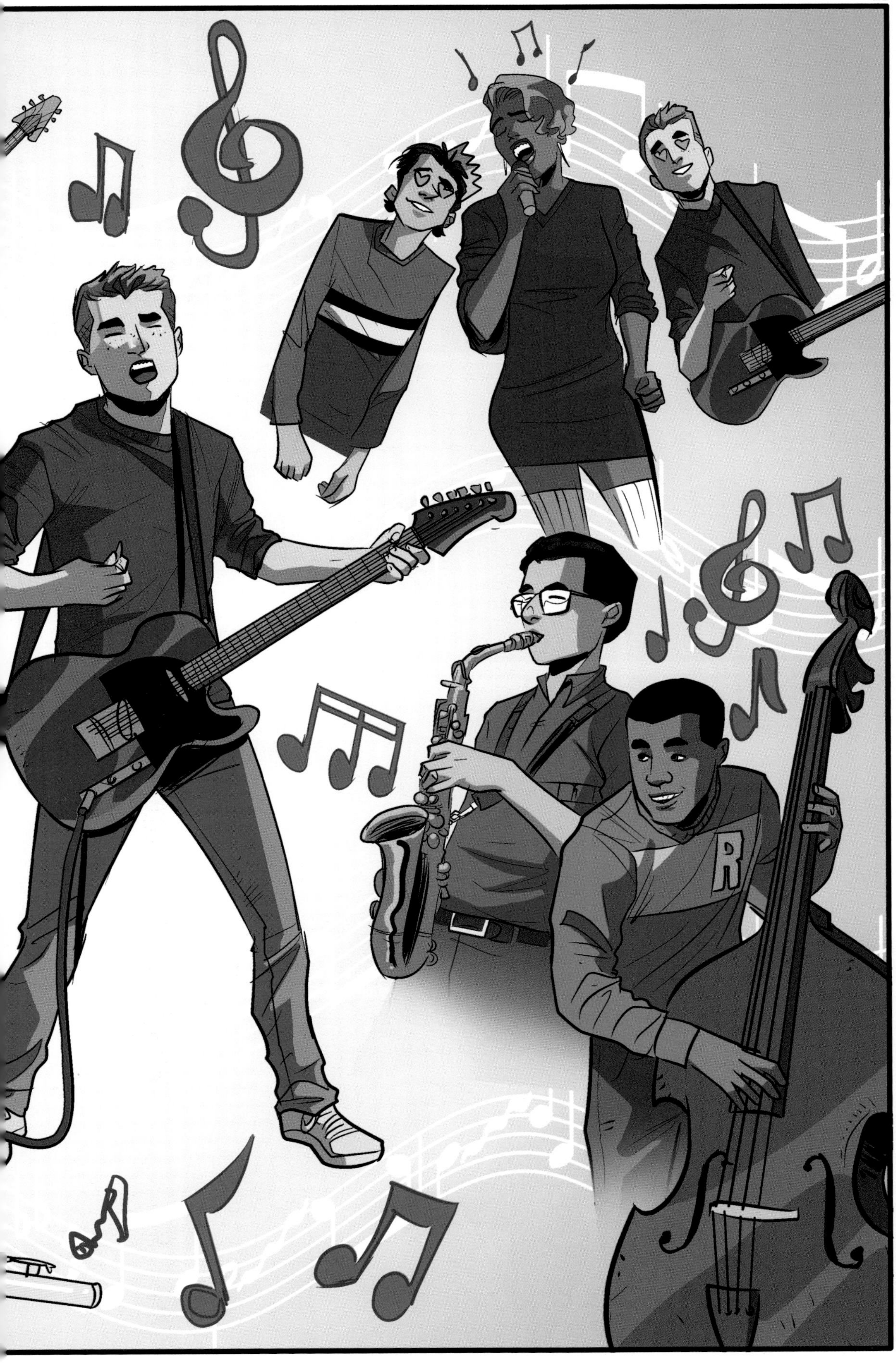

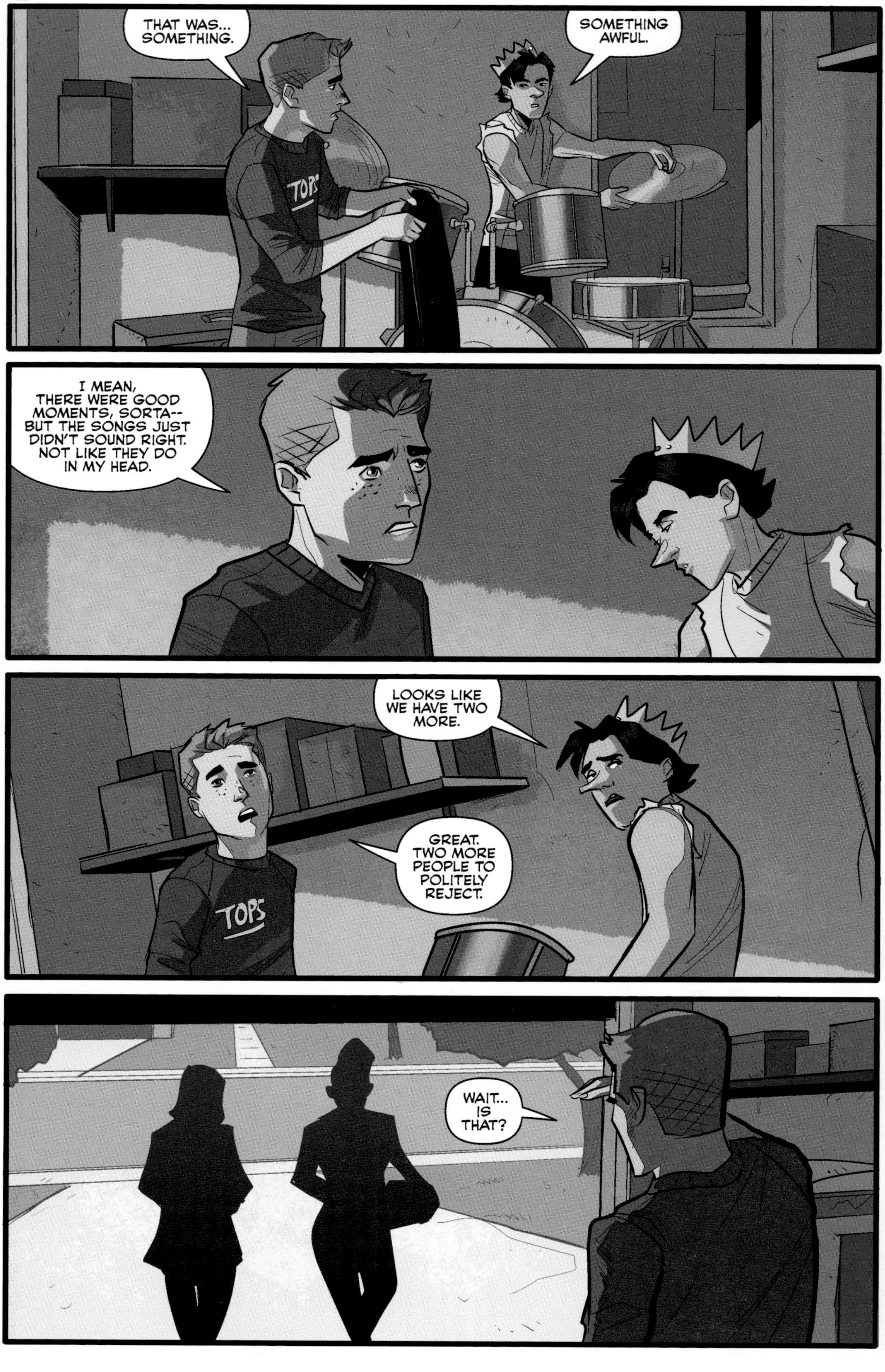
THAT WAS... SOMETHING.
SOMETHING AWFUL.
TOPS
I MEAN, THERE WERE GOOD MOMENTS, SORTA-- BUT THE SONGS JUST DIDN'T SOUND RIGHT. NOT LIKE THEY DO IN MY HEAD.
LOOKS LIKE WE HAVE TWO MORE.
GREAT. TWO MORE PEOPLE TO POLITELY REJECT.
TOPS
WAIT... IS THAT?

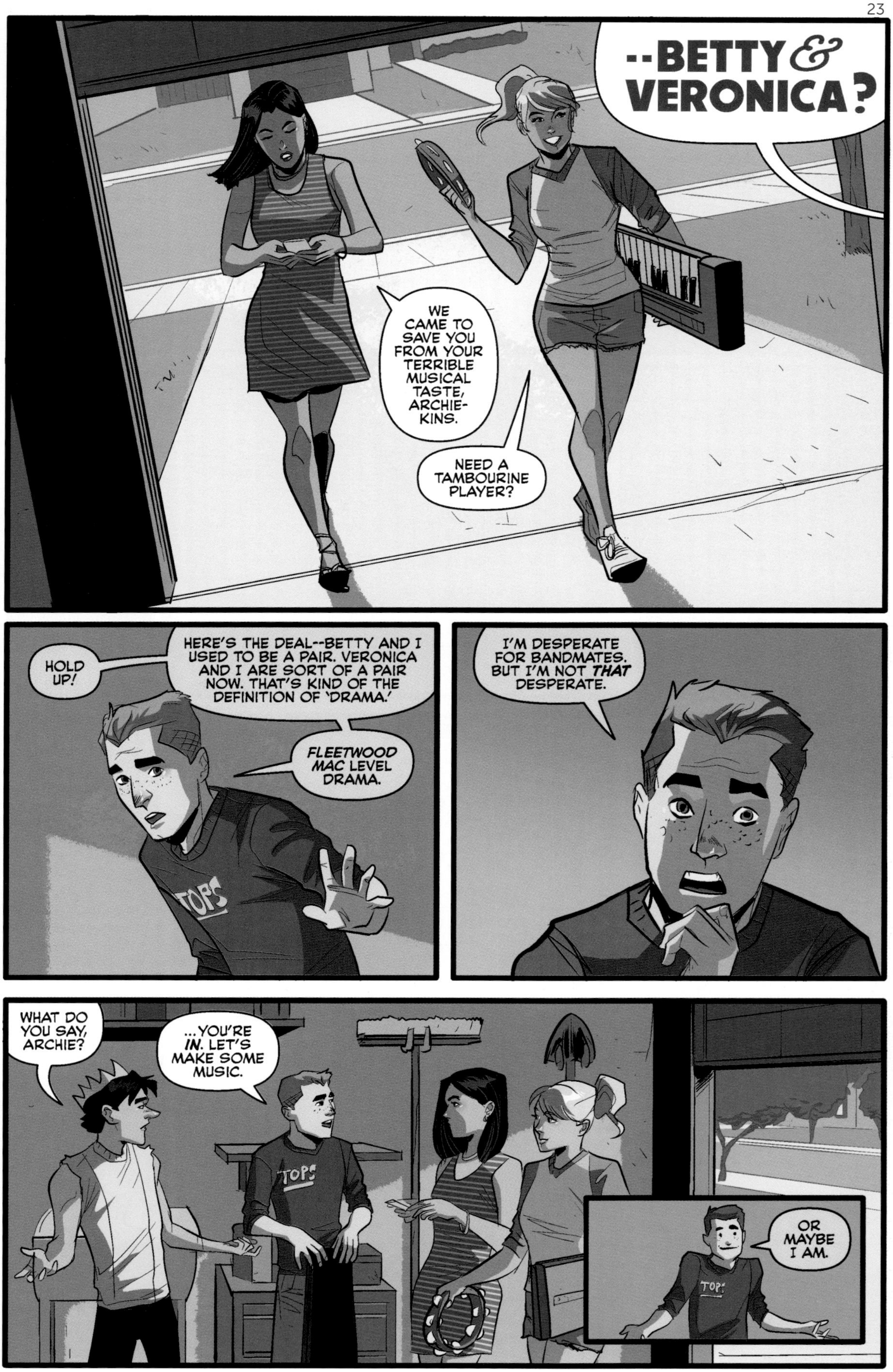
--BETTY & VERONICA?
WE CAME TO SAVE YOU FROM YOUR TERRIBLE MUSICAL TASTE, ARCHIE-KINS.
NEED A TAMBOURINE PLAYER?
HOLD UP!
HERE'S THE DEAL--BETTY AND I USED TO BE A PAIR. VERONICA AND I ARE SORT OF A PAIR NOW. THAT'S KIND OF THE DEFINITION OF 'DRAMA.'
FLEETWOOD MAC LEVEL DRAMA.
TOPS
I'M DESPERATE FOR BANDMATES. BUT I'M NOT THAT DESPERATE.
WHAT DO YOU SAY, ARCHIE?
...YOU'RE IN. LET'S MAKE SOME MUSIC.
TOPS
OR MAYBE I AM.
TOPS

ONLY ONE WAY TO LEARN TO FLY...

EVERYONE GOT THE MUSIC? THIS SONG'S CALLED 'CRASH AND BURN.'

ONE, TWO, THREE, FOUR!

TIK TIK TIK TIK

TAKE ME HOME--I'LL GO UNDERGROUND --ON A RADIO TO NOWHERE

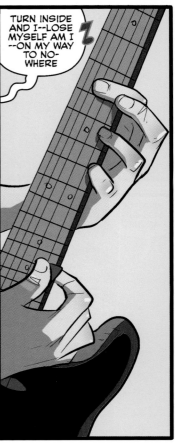

TURN INSIDE AND I--LOSE MYSELF AM I --ON MY WAY TO NO-WHERE

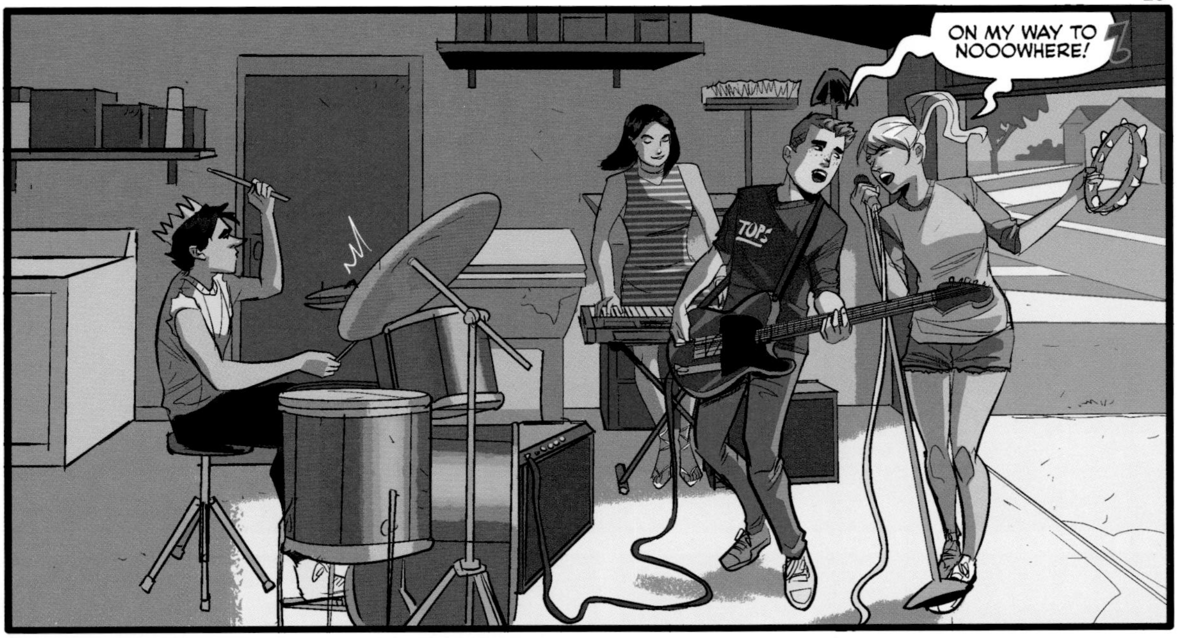
ON MY WAY TO NOOOWHERE!
TOPS

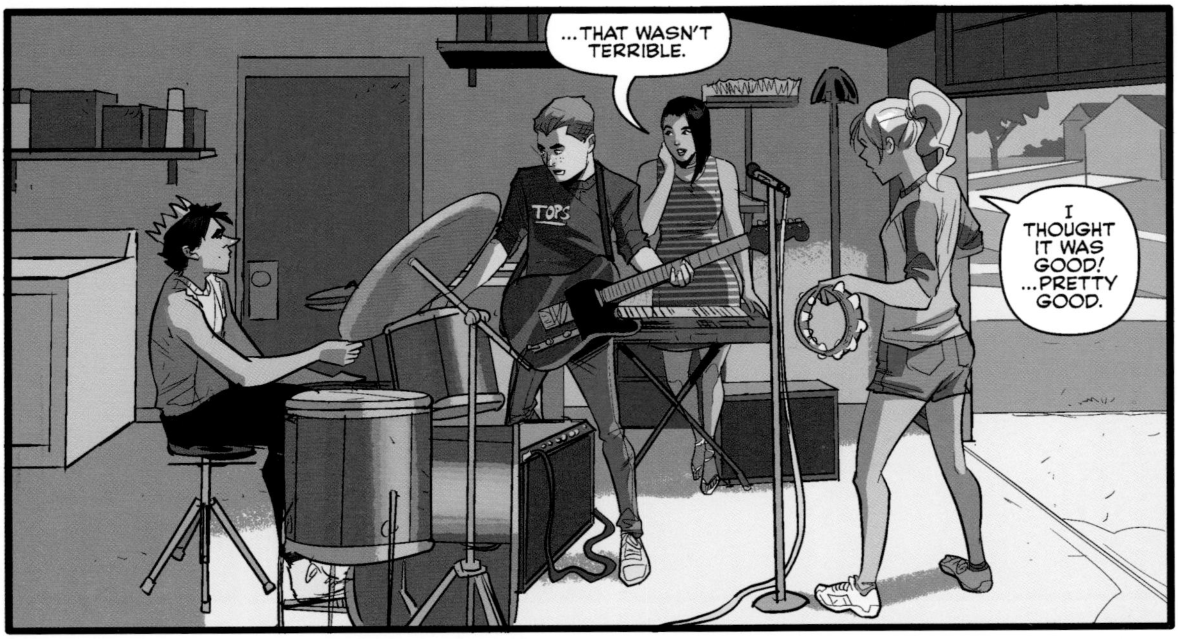
...THAT WASN'T TERRIBLE.
TOPS
I THOUGHT IT WAS GOOD! ...PRETTY GOOD.

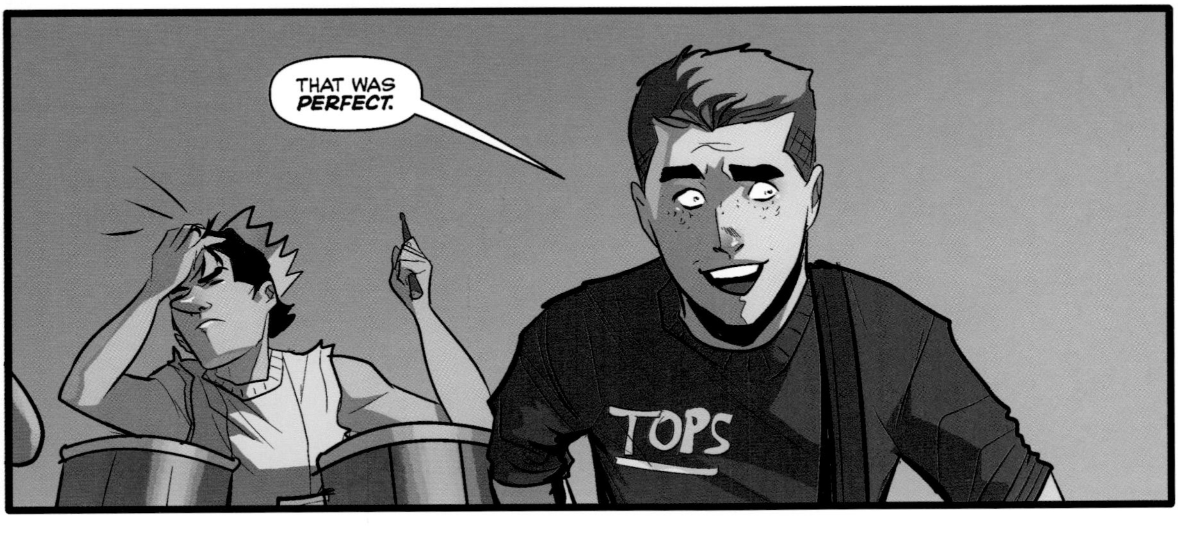
THAT WAS ***PERFECT.***
TOPS

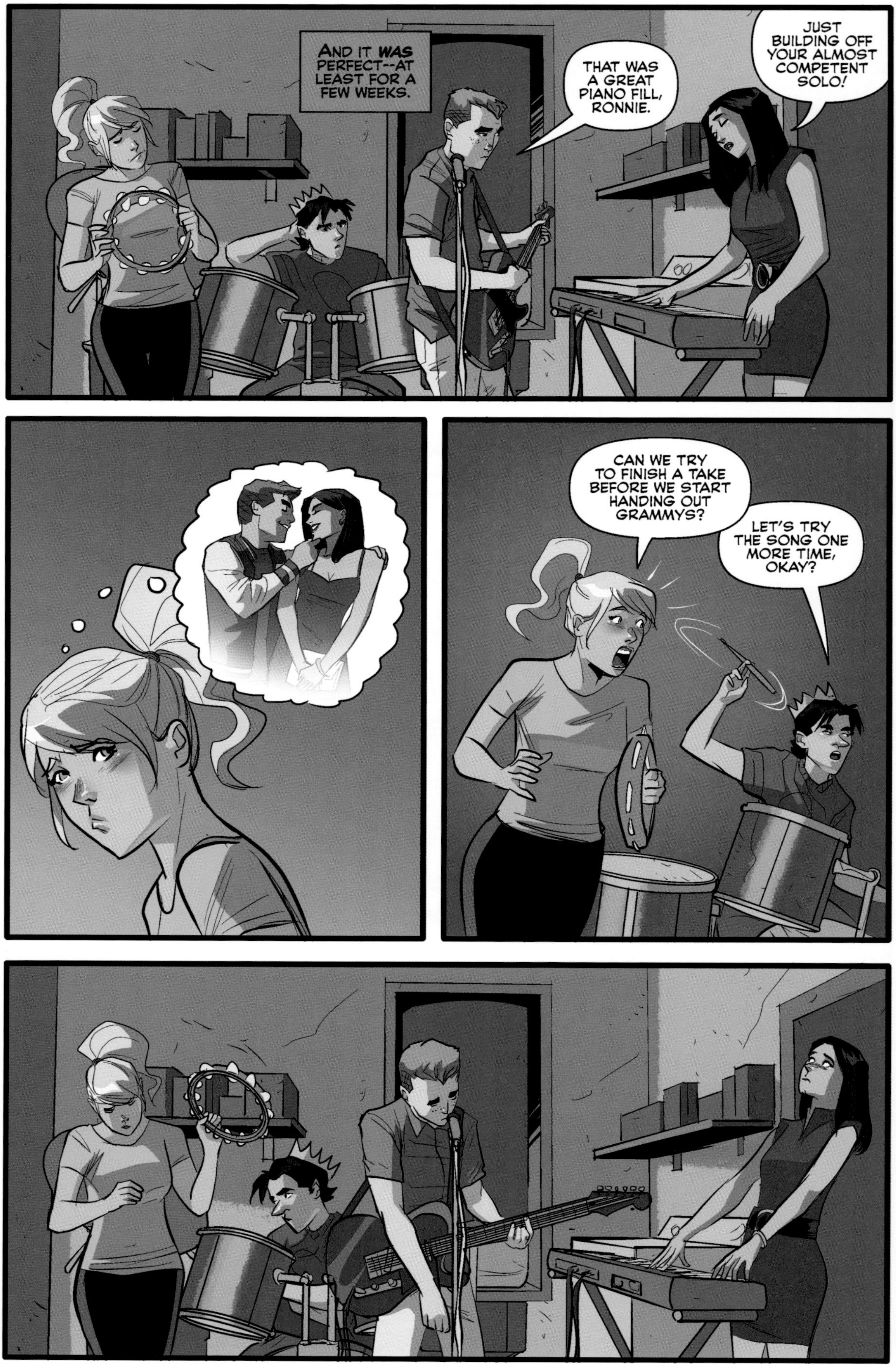
AND IT WAS PERFECT--AT LEAST FOR A FEW WEEKS.
THAT WAS A GREAT PIANO FILL, RONNIE.
JUST BUILDING OFF YOUR ALMOST COMPETENT SOLO!
CAN WE TRY TO FINISH A TAKE BEFORE WE START HANDING OUT GRAMMYS?
LET'S TRY THE SONG ONE MORE TIME, OKAY?

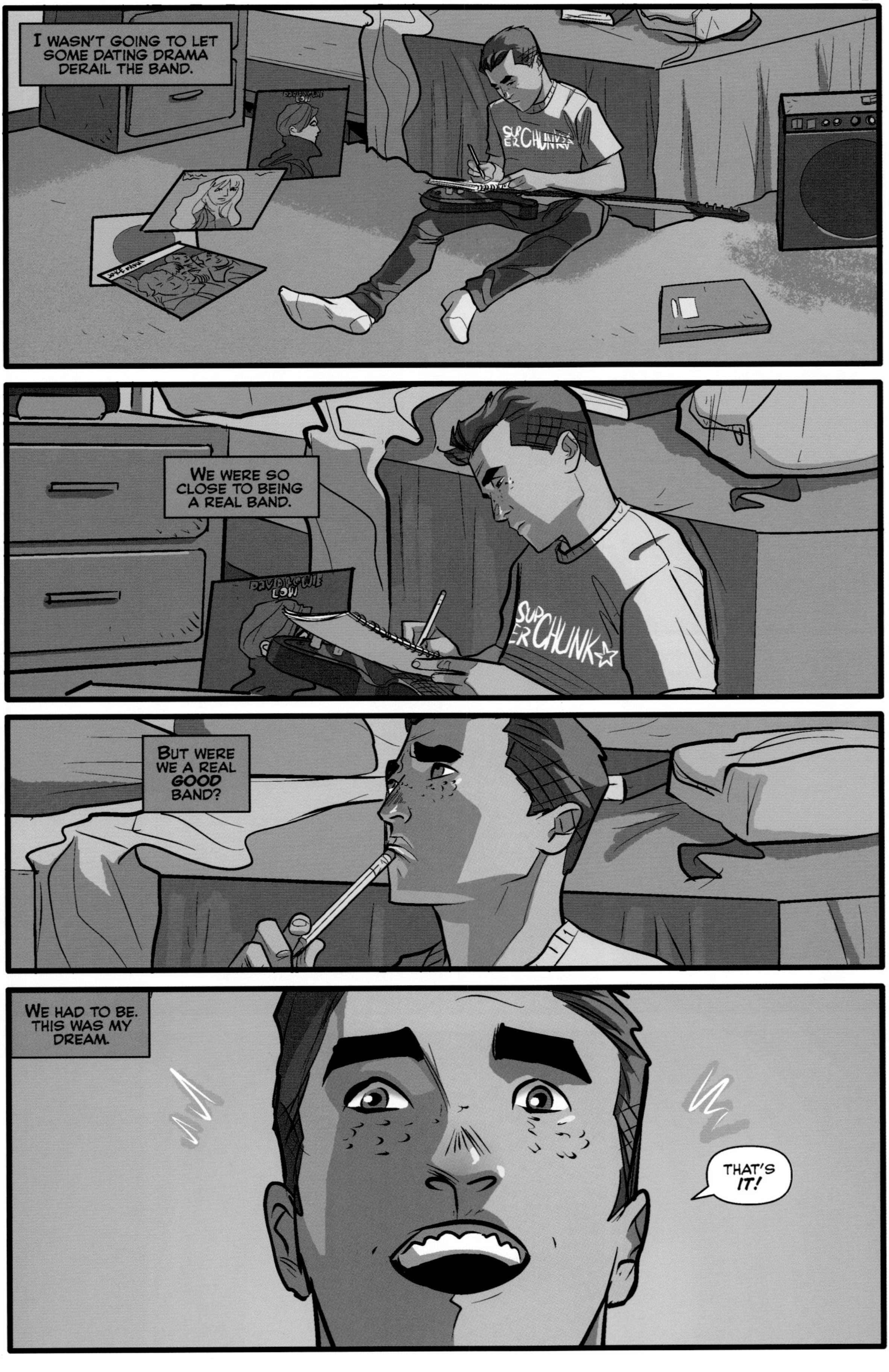
I WASN'T GOING TO LET SOME DATING DRAMA DERAIL THE BAND.
WE WERE SO CLOSE TO BEING A REAL BAND.
BUT WERE WE A REAL **GOOD** BAND?
WE HAD TO BE. THIS WAS MY DREAM.
THAT'S *IT!*

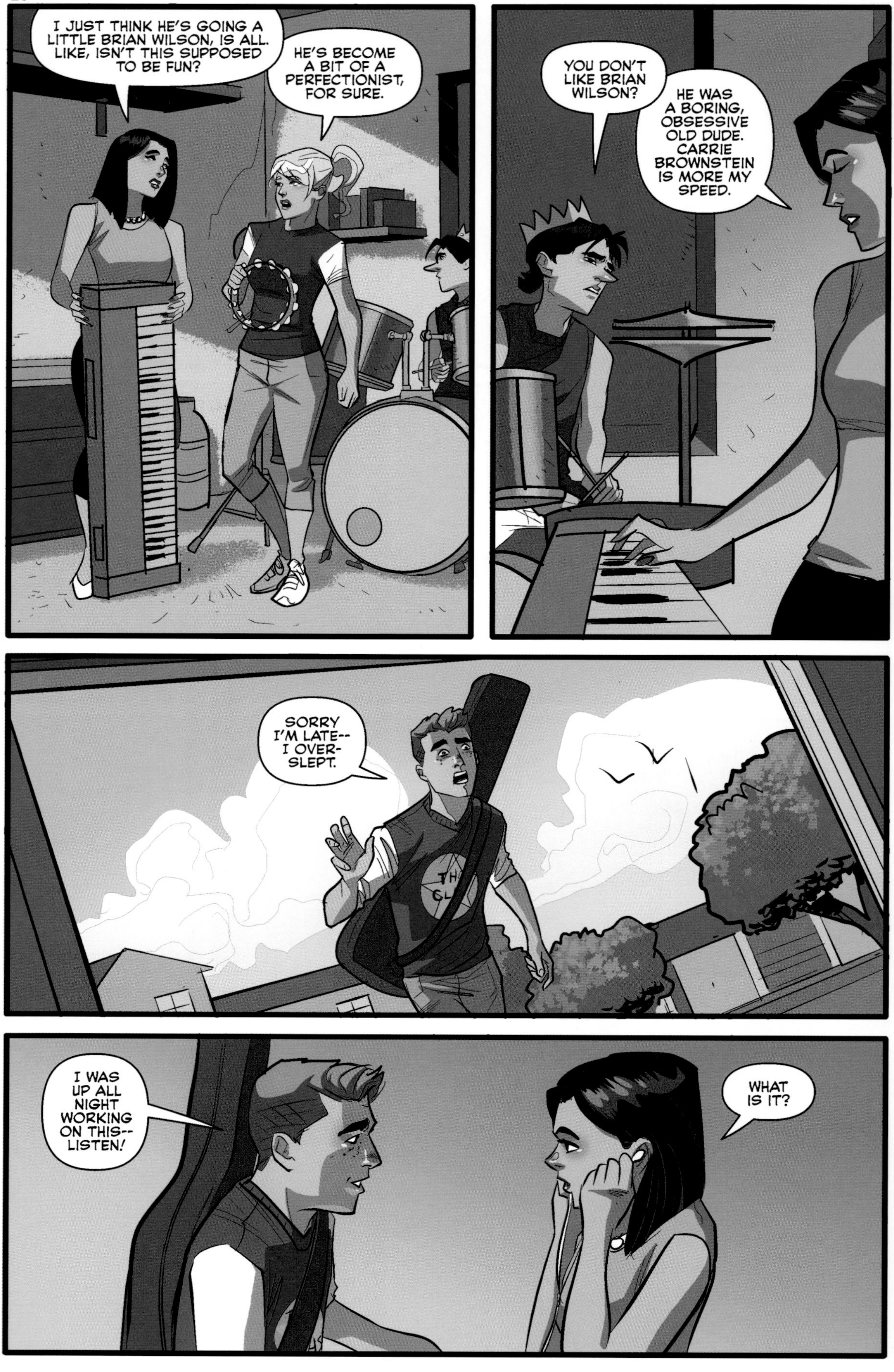
I JUST THINK HE'S GOING A LITTLE BRIAN WILSON, IS ALL. LIKE, ISN'T THIS SUPPOSED TO BE FUN?
HE'S BECOME A BIT OF A PERFECTIONIST, FOR SURE.
YOU DON'T LIKE BRIAN WILSON?
HE WAS A BORING, OBSESSIVE OLD DUDE. CARRIE BROWNSTEIN IS MORE MY SPEED.
SORRY I'M LATE-- I OVER-SLEPT.
I WAS UP ALL NIGHT WORKING ON THIS-- LISTEN!
WHAT IS IT?

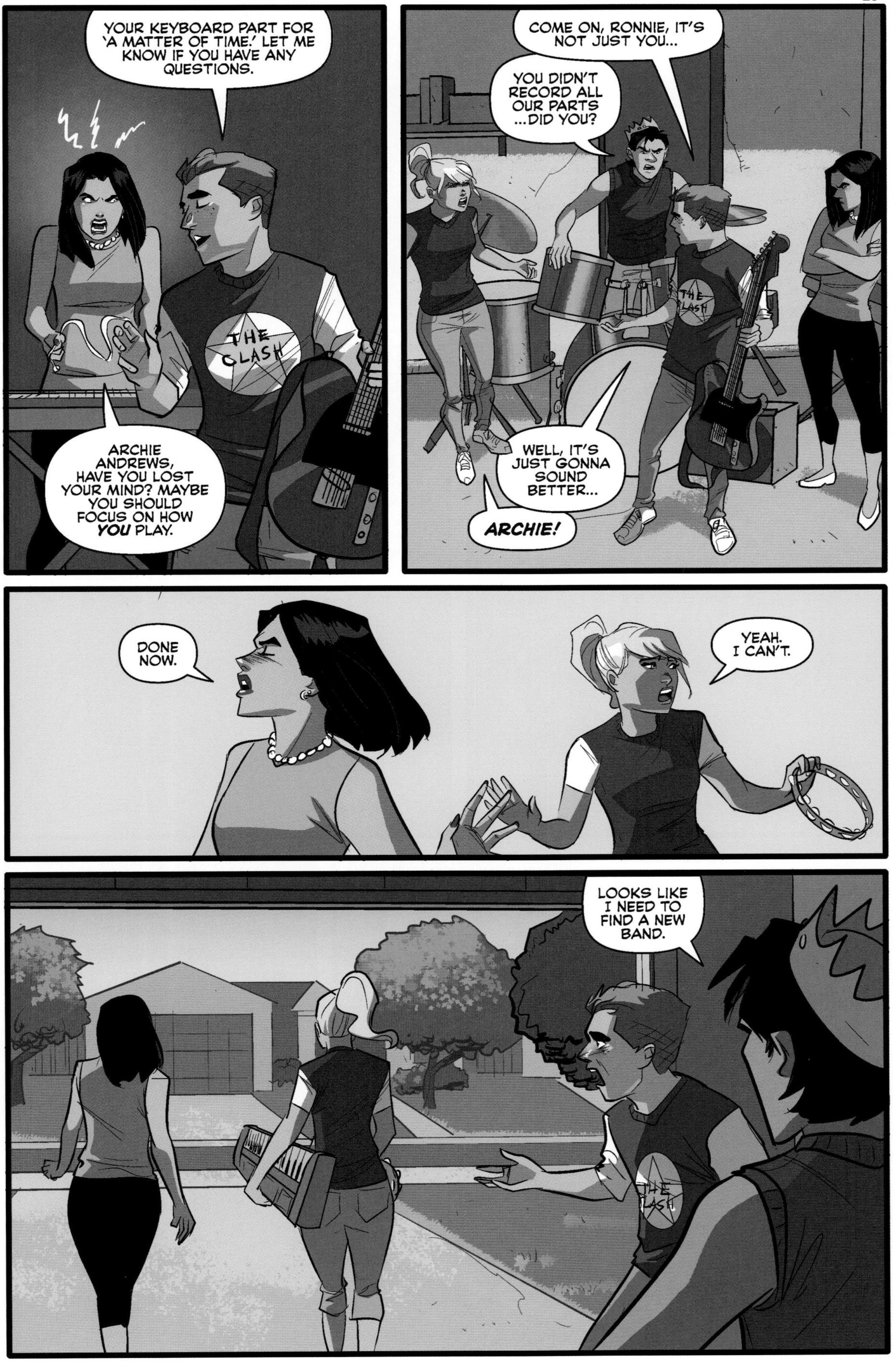
YOUR KEYBOARD PART FOR 'A MATTER OF TIME.' LET ME KNOW IF YOU HAVE ANY QUESTIONS.
ARCHIE ANDREWS, HAVE YOU LOST YOUR MIND? MAYBE YOU SHOULD FOCUS ON HOW *YOU* PLAY.
COME ON, RONNIE, IT'S NOT JUST YOU...
YOU DIDN'T RECORD ALL OUR PARTS ...DID YOU?
WELL, IT'S JUST GONNA SOUND BETTER...
ARCHIE!
DONE NOW.
YEAH. I CAN'T.
LOOKS LIKE I NEED TO FIND A NEW BAND.
THE CLASH

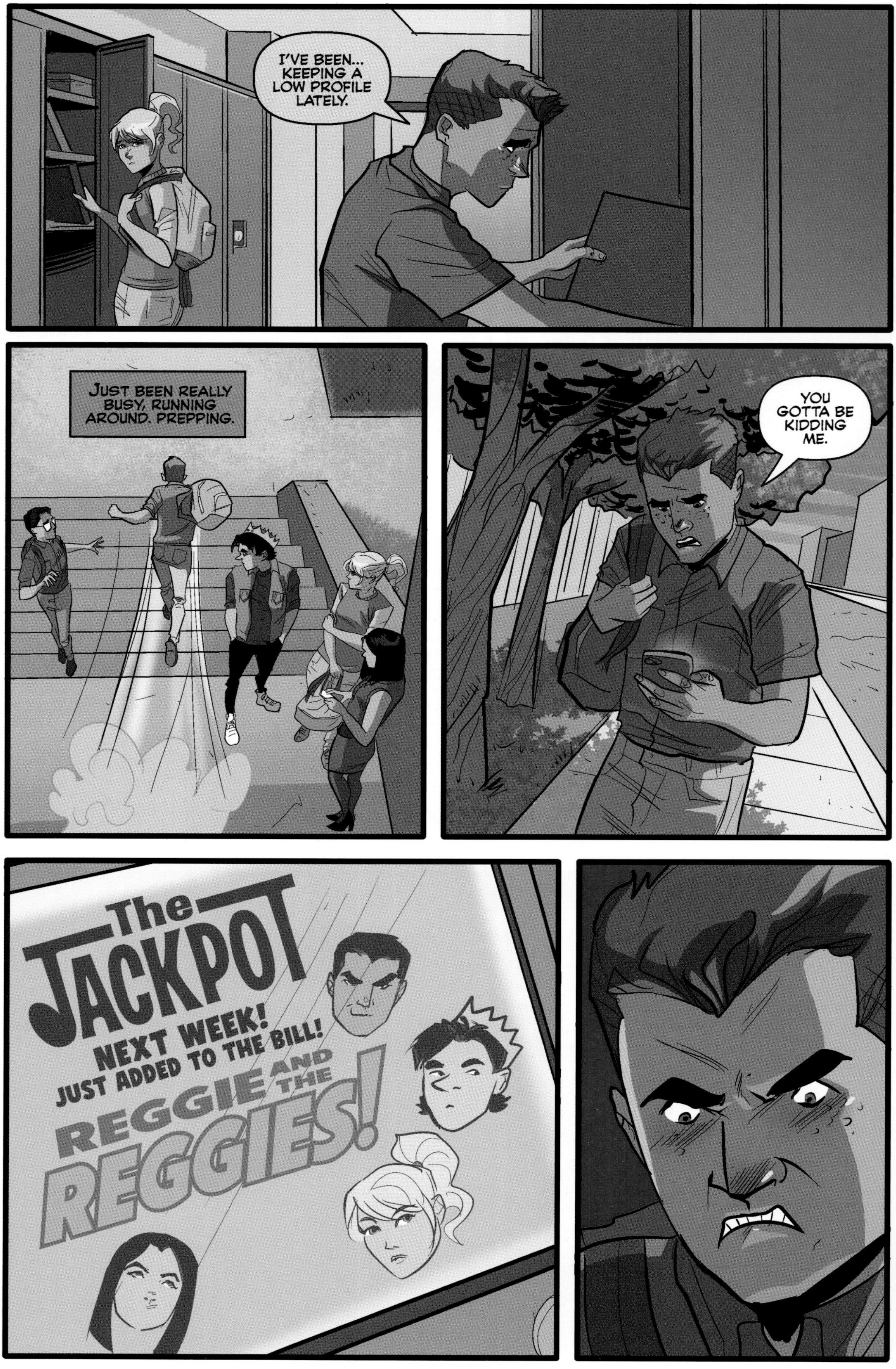
I'VE BEEN... KEEPING A LOW PROFILE LATELY.
JUST BEEN REALLY BUSY, RUNNING AROUND. PREPPING.
YOU GOTTA BE KIDDING ME.
The JACKPOT
NEXT WEEK!
JUST ADDED TO THE BILL!
REGGIE AND THE REGGIES!

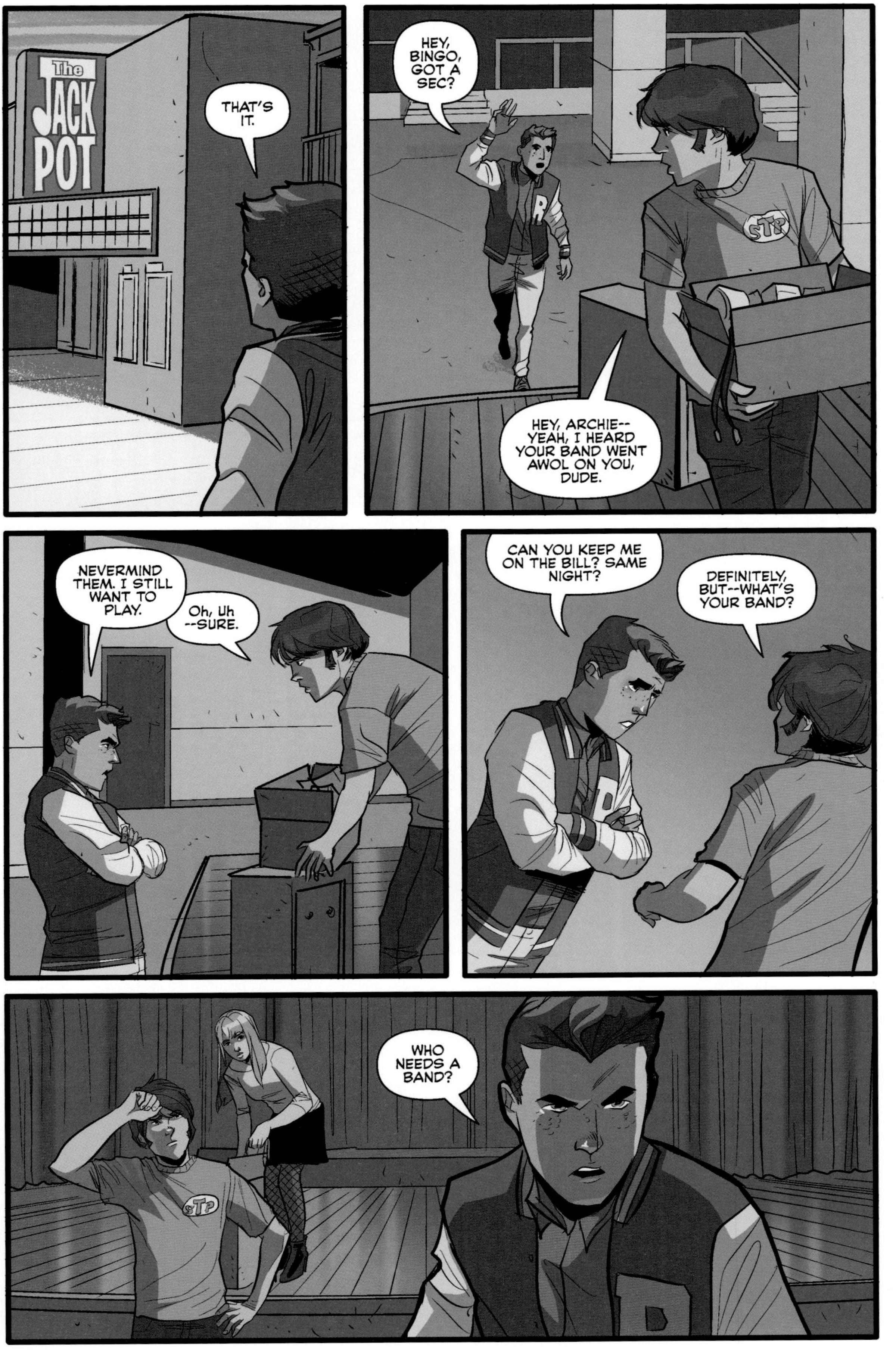
The JACK POT
THAT'S IT.
HEY, BINGO, GOT A SEC?
HEY, ARCHIE--YEAH, I HEARD YOUR BAND WENT AWOL ON YOU, DUDE.
NEVERMIND THEM. I STILL WANT TO PLAY.
Oh, uh --SURE.
CAN YOU KEEP ME ON THE BILL? SAME NIGHT?
DEFINITELY, BUT--WHAT'S YOUR BAND?
WHO NEEDS A BAND?

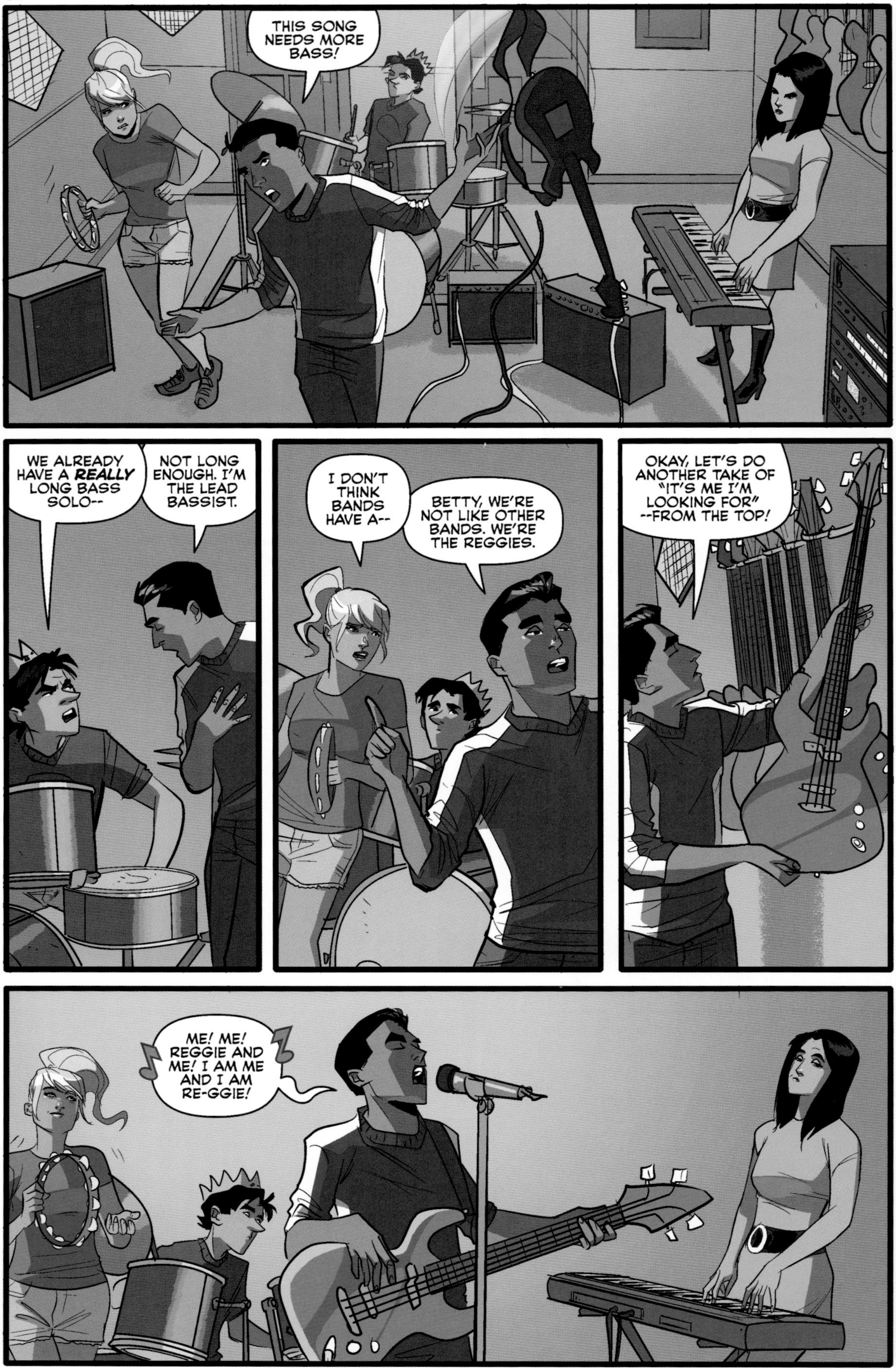
THIS SONG NEEDS MORE BASS!
WE ALREADY HAVE A ***REALLY*** LONG BASS SOLO--
NOT LONG ENOUGH. I'M THE LEAD BASSIST.
I DON'T THINK BANDS HAVE A--
BETTY, WE'RE NOT LIKE OTHER BANDS. WE'RE THE REGGIES.
OKAY, LET'S DO ANOTHER TAKE OF "IT'S ME I'M LOOKING FOR" --FROM THE TOP!
ME! ME! REGGIE AND ME! I AM ME AND I AM RE-GGIE!

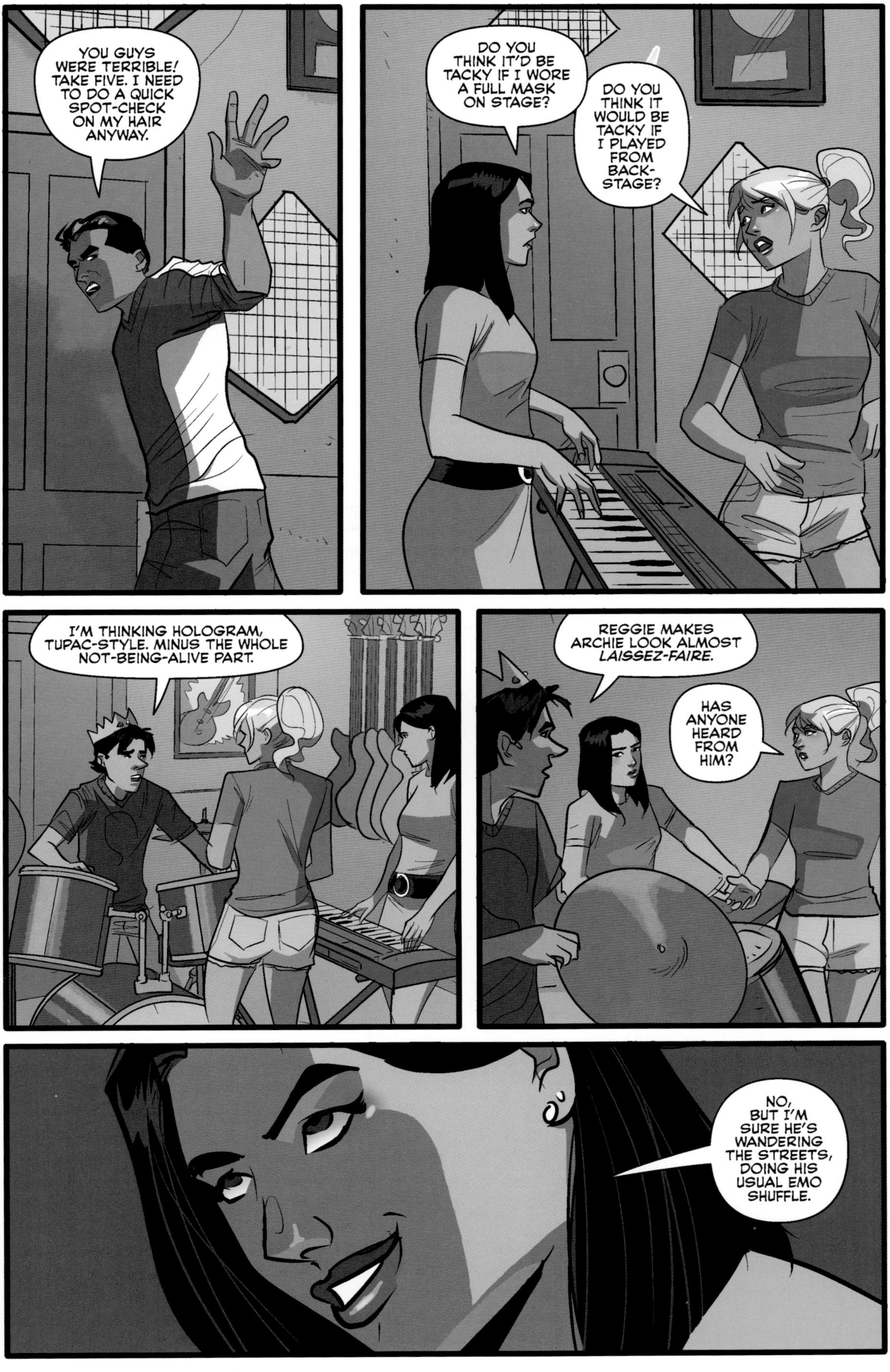
YOU GUYS WERE TERRIBLE! TAKE FIVE. I NEED TO DO A QUICK SPOT-CHECK ON MY HAIR ANYWAY.
DO YOU THINK IT'D BE TACKY IF I WORE A FULL MASK ON STAGE?
DO YOU THINK IT WOULD BE TACKY IF I PLAYED FROM BACK-STAGE?
I'M THINKING HOLOGRAM, TUPAC-STYLE. MINUS THE WHOLE NOT-BEING-ALIVE PART.
REGGIE MAKES ARCHIE LOOK ALMOST *LAISSEZ-FAIRE*.
HAS ANYONE HEARD FROM HIM?
NO, BUT I'M SURE HE'S WANDERING THE STREETS, DOING HIS USUAL EMO SHUFFLE.

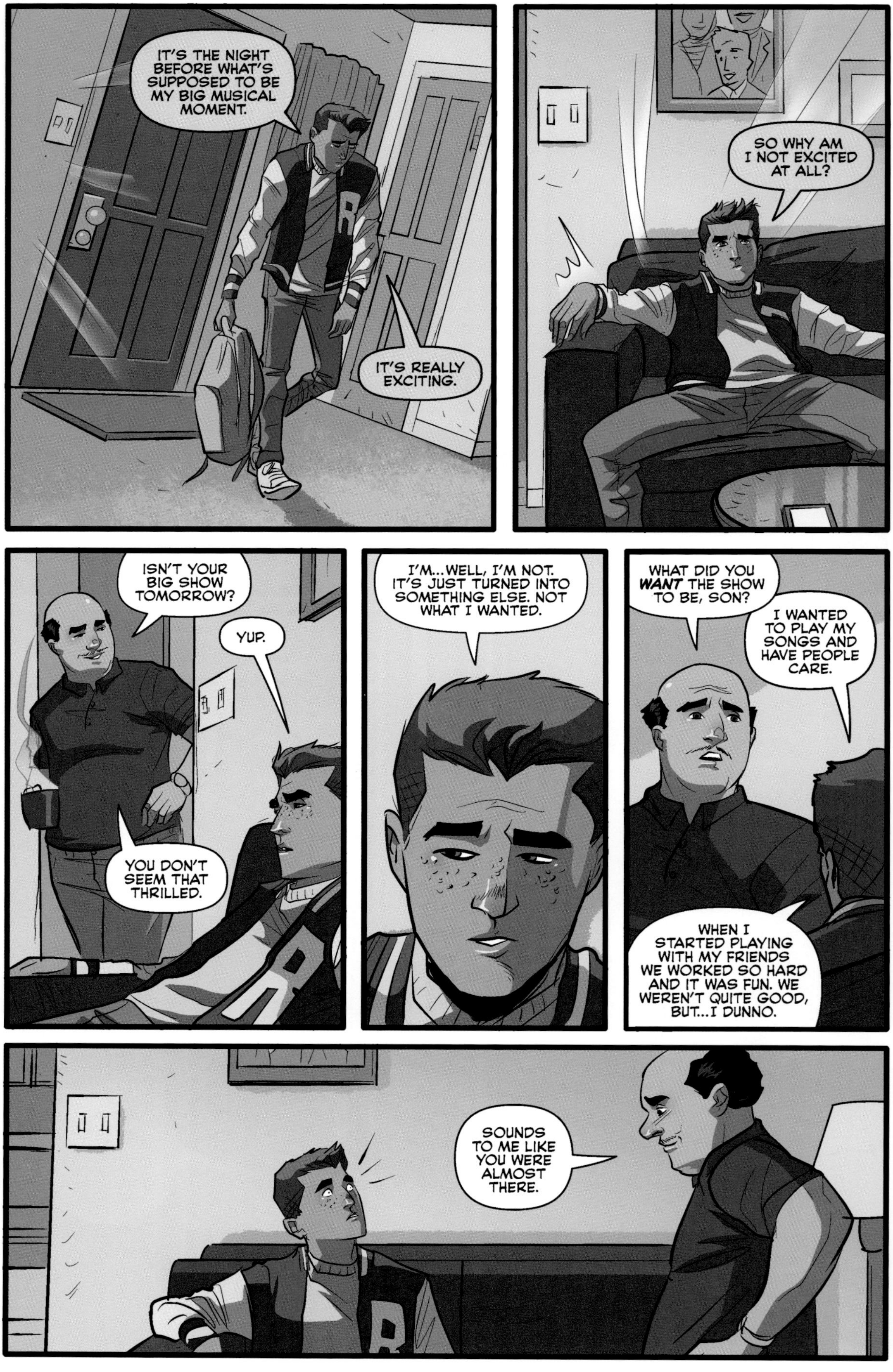
IT'S THE NIGHT BEFORE WHAT'S SUPPOSED TO BE MY BIG MUSICAL MOMENT.
IT'S REALLY EXCITING.
SO WHY AM I NOT EXCITED AT ALL?
ISN'T YOUR BIG SHOW TOMORROW?
YUP.
YOU DON'T SEEM THAT THRILLED.
I'M...WELL, I'M NOT. IT'S JUST TURNED INTO SOMETHING ELSE. NOT WHAT I WANTED.
WHAT DID YOU *WANT* THE SHOW TO BE, SON?
I WANTED TO PLAY MY SONGS AND HAVE PEOPLE CARE.
WHEN I STARTED PLAYING WITH MY FRIENDS WE WORKED SO HARD AND IT WAS FUN. WE WEREN'T QUITE GOOD, BUT...I DUNNO.
SOUNDS TO ME LIKE YOU WERE ALMOST THERE.

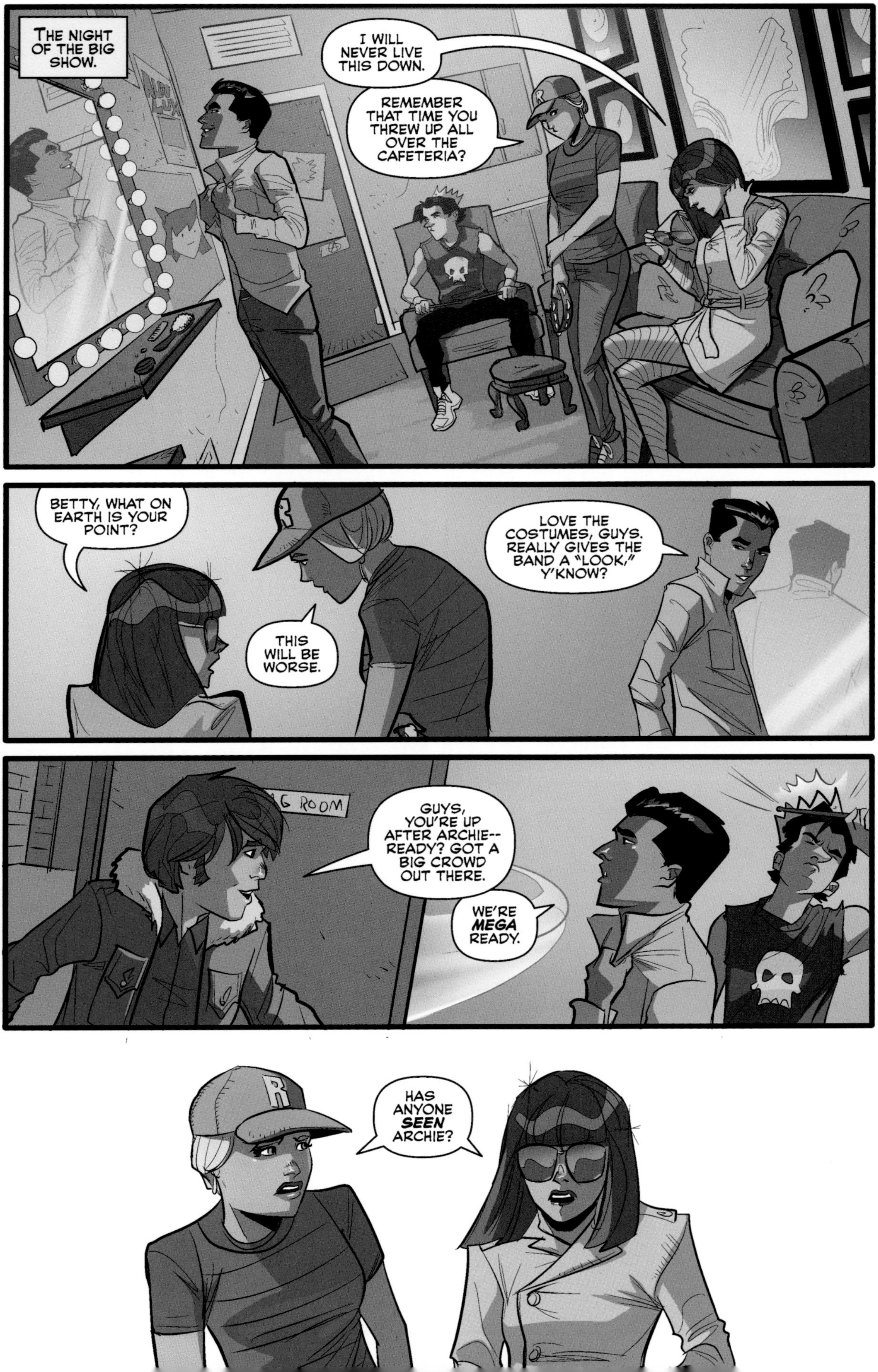
THE NIGHT OF THE BIG SHOW.
I WILL NEVER LIVE THIS DOWN.
REMEMBER THAT TIME YOU THREW UP ALL OVER THE CAFETERIA?
BETTY, WHAT ON EARTH IS YOUR POINT?
THIS WILL BE WORSE.
LOVE THE COSTUMES, GUYS. REALLY GIVES THE BAND A "LOOK," Y'KNOW?
GUYS, YOU'RE UP AFTER ARCHIE-- READY? GOT A BIG CROWD OUT THERE.
WE'RE **MEGA** READY.
HAS ANYONE **SEEN** ARCHIE?

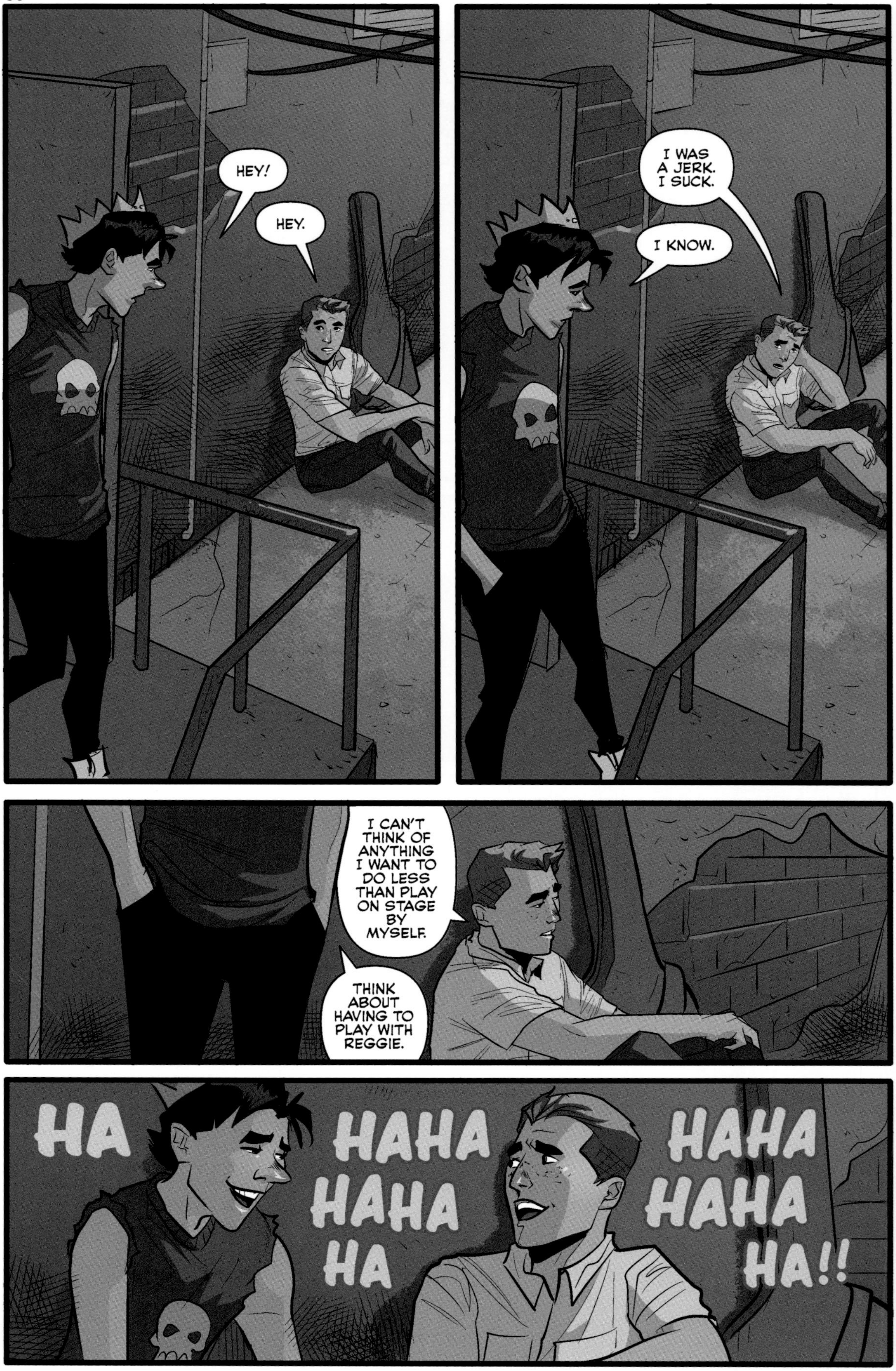
HEY!
HEY.
I WAS A JERK. I SUCK.
I KNOW.
I CAN'T THINK OF ANYTHING I WANT TO DO LESS THAN PLAY ON STAGE BY MYSELF.
THINK ABOUT HAVING TO PLAY WITH REGGIE.
HA
HAHA HAHA HA
HAHA HAHA HA!!

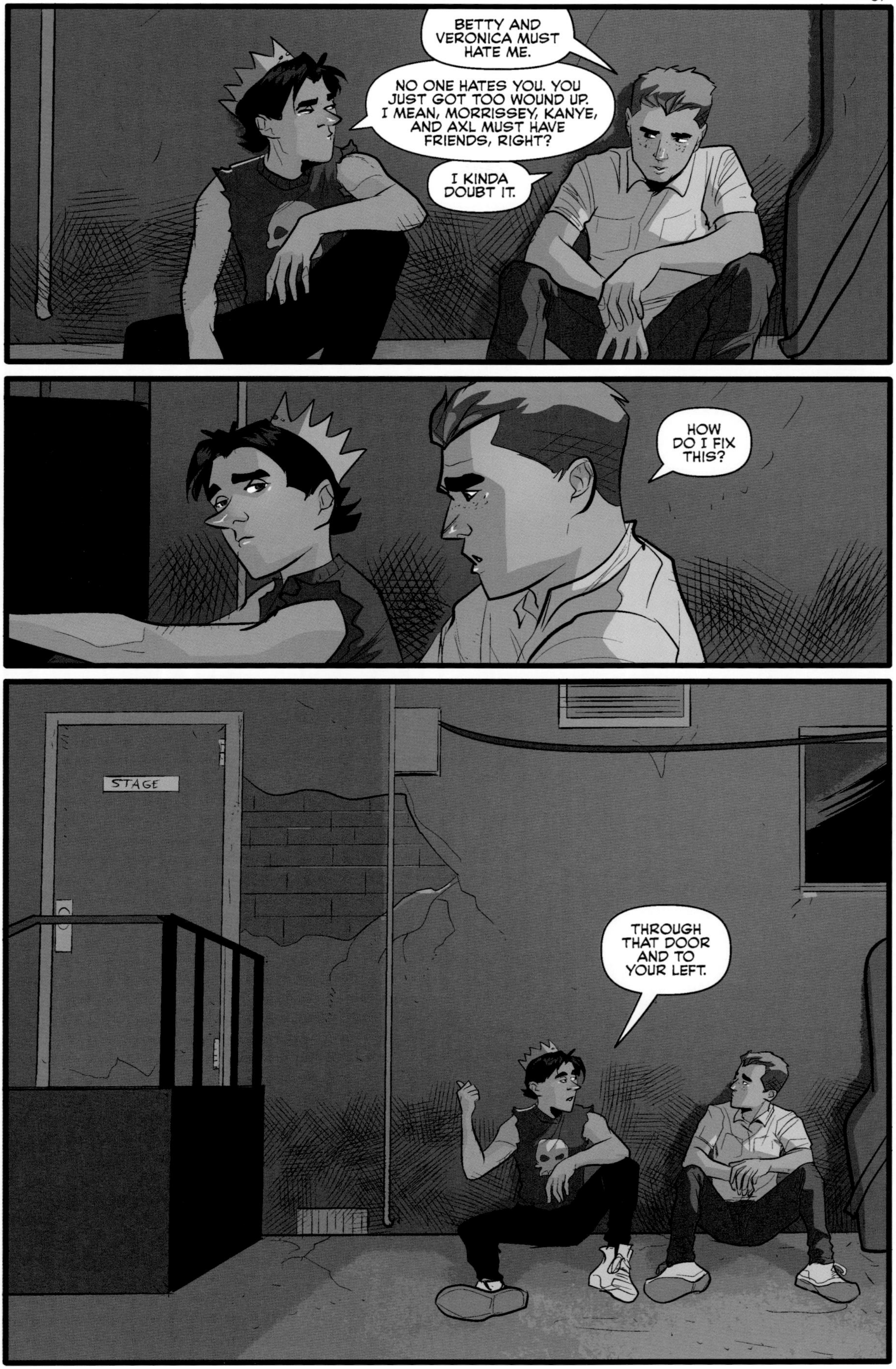
BETTY AND VERONICA MUST HATE ME.
NO ONE HATES YOU. YOU JUST GOT TOO WOUND UP. I MEAN, MORRISSEY, KANYE, AND AXL MUST HAVE FRIENDS, RIGHT?
I KINDA DOUBT IT.
HOW DO I FIX THIS?
STAGE
THROUGH THAT DOOR AND TO YOUR LEFT.

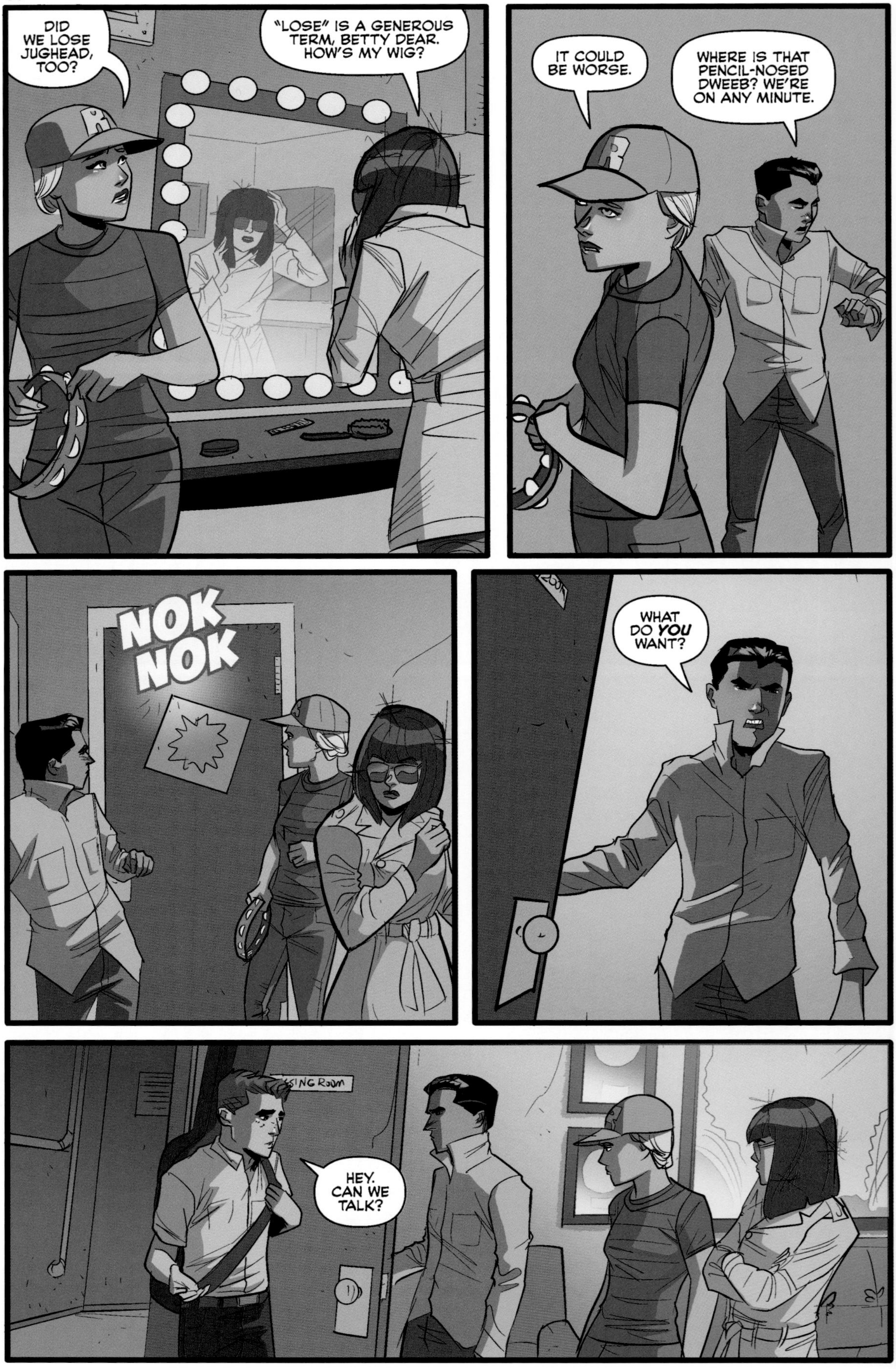
DID WE LOSE JUGHEAD, TOO?
"LOSE" IS A GENEROUS TERM, BETTY DEAR. HOW'S MY WIG?
IT COULD BE WORSE.
WHERE IS THAT PENCIL-NOSED DWEEB? WE'RE ON ANY MINUTE.
NOK NOK
WHAT DO *YOU* WANT?
HEY. CAN WE TALK?

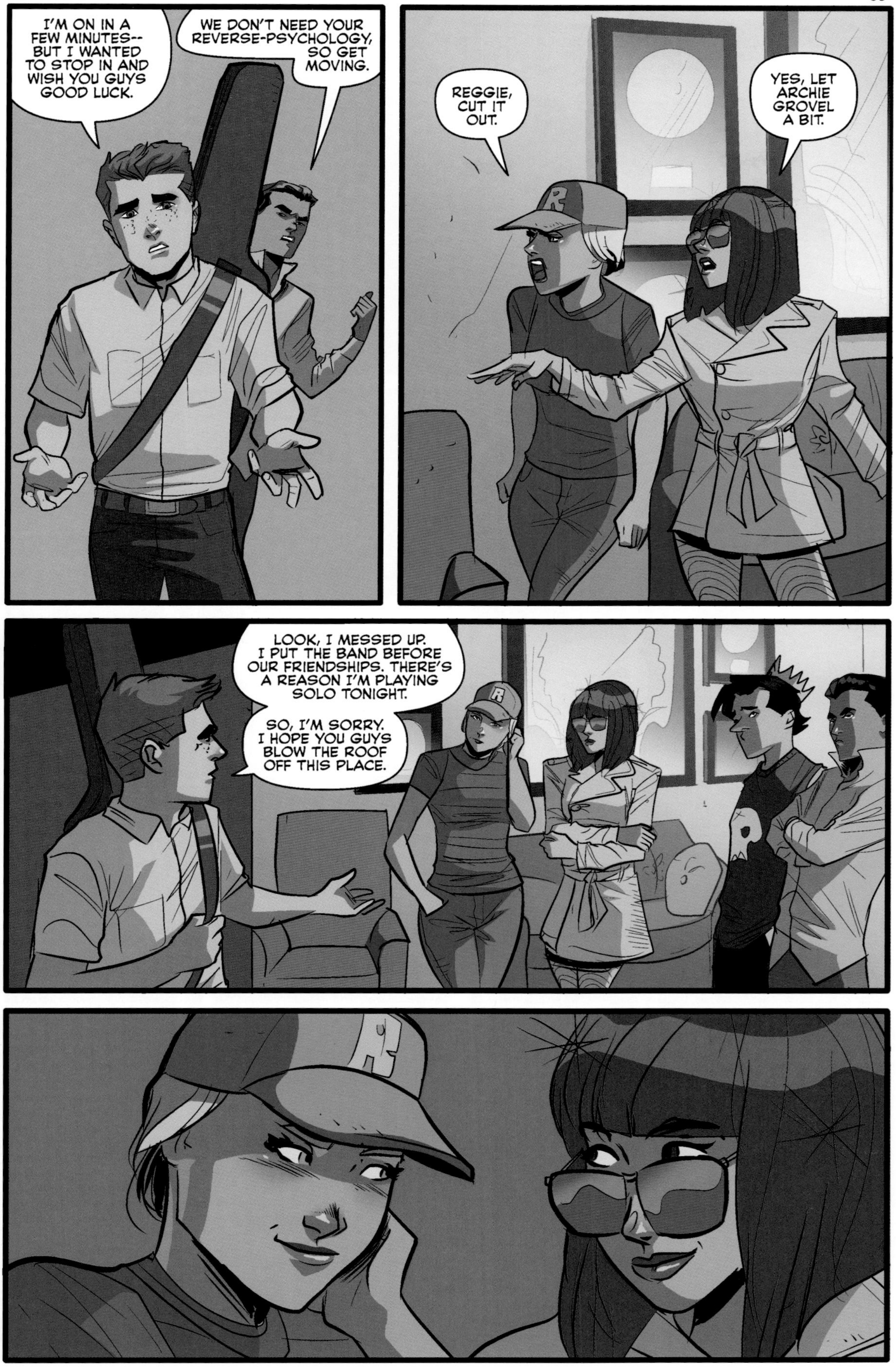
I'M ON IN A FEW MINUTES-- BUT I WANTED TO STOP IN AND WISH YOU GUYS GOOD LUCK.
WE DON'T NEED YOUR REVERSE-PSYCHOLOGY, SO GET MOVING.
REGGIE, CUT IT OUT.
YES, LET ARCHIE GROVEL A BIT.
LOOK, I MESSED UP. I PUT THE BAND BEFORE OUR FRIENDSHIPS. THERE'S A REASON I'M PLAYING SOLO TONIGHT.
SO, I'M SORRY. I HOPE YOU GUYS BLOW THE ROOF OFF THIS PLACE.

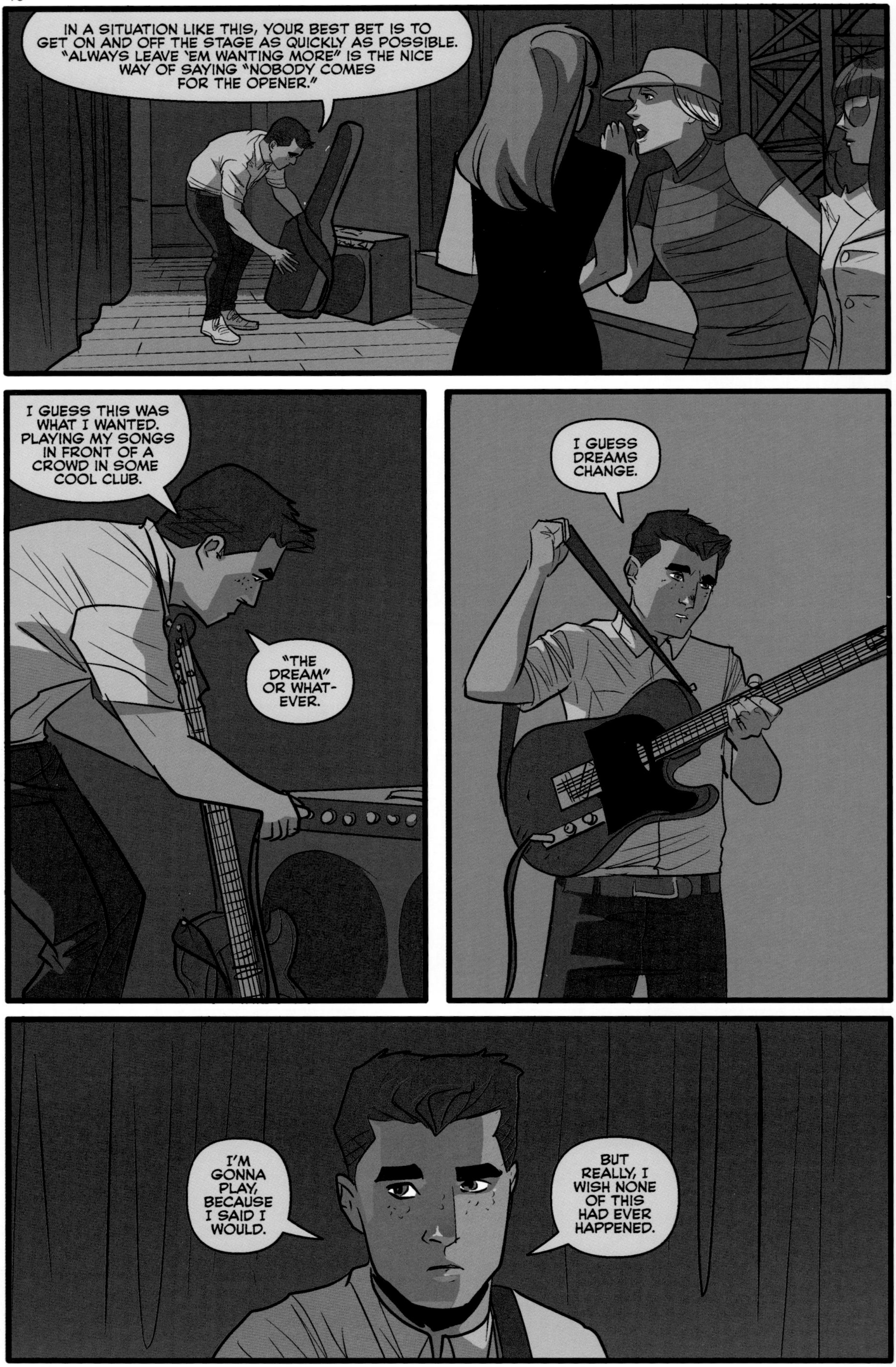
IN A SITUATION LIKE THIS, YOUR BEST BET IS TO GET ON AND OFF THE STAGE AS QUICKLY AS POSSIBLE. "ALWAYS LEAVE 'EM WANTING MORE" IS THE NICE WAY OF SAYING "NOBODY COMES FOR THE OPENER."
I GUESS THIS WAS WHAT I WANTED. PLAYING MY SONGS IN FRONT OF A CROWD IN SOME COOL CLUB.
"THE DREAM" OR WHAT-EVER.
I GUESS DREAMS CHANGE.
I'M GONNA PLAY, BECAUSE I SAID I WOULD.
BUT REALLY, I WISH NONE OF THIS HAD EVER HAPPENED.

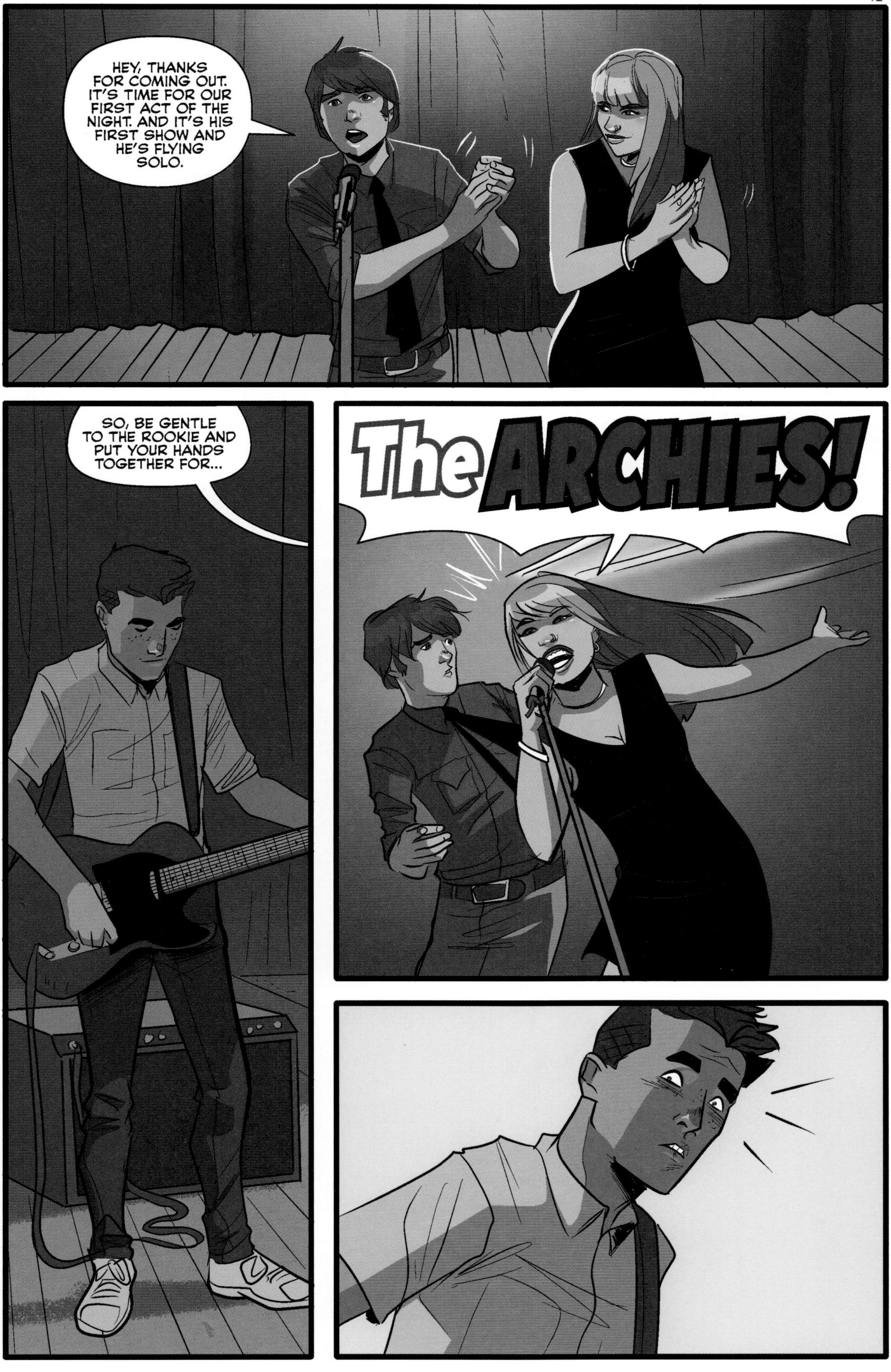
HEY, THANKS FOR COMING OUT. IT'S TIME FOR OUR FIRST ACT OF THE NIGHT. AND IT'S HIS FIRST SHOW AND HE'S FLYING SOLO.
SO, BE GENTLE TO THE ROOKIE AND PUT YOUR HANDS TOGETHER FOR...
The ARCHIES!

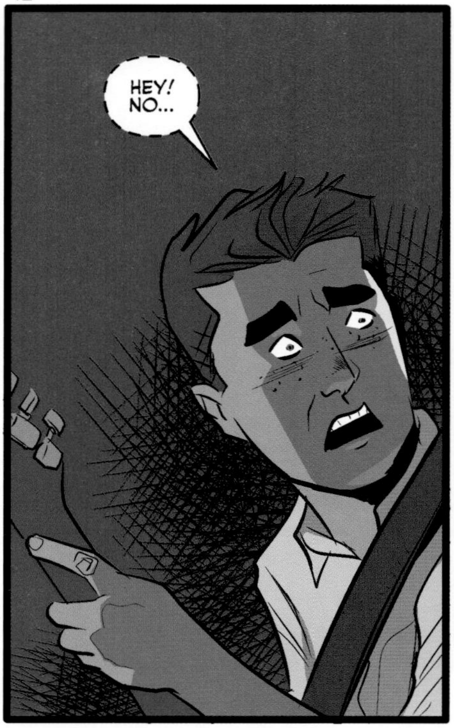
HEY!
NO...

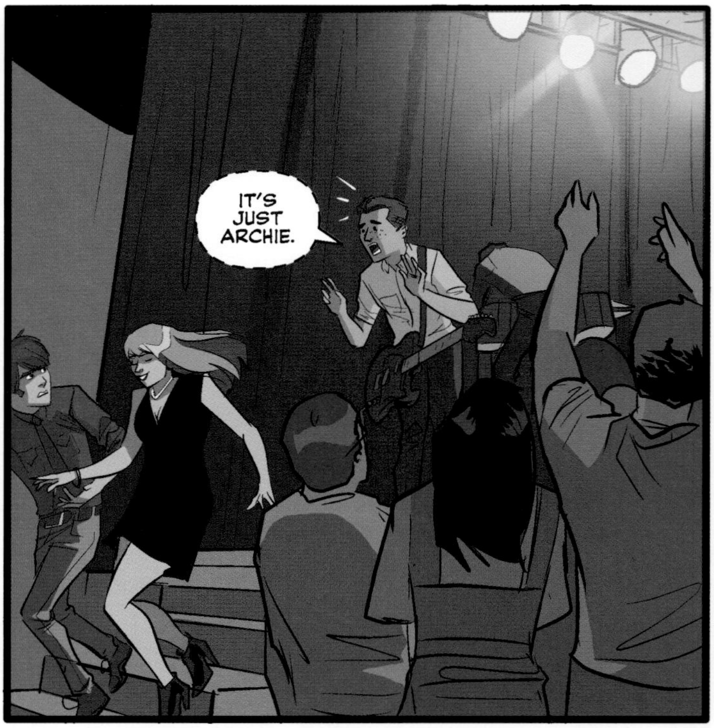
IT'S
JUST
ARCHIE.

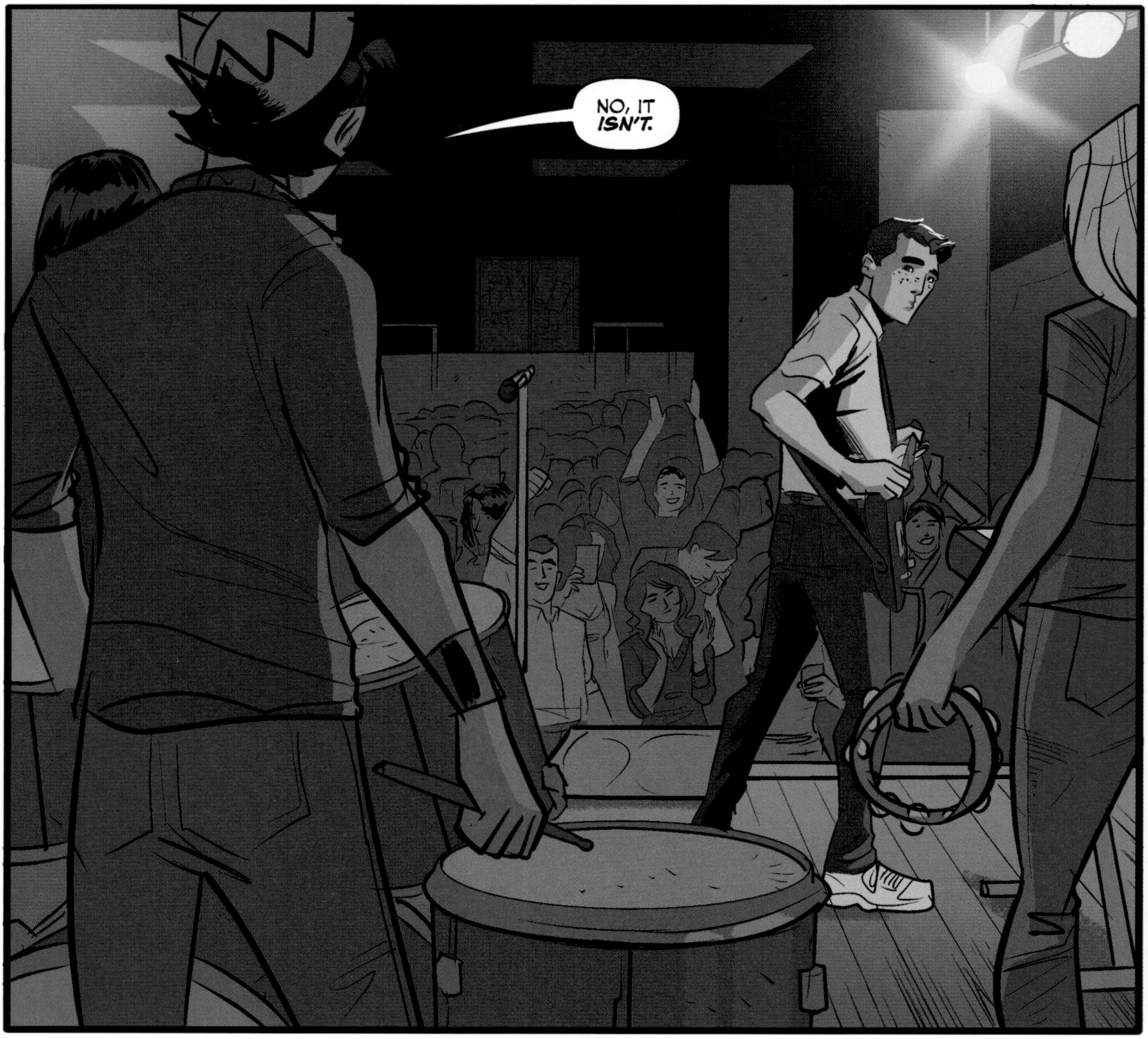
NO, IT
ISN'T.

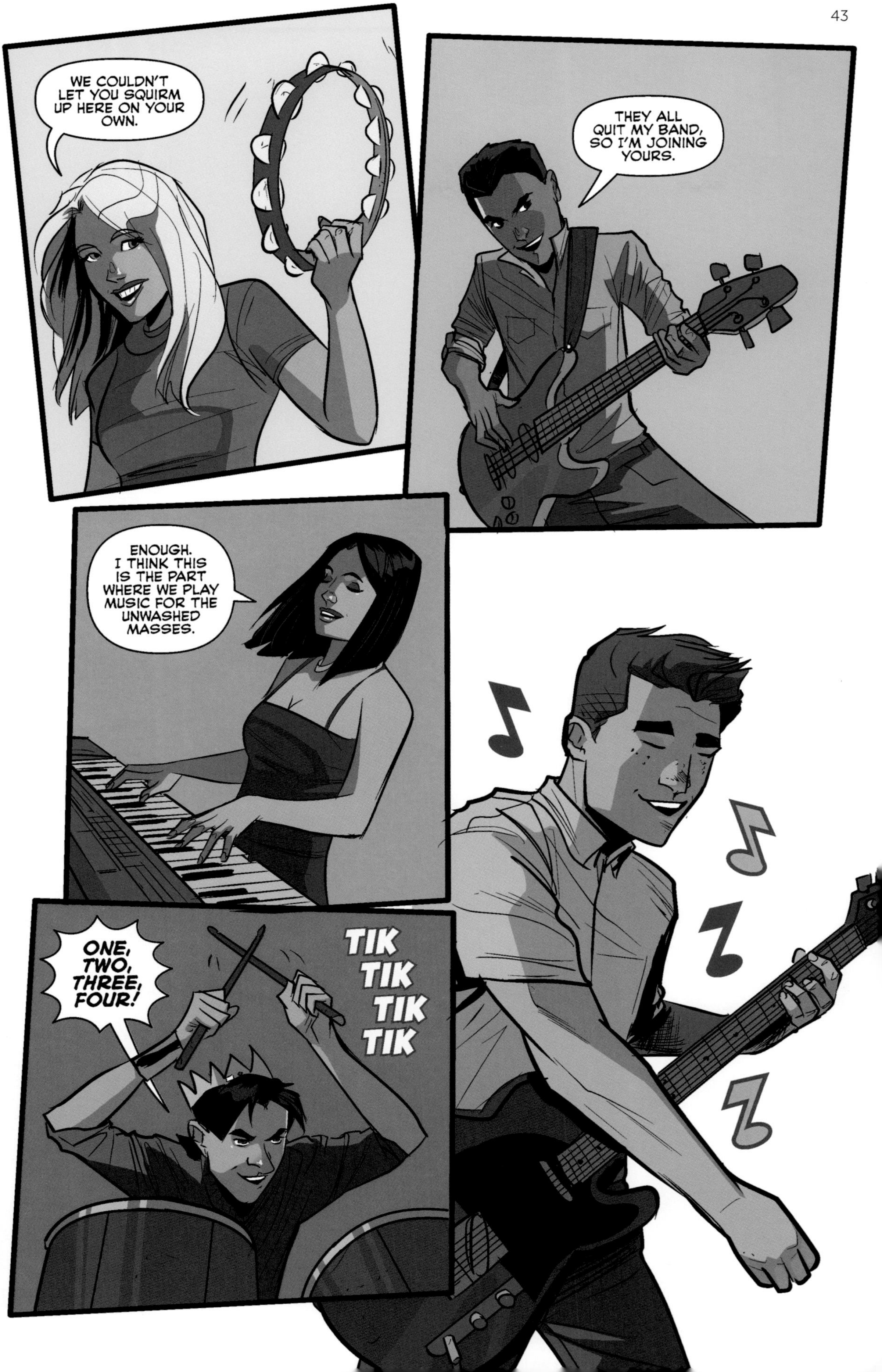
WE COULDN'T LET YOU SQUIRM UP HERE ON YOUR OWN.
THEY ALL QUIT MY BAND, SO I'M JOINING YOURS.
ENOUGH. I THINK THIS IS THE PART WHERE WE PLAY MUSIC FOR THE UNWASHED MASSES.
ONE, TWO, THREE, FOUR!
TIK TIK TIK TIK

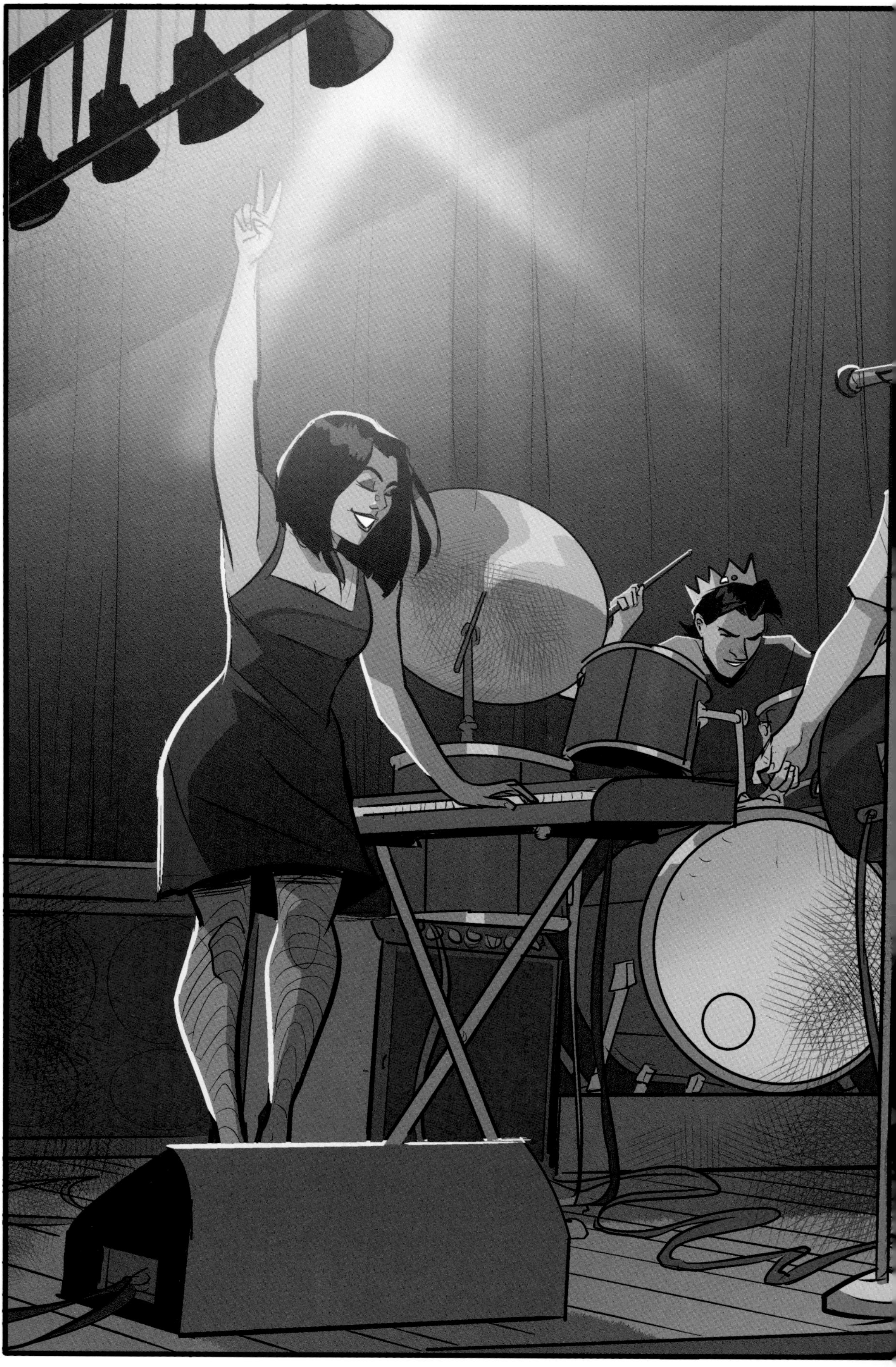

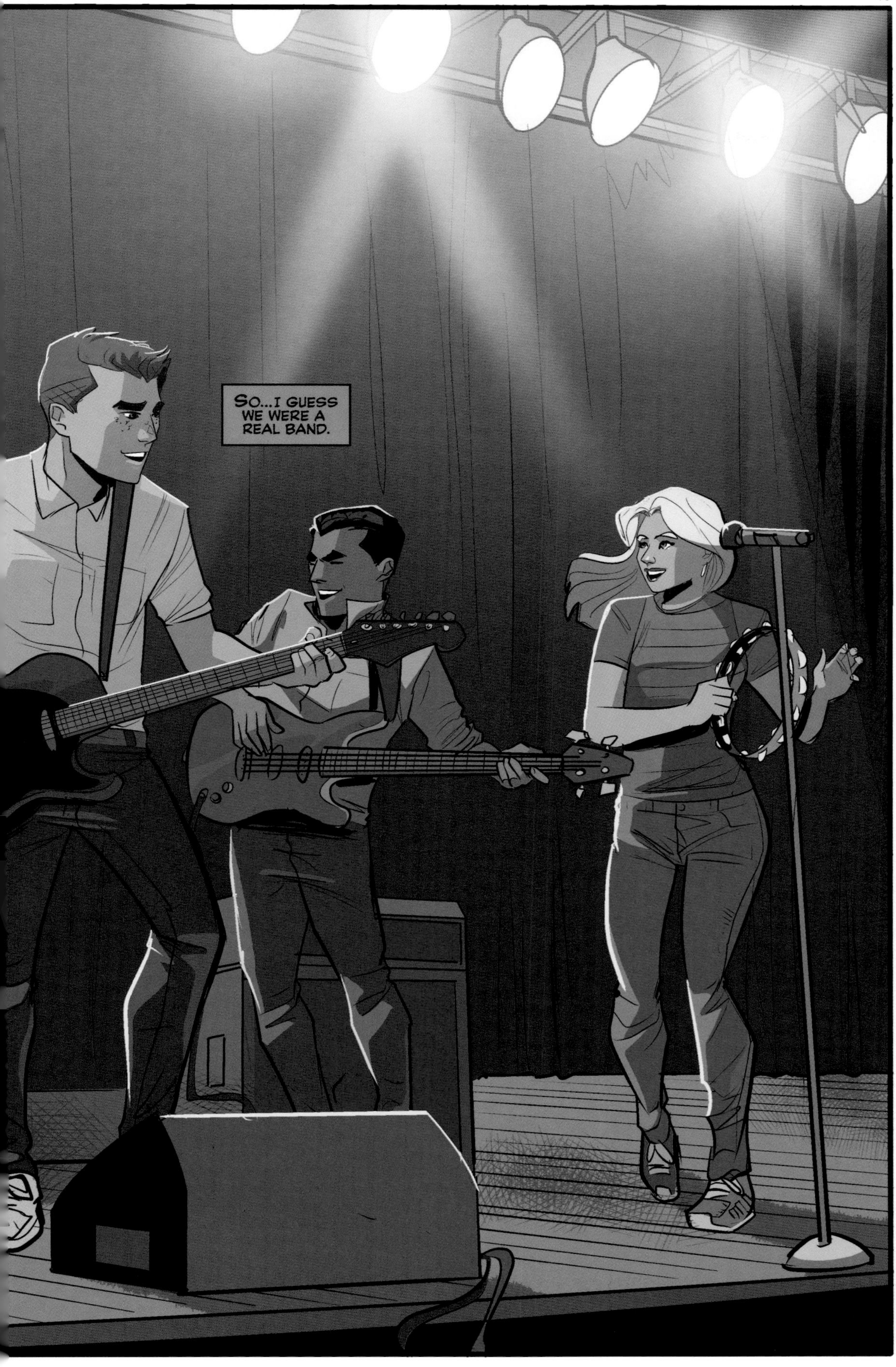
So...I guess we were a real band.

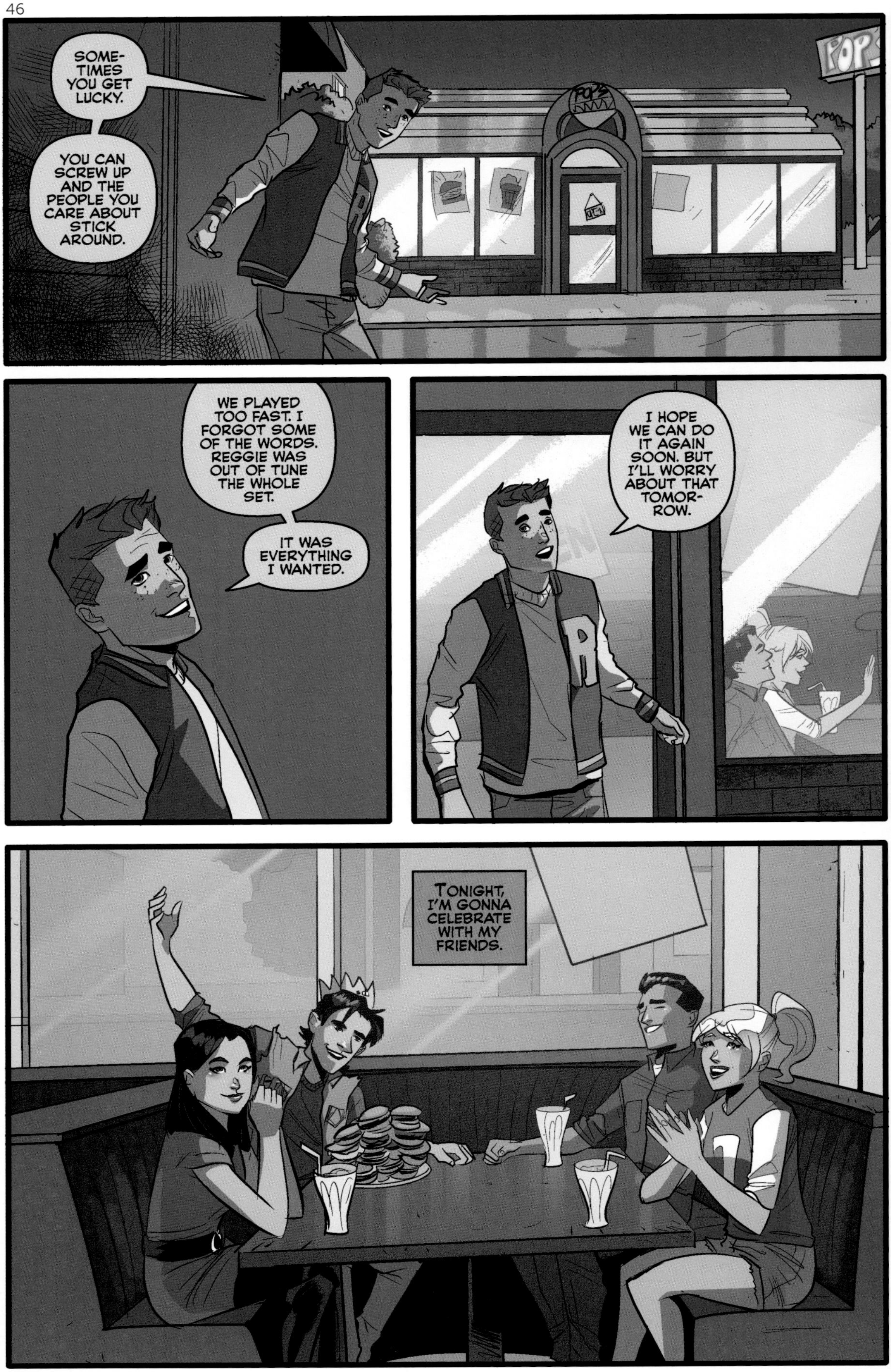
SOME-TIMES YOU GET LUCKY.
YOU CAN SCREW UP AND THE PEOPLE YOU CARE ABOUT STICK AROUND.
WE PLAYED TOO FAST. I FORGOT SOME OF THE WORDS. REGGIE WAS OUT OF TUNE THE WHOLE SET.
IT WAS EVERYTHING I WANTED.
I HOPE WE CAN DO IT AGAIN SOON. BUT I'LL WORRY ABOUT THAT TOMOR-ROW.
TONIGHT, I'M GONNA CELEBRATE WITH MY FRIENDS.

THE
ARCHIES

1: Jaime Hernandez

2: David Mack

3: Audrey Mok

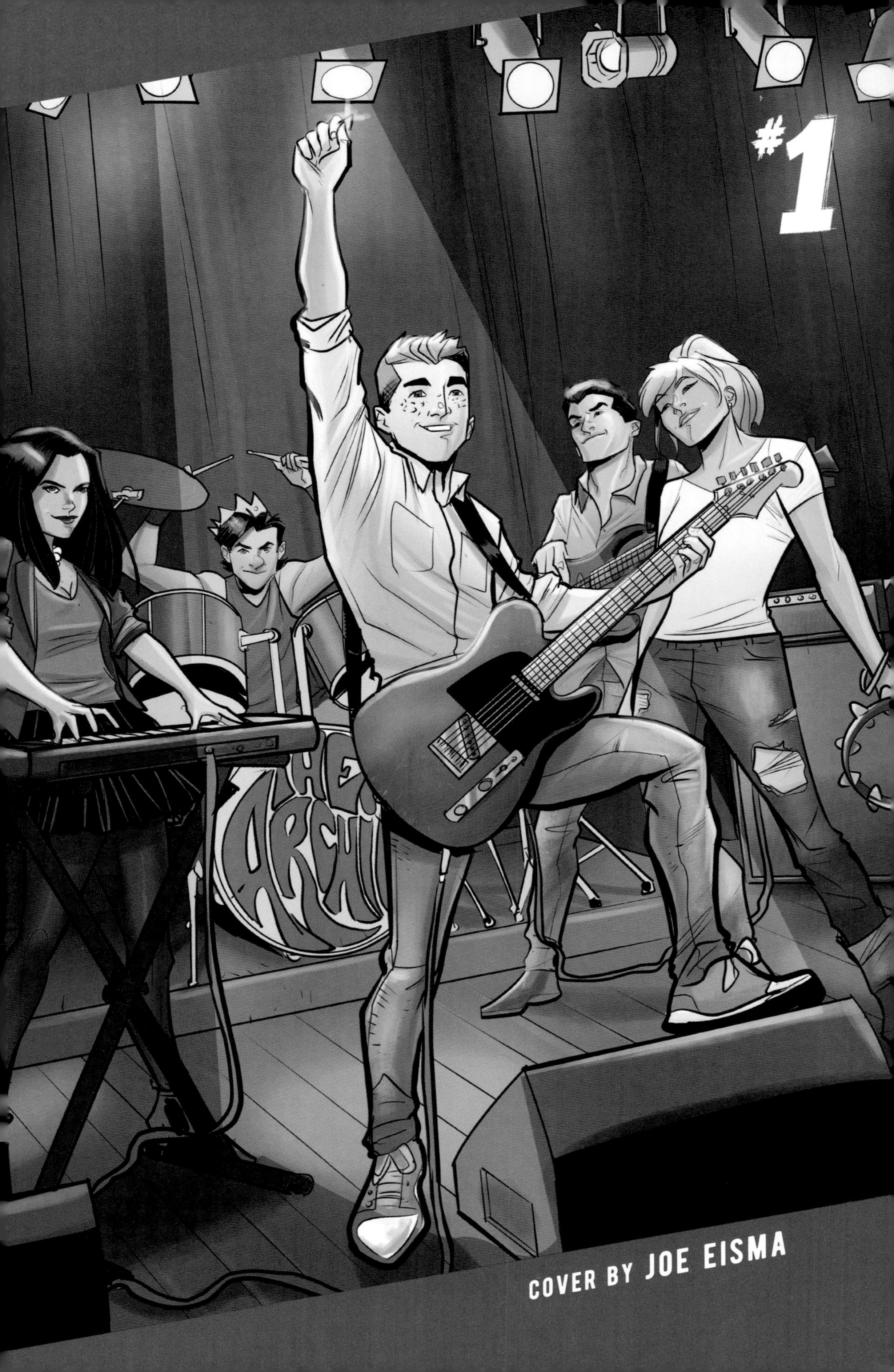
#1

COVER BY JOE EISMA

CHAPTER TWO

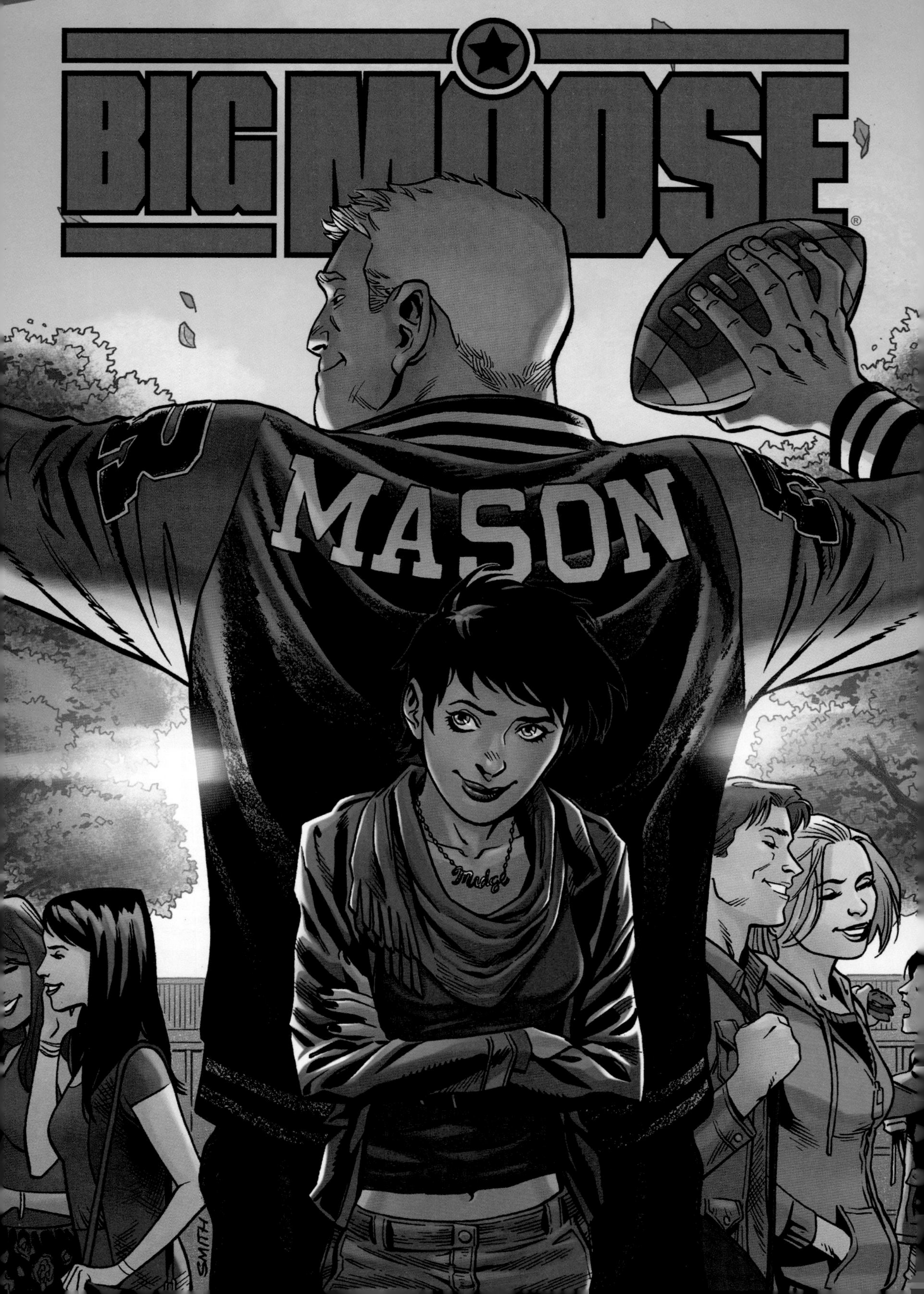

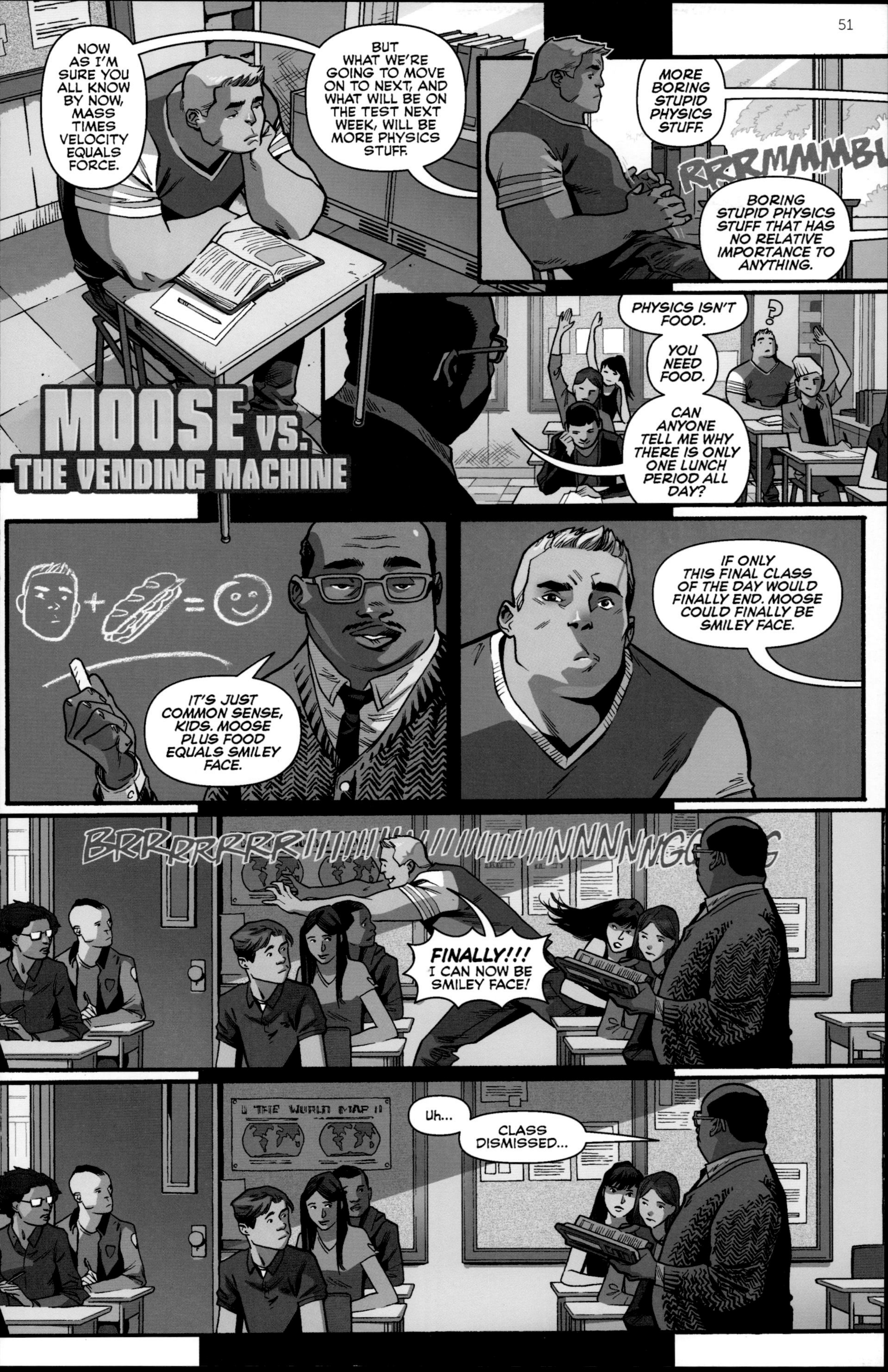
MOOSE VS. THE VENDING MACHINE
NOW AS I'M SURE YOU ALL KNOW BY NOW, MASS TIMES VELOCITY EQUALS FORCE.
BUT WHAT WE'RE GOING TO MOVE ON TO NEXT, AND WHAT WILL BE ON THE TEST NEXT WEEK, WILL BE MORE PHYSICS STUFF.
MORE BORING STUPID PHYSICS STUFF.
RRRMMMBL
BORING STUPID PHYSICS STUFF THAT HAS NO RELATIVE IMPORTANCE TO ANYTHING.
PHYSICS ISN'T FOOD.
YOU NEED FOOD.
CAN ANYONE TELL ME WHY THERE IS ONLY ONE LUNCH PERIOD ALL DAY?
?
IT'S JUST COMMON SENSE, KIDS. MOOSE PLUS FOOD EQUALS SMILEY FACE.
IF ONLY THIS FINAL CLASS OF THE DAY WOULD FINALLY END. MOOSE COULD FINALLY BE SMILEY FACE.
BRRRRRRRIIIIIIIIIIIIIIIIIIIIINNNNNNGG
FINALLY!!! I CAN NOW BE SMILEY FACE!
THE WORLD MAP
Uh...
CLASS DISMISSED...

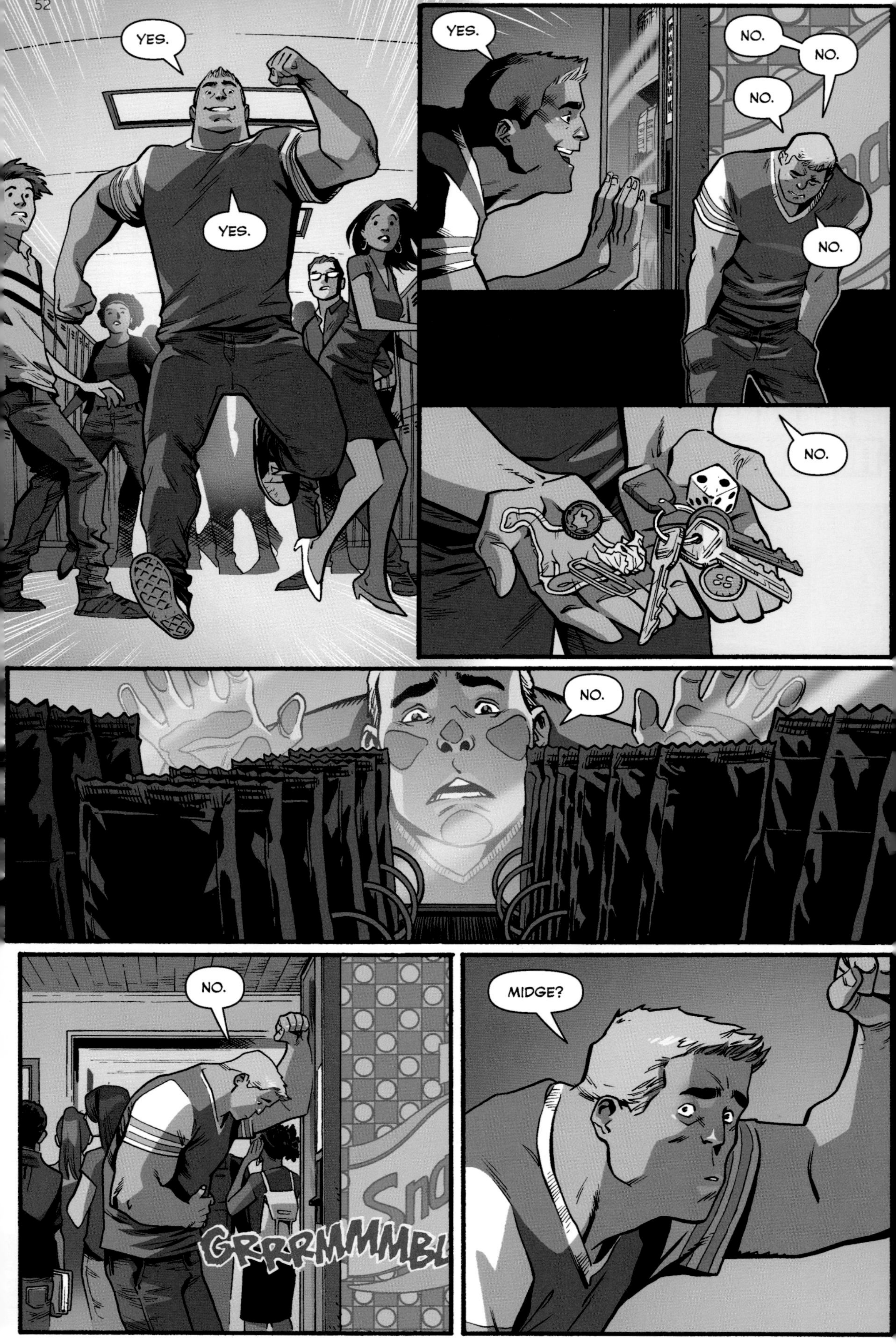
YES.
YES.
YES.
NO.
NO.
NO.
NO.
NO.
NO.
NO.
GRRRMMMMBL
MIDGE?

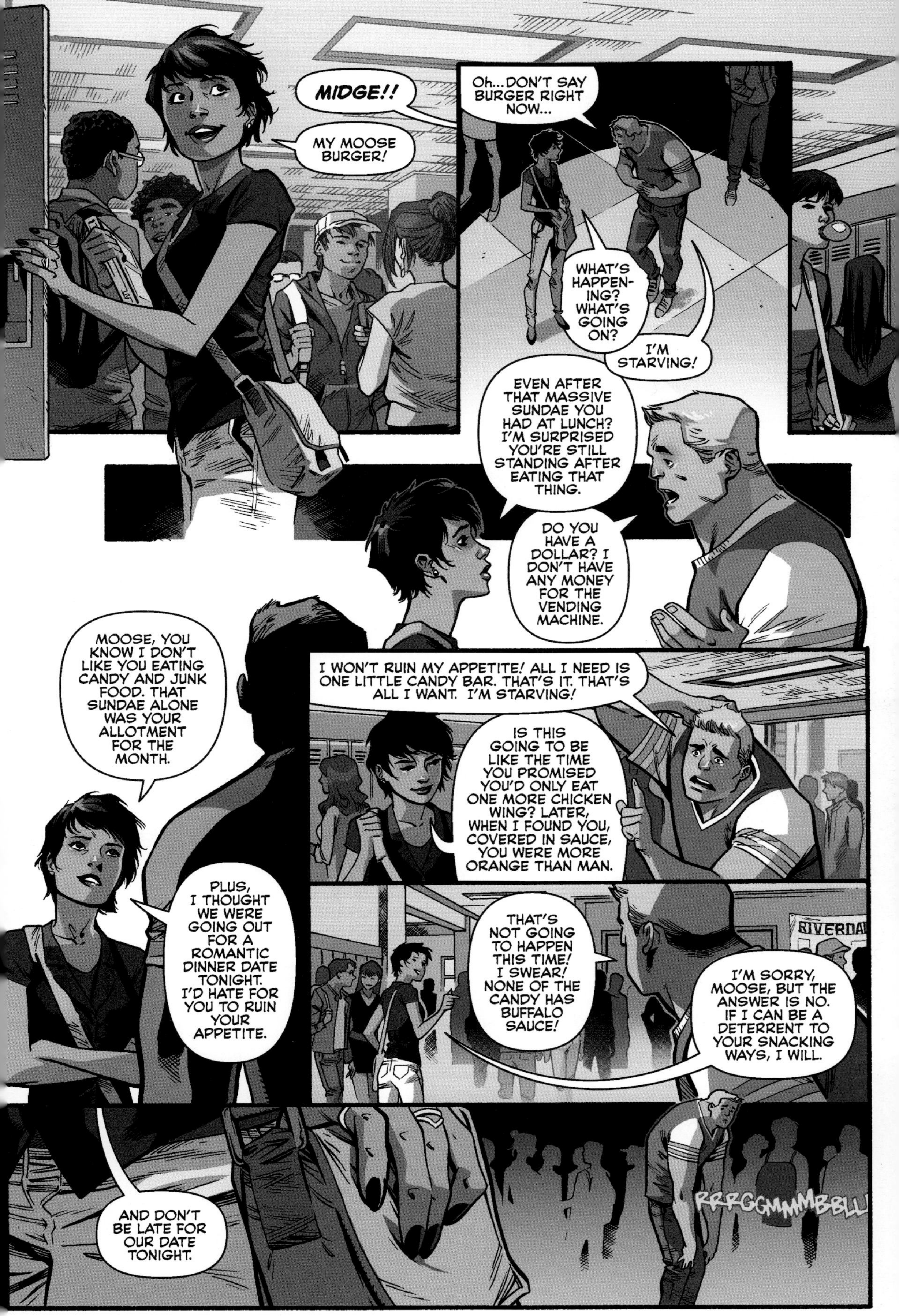
MIDGE!!
MY MOOSE BURGER!
Oh...DON'T SAY BURGER RIGHT NOW...
WHAT'S HAPPEN-ING? WHAT'S GOING ON?
I'M STARVING!
EVEN AFTER THAT MASSIVE SUNDAE YOU HAD AT LUNCH? I'M SURPRISED YOU'RE STILL STANDING AFTER EATING THAT THING.
DO YOU HAVE A DOLLAR? I DON'T HAVE ANY MONEY FOR THE VENDING MACHINE.
MOOSE, YOU KNOW I DON'T LIKE YOU EATING CANDY AND JUNK FOOD. THAT SUNDAE ALONE WAS YOUR ALLOTMENT FOR THE MONTH.
PLUS, I THOUGHT WE WERE GOING OUT FOR A ROMANTIC DINNER DATE TONIGHT. I'D HATE FOR YOU TO RUIN YOUR APPETITE.
I WON'T RUIN MY APPETITE! ALL I NEED IS ONE LITTLE CANDY BAR. THAT'S IT. THAT'S ALL I WANT. I'M STARVING!
IS THIS GOING TO BE LIKE THE TIME YOU PROMISED YOU'D ONLY EAT ONE MORE CHICKEN WING? LATER, WHEN I FOUND YOU, COVERED IN SAUCE, YOU WERE MORE ORANGE THAN MAN.
THAT'S NOT GOING TO HAPPEN THIS TIME! I SWEAR! NONE OF THE CANDY HAS BUFFALO SAUCE!
I'M SORRY, MOOSE, BUT THE ANSWER IS NO. IF I CAN BE A DETERRENT TO YOUR SNACKING WAYS, I WILL.
AND DON'T BE LATE FOR OUR DATE TONIGHT.
RRRGGMMMBBLL

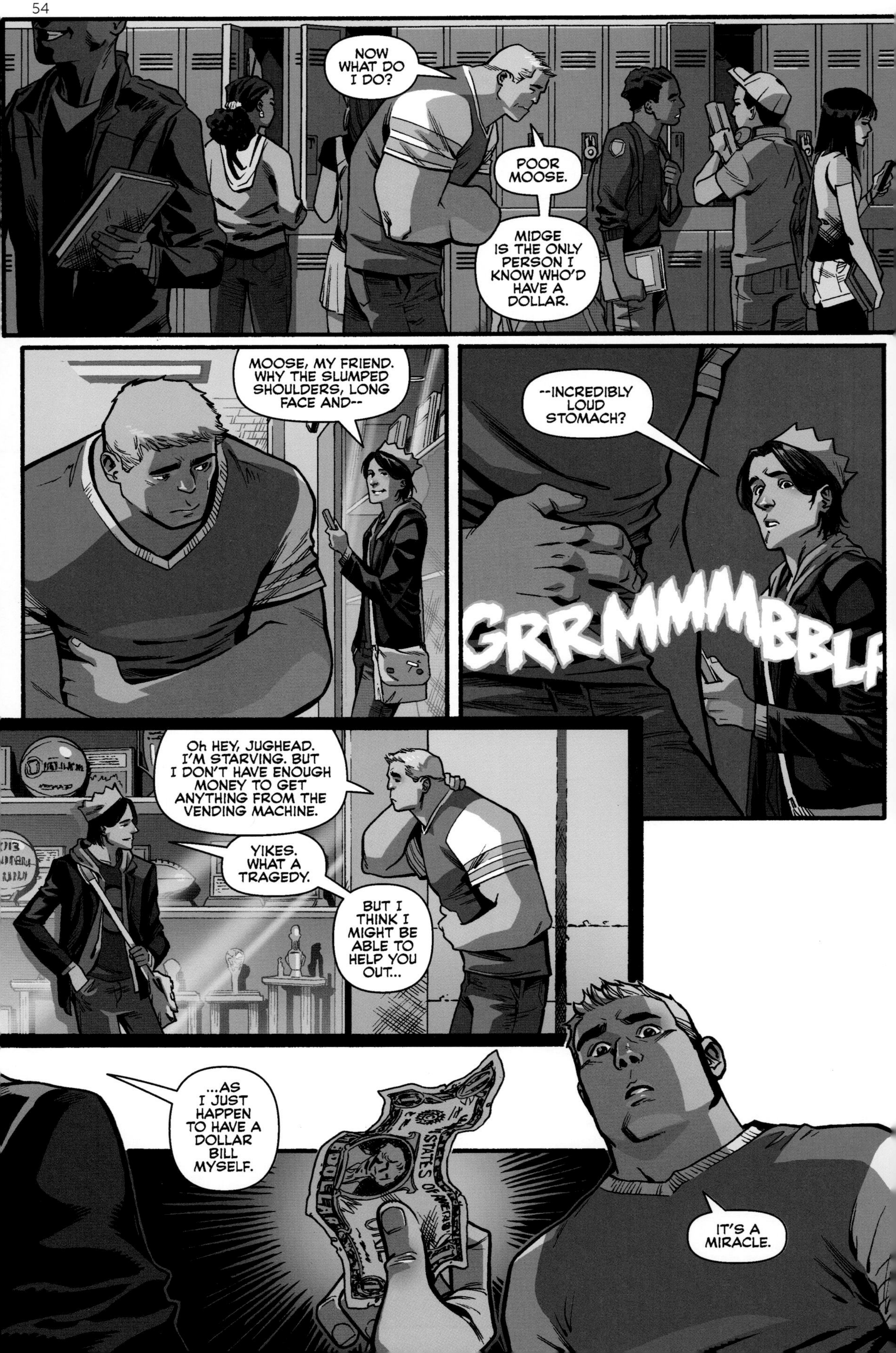
NOW WHAT DO I DO?
POOR MOOSE.
MIDGE IS THE ONLY PERSON I KNOW WHO'D HAVE A DOLLAR.
MOOSE, MY FRIEND. WHY THE SLUMPED SHOULDERS, LONG FACE AND--
--INCREDIBLY LOUD STOMACH?
GRRMMMMBBLF
Oh HEY, JUGHEAD. I'M STARVING. BUT I DON'T HAVE ENOUGH MONEY TO GET ANYTHING FROM THE VENDING MACHINE.
YIKES. WHAT A TRAGEDY.
BUT I THINK I MIGHT BE ABLE TO HELP YOU OUT...
...AS I JUST HAPPEN TO HAVE A DOLLAR BILL MYSELF.
IT'S A MIRACLE.

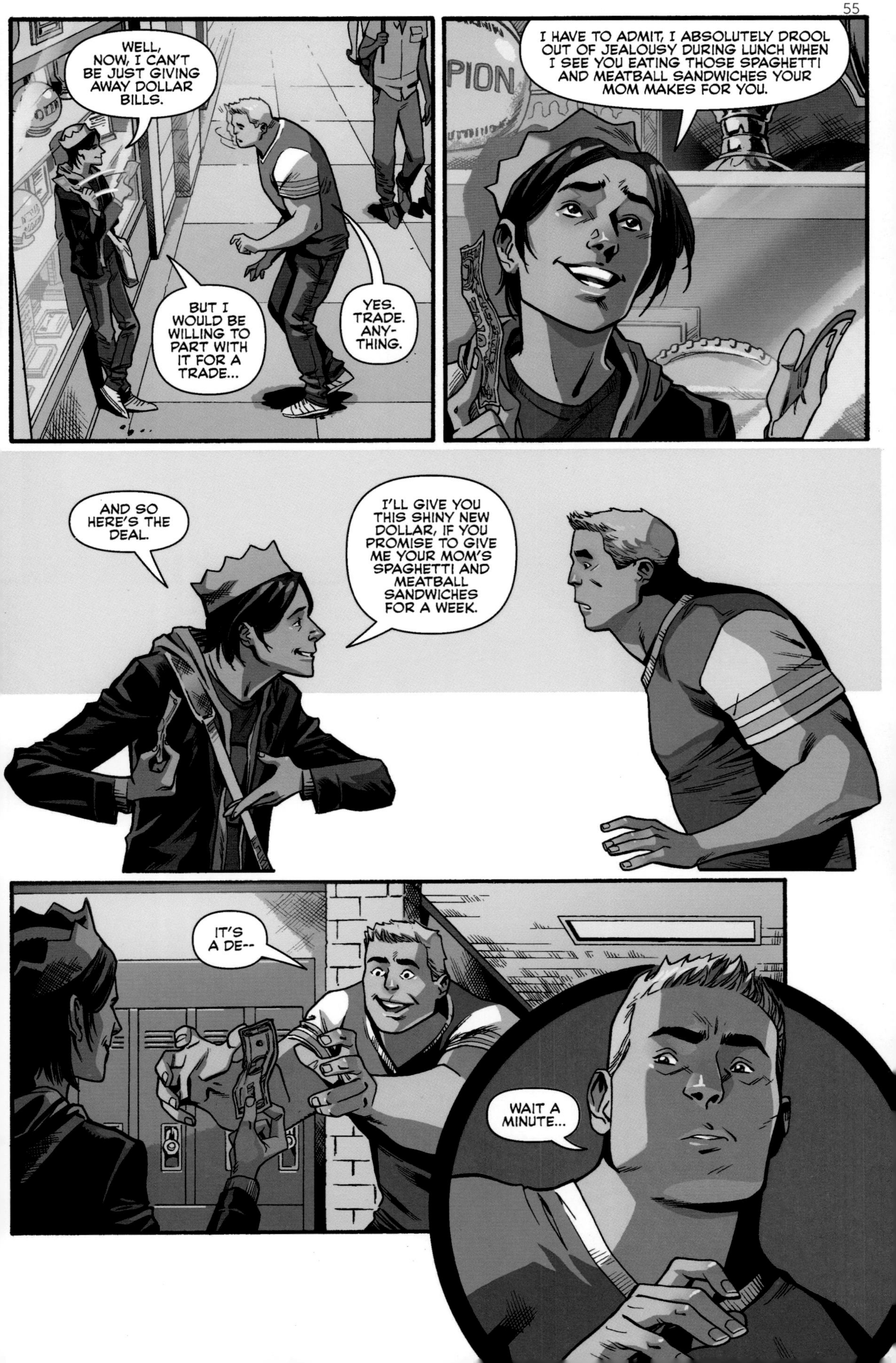
WELL, NOW, I CAN'T BE JUST GIVING AWAY DOLLAR BILLS.
BUT I WOULD BE WILLING TO PART WITH IT FOR A TRADE...
YES. TRADE. ANY-THING.
I HAVE TO ADMIT, I ABSOLUTELY DROOL OUT OF JEALOUSY DURING LUNCH WHEN I SEE YOU EATING THOSE SPAGHETTI AND MEATBALL SANDWICHES YOUR MOM MAKES FOR YOU.
AND SO HERE'S THE DEAL.
I'LL GIVE YOU THIS SHINY NEW DOLLAR, IF YOU PROMISE TO GIVE ME YOUR MOM'S SPAGHETTI AND MEATBALL SANDWICHES FOR A WEEK.
IT'S A DE--
WAIT A MINUTE...

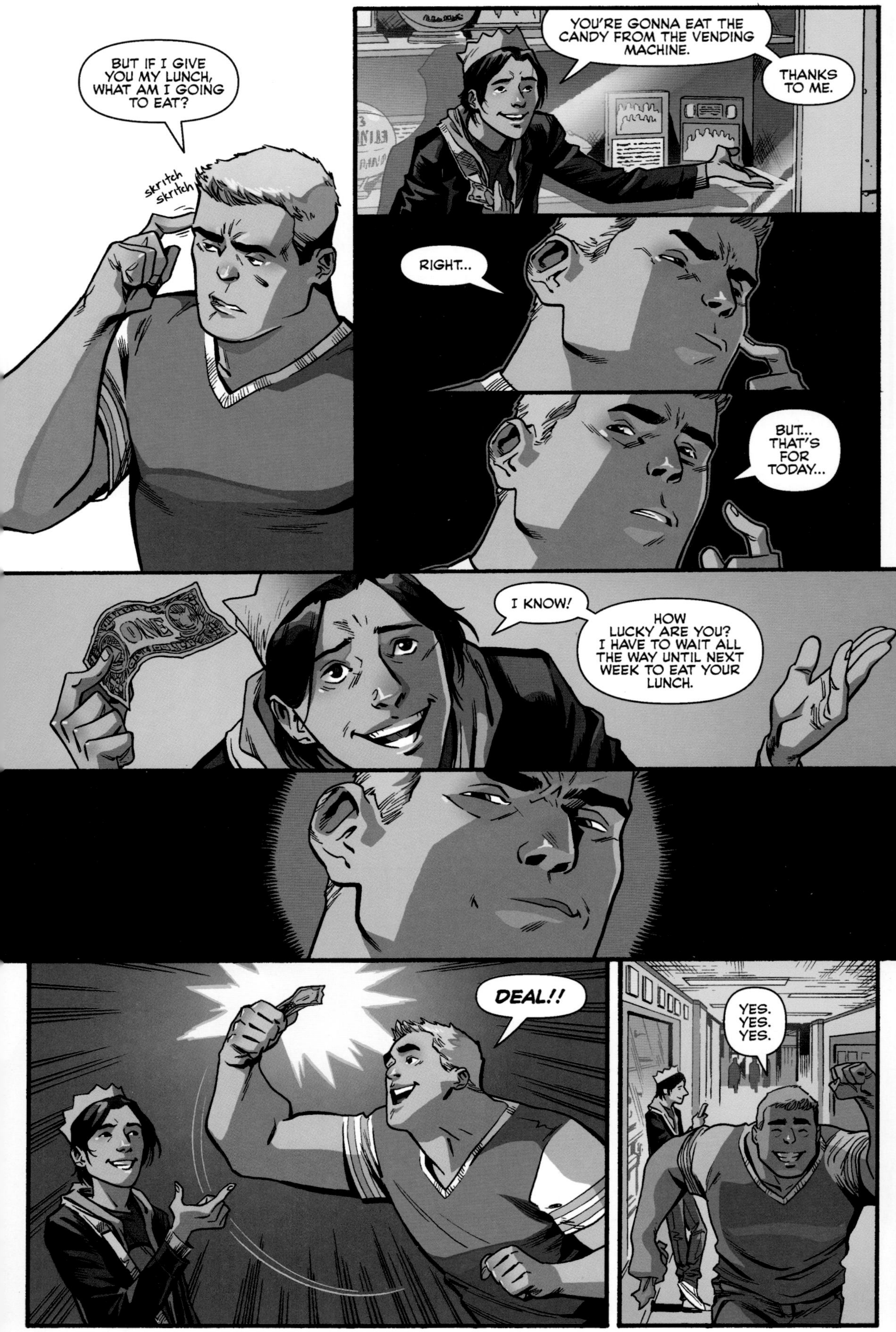
BUT IF I GIVE YOU MY LUNCH, WHAT AM I GOING TO EAT?
skritch skritch
YOU'RE GONNA EAT THE CANDY FROM THE VENDING MACHINE.
THANKS TO ME.
RIGHT...
BUT... THAT'S FOR TODAY...
I KNOW!
HOW LUCKY ARE YOU? I HAVE TO WAIT ALL THE WAY UNTIL NEXT WEEK TO EAT YOUR LUNCH.
DEAL!!
YES. YES. YES.

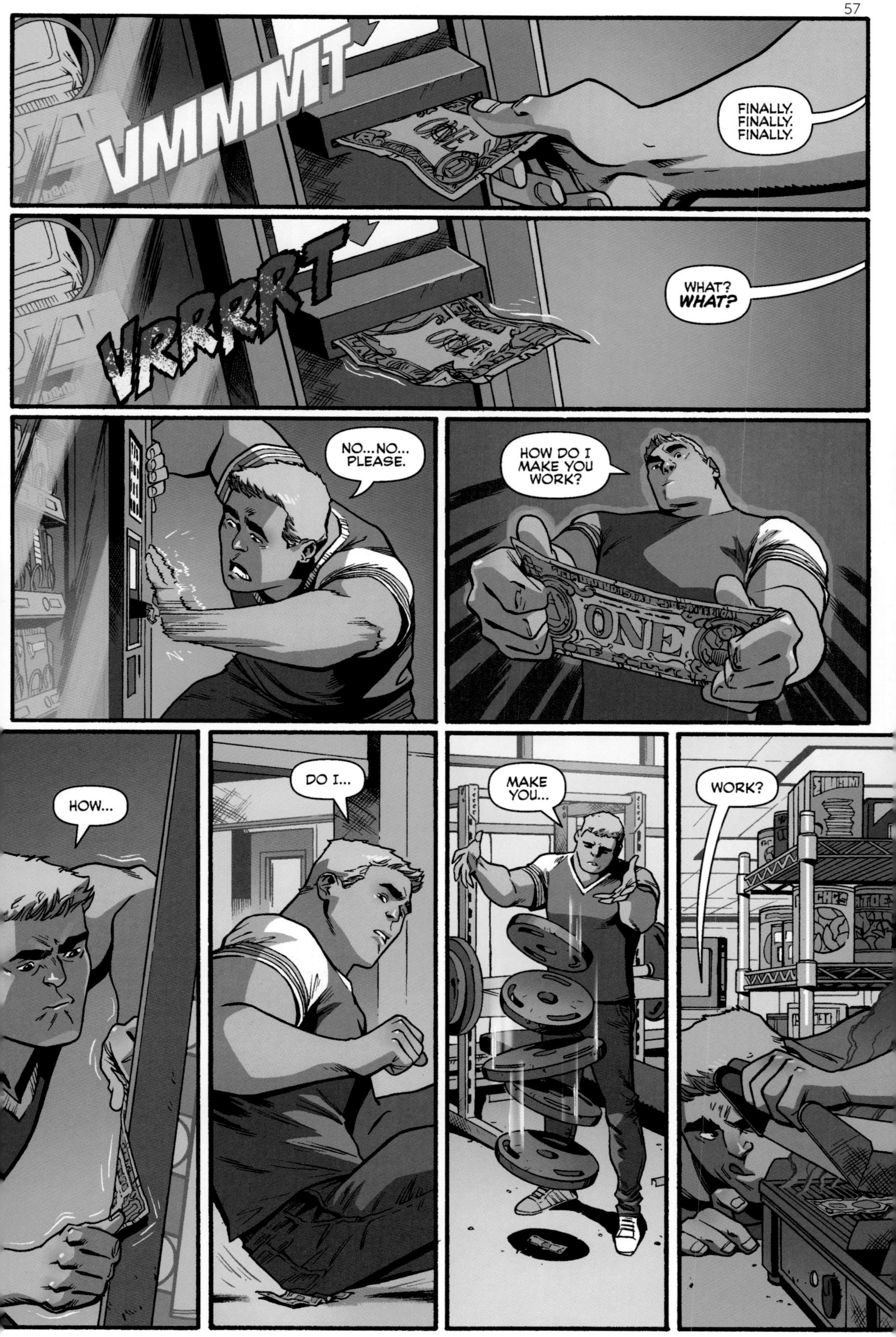
VMMMT
FINALLY. FINALLY. FINALLY.
VRRRRT
WHAT? *WHAT?*
NO...NO... PLEASE.
HOW DO I MAKE YOU WORK?
ONE
HOW...
DO I...
MAKE YOU...
WORK?

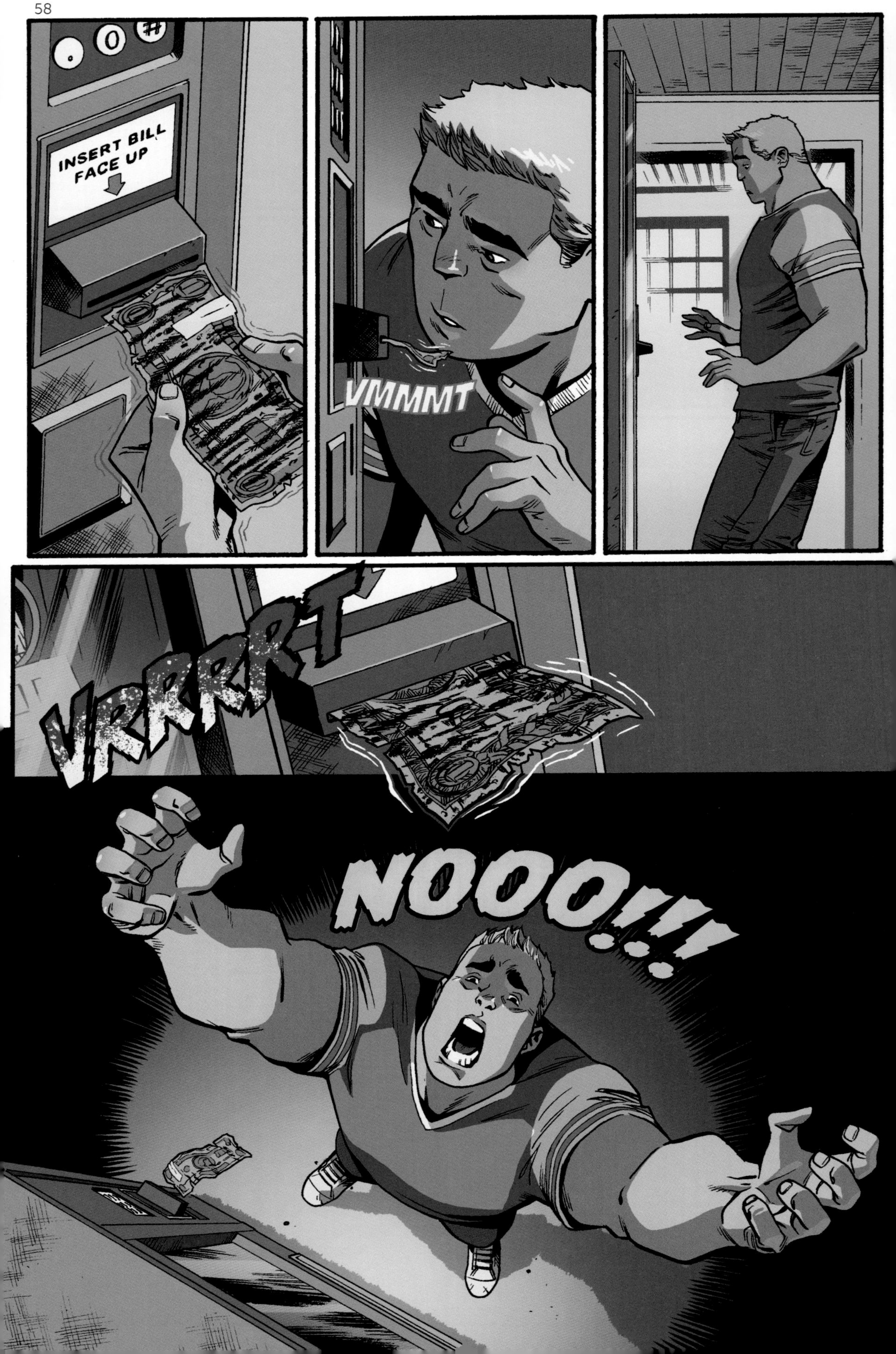
INSERT BILL
FACE UP
VMMMT
VRRRRT
NOOO!!!

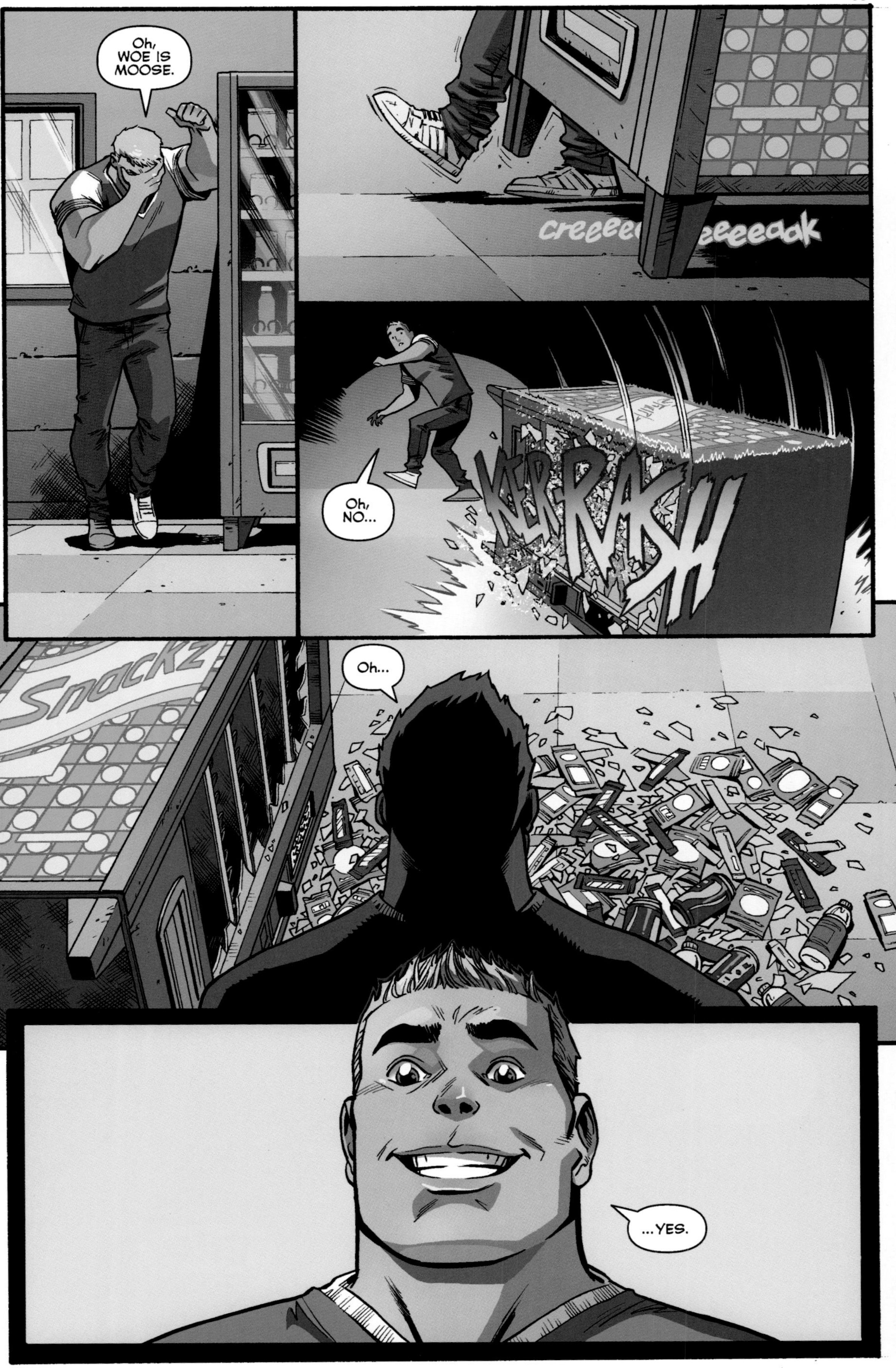
Oh, WOE IS MOOSE.
creeee
eeeeeaak
Oh, NO...
KER-RASH
Snackz
Oh...
...YES.

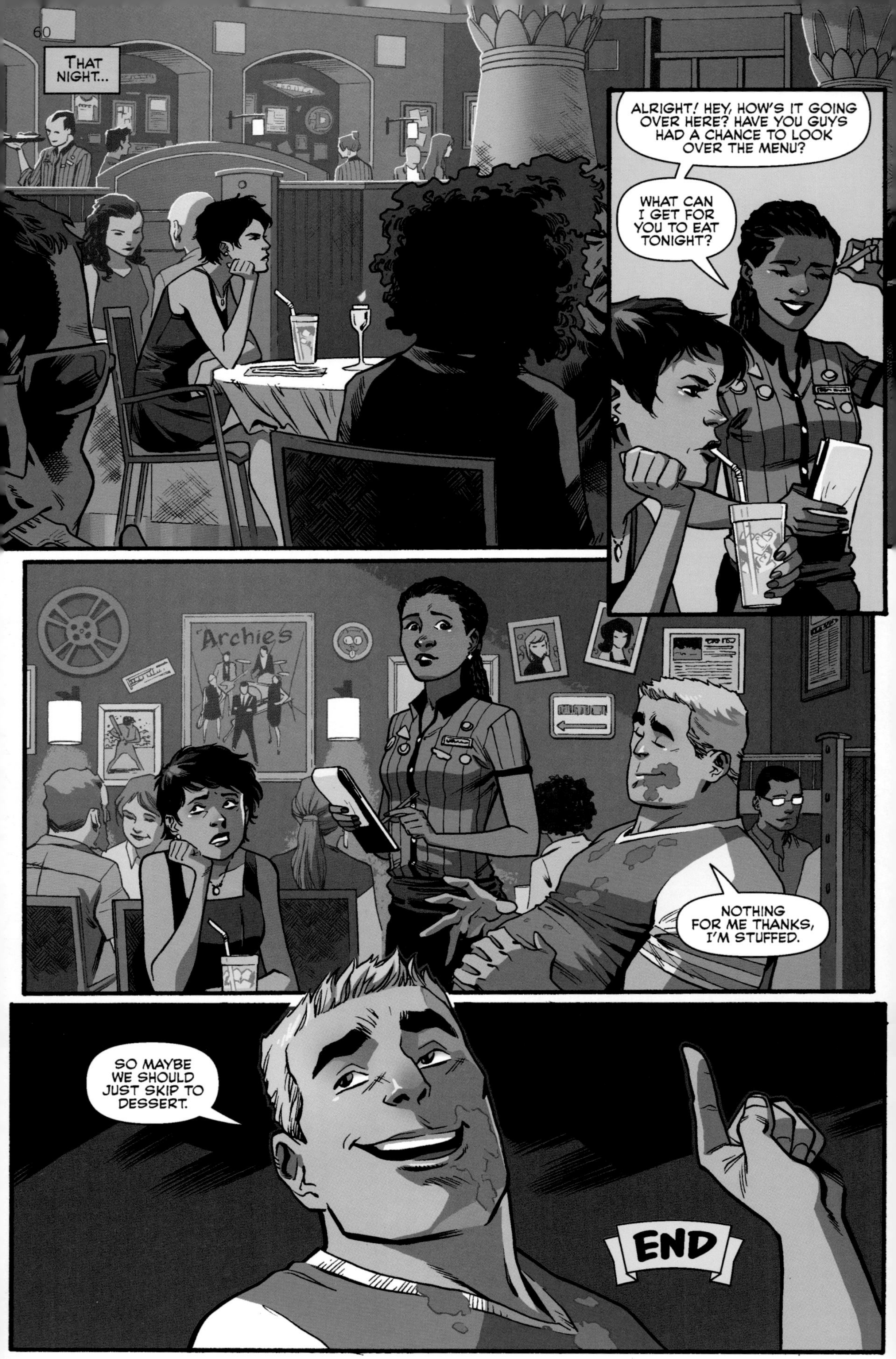
THAT NIGHT...
ALRIGHT! HEY, HOW'S IT GOING OVER HERE? HAVE YOU GUYS HAD A CHANCE TO LOOK OVER THE MENU?
WHAT CAN I GET FOR YOU TO EAT TONIGHT?
Archie's
NOTHING FOR ME THANKS, I'M STUFFED.
SO MAYBE WE SHOULD JUST SKIP TO DESSERT.
END

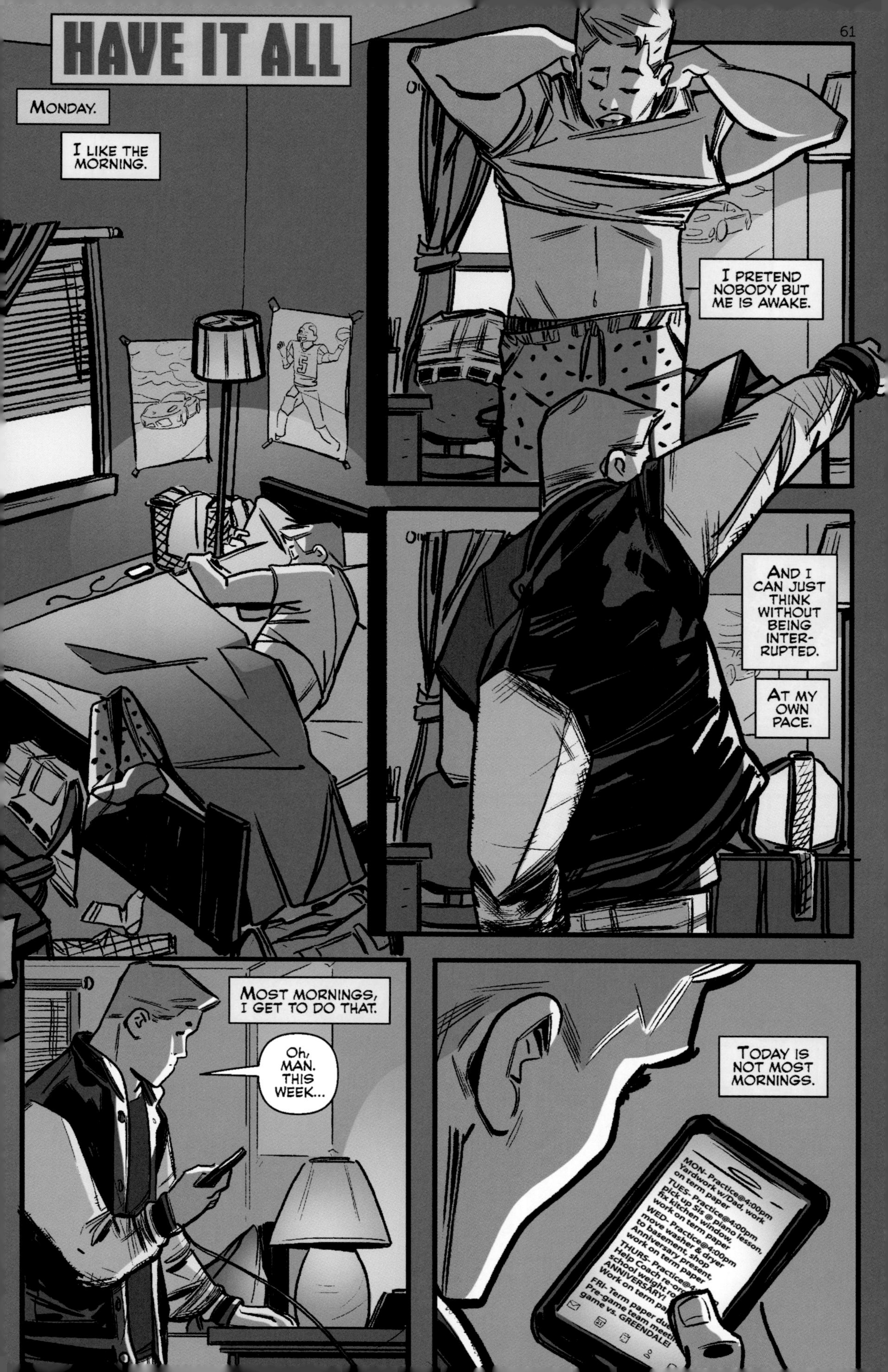
HAVE IT ALL
MONDAY.
I LIKE THE MORNING.
I PRETEND NOBODY BUT ME IS AWAKE.
AND I CAN JUST THINK WITHOUT BEING INTER-RUPTED.
AT MY OWN PACE.
MOST MORNINGS, I GET TO DO THAT.
OH, MAN. THIS WEEK...
TODAY IS NOT MOST MORNINGS.
MON- Practice@4:00pm
Yardwork w/Dad, work on term paper
TUES- Practice@4:00pm
pick up Sis @ piano lesson,
fix kitchen window,
work on term paper
WED- Practice@4:00pm
move washer & dryer to basement, shop
Anniversary present,
work on term paper
ANNIVERSARY!
Pre-game team meeti
game vs. GREENDALE!

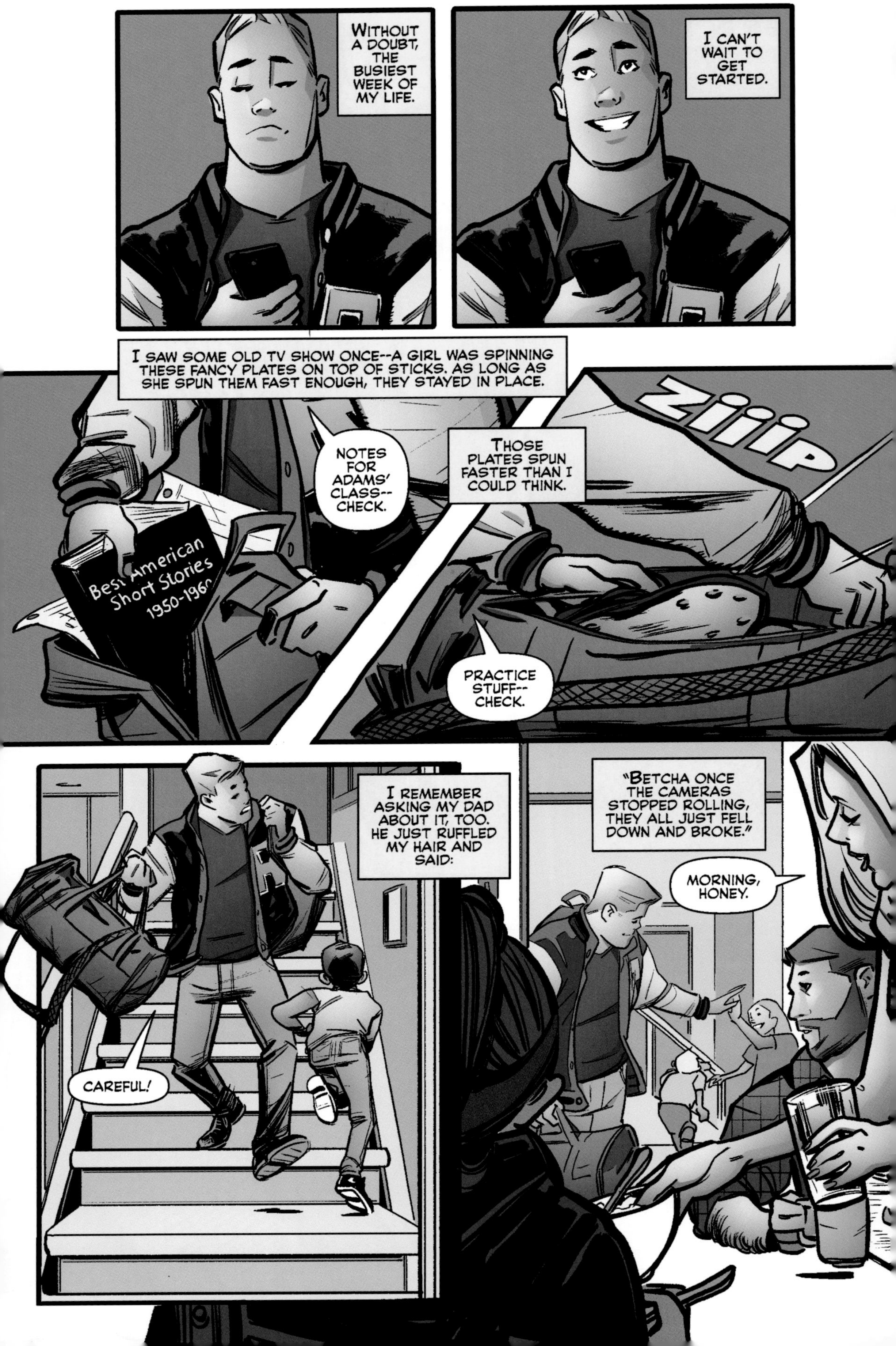
WITHOUT A DOUBT, THE BUSIEST WEEK OF MY LIFE.
I CAN'T WAIT TO GET STARTED.
I SAW SOME OLD TV SHOW ONCE--A GIRL WAS SPINNING THESE FANCY PLATES ON TOP OF STICKS. AS LONG AS SHE SPUN THEM FAST ENOUGH, THEY STAYED IN PLACE.
NOTES FOR ADAMS' CLASS--CHECK.
Best American Short Stories 1950-1960
THOSE PLATES SPUN FASTER THAN I COULD THINK.
ZIIIP
PRACTICE STUFF--CHECK.
I REMEMBER ASKING MY DAD ABOUT IT, TOO. HE JUST RUFFLED MY HAIR AND SAID:
CAREFUL!
"BETCHA ONCE THE CAMERAS STOPPED ROLLING, THEY ALL JUST FELL DOWN AND BROKE."
MORNING, HONEY.

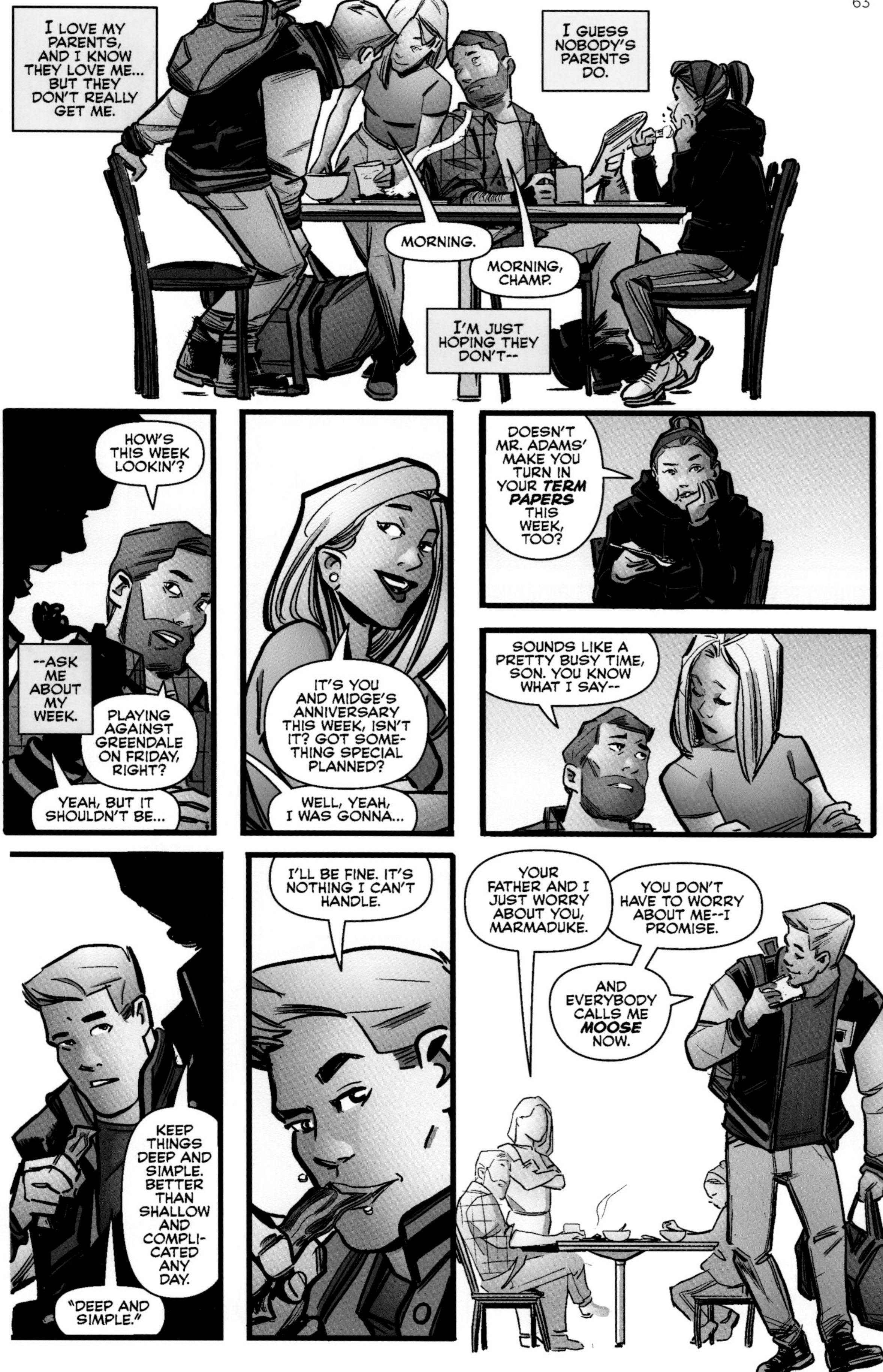
I LOVE MY PARENTS, AND I KNOW THEY LOVE ME... BUT THEY DON'T REALLY GET ME.
I GUESS NOBODY'S PARENTS DO.
MORNING.
MORNING, CHAMP.
I'M JUST HOPING THEY DON'T--
HOW'S THIS WEEK LOOKIN'?
--ASK ME ABOUT MY WEEK.
PLAYING AGAINST GREENDALE ON FRIDAY, RIGHT?
YEAH, BUT IT SHOULDN'T BE...
IT'S YOU AND MIDGE'S ANNIVERSARY THIS WEEK, ISN'T IT? GOT SOMETHING SPECIAL PLANNED?
WELL, YEAH, I WAS GONNA...
DOESN'T MR. ADAMS' MAKE YOU TURN IN YOUR ***TERM PAPERS*** THIS WEEK, TOO?
SOUNDS LIKE A PRETTY BUSY TIME, SON. YOU KNOW WHAT I SAY--
KEEP THINGS DEEP AND SIMPLE. BETTER THAN SHALLOW AND COMPLICATED ANY DAY.
"DEEP AND SIMPLE."
I'LL BE FINE. IT'S NOTHING I CAN'T HANDLE.
YOUR FATHER AND I JUST WORRY ABOUT YOU, MARMADUKE.
YOU DON'T HAVE TO WORRY ABOUT ME--I PROMISE.
AND EVERYBODY CALLS ME ***MOOSE*** NOW.

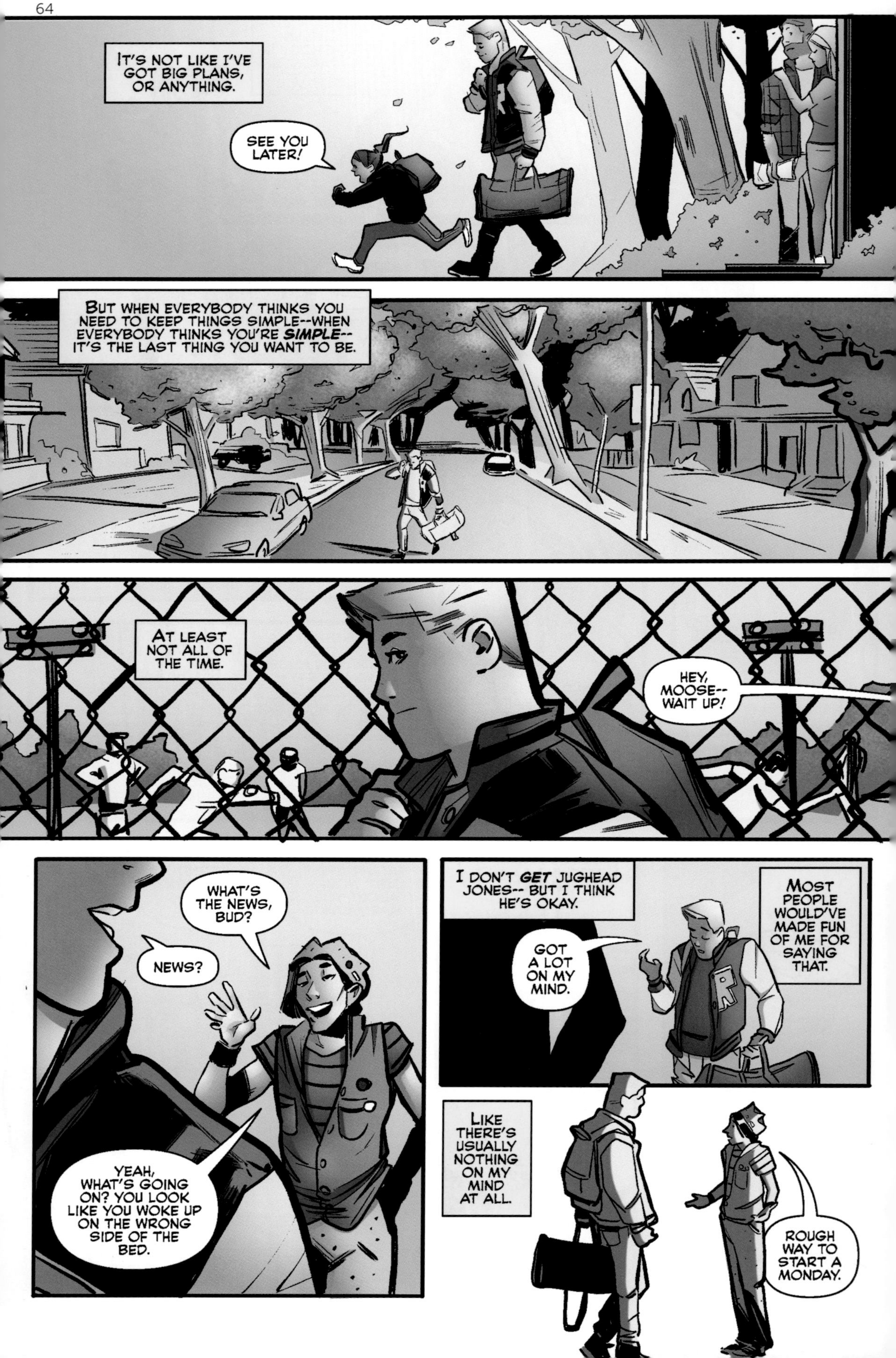
IT'S NOT LIKE I'VE GOT BIG PLANS, OR ANYTHING.
SEE YOU LATER!
BUT WHEN EVERYBODY THINKS YOU NEED TO KEEP THINGS SIMPLE--WHEN EVERYBODY THINKS YOU'RE *SIMPLE*-- IT'S THE LAST THING YOU WANT TO BE.
AT LEAST NOT ALL OF THE TIME.
HEY, MOOSE-- WAIT UP!
WHAT'S THE NEWS, BUD?
NEWS?
YEAH, WHAT'S GOING ON? YOU LOOK LIKE YOU WOKE UP ON THE WRONG SIDE OF THE BED.
I DON'T *GET* JUGHEAD JONES-- BUT I THINK HE'S OKAY.
GOT A LOT ON MY MIND.
MOST PEOPLE WOULD'VE MADE FUN OF ME FOR SAYING THAT.
LIKE THERE'S USUALLY NOTHING ON MY MIND AT ALL.
ROUGH WAY TO START A MONDAY.

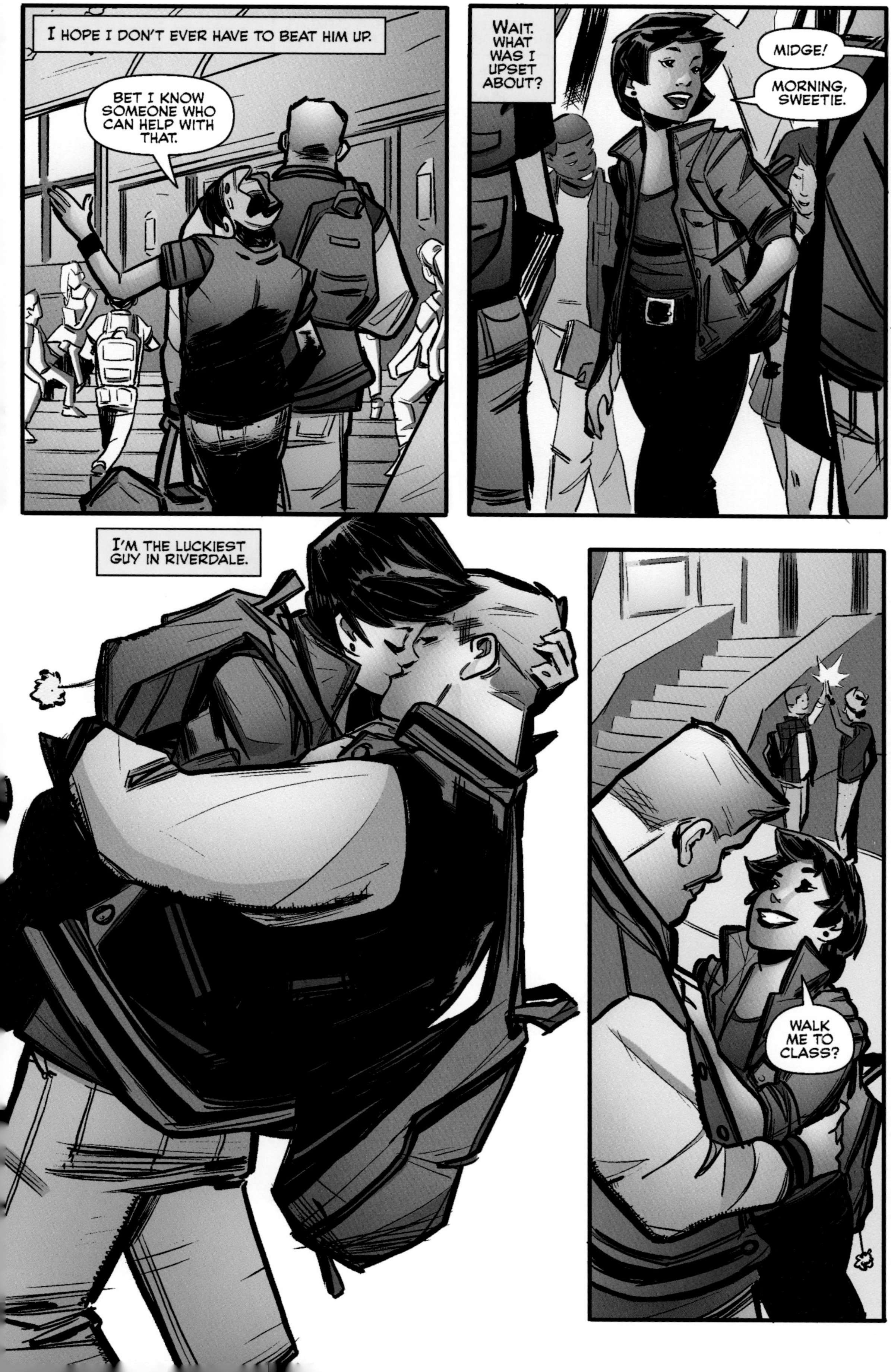
I HOPE I DON'T EVER HAVE TO BEAT HIM UP.
BET I KNOW SOMEONE WHO CAN HELP WITH THAT.
WAIT. WHAT WAS I UPSET ABOUT?
MIDGE!
MORNING, SWEETIE.
I'M THE LUCKIEST GUY IN RIVERDALE.
WALK ME TO CLASS?

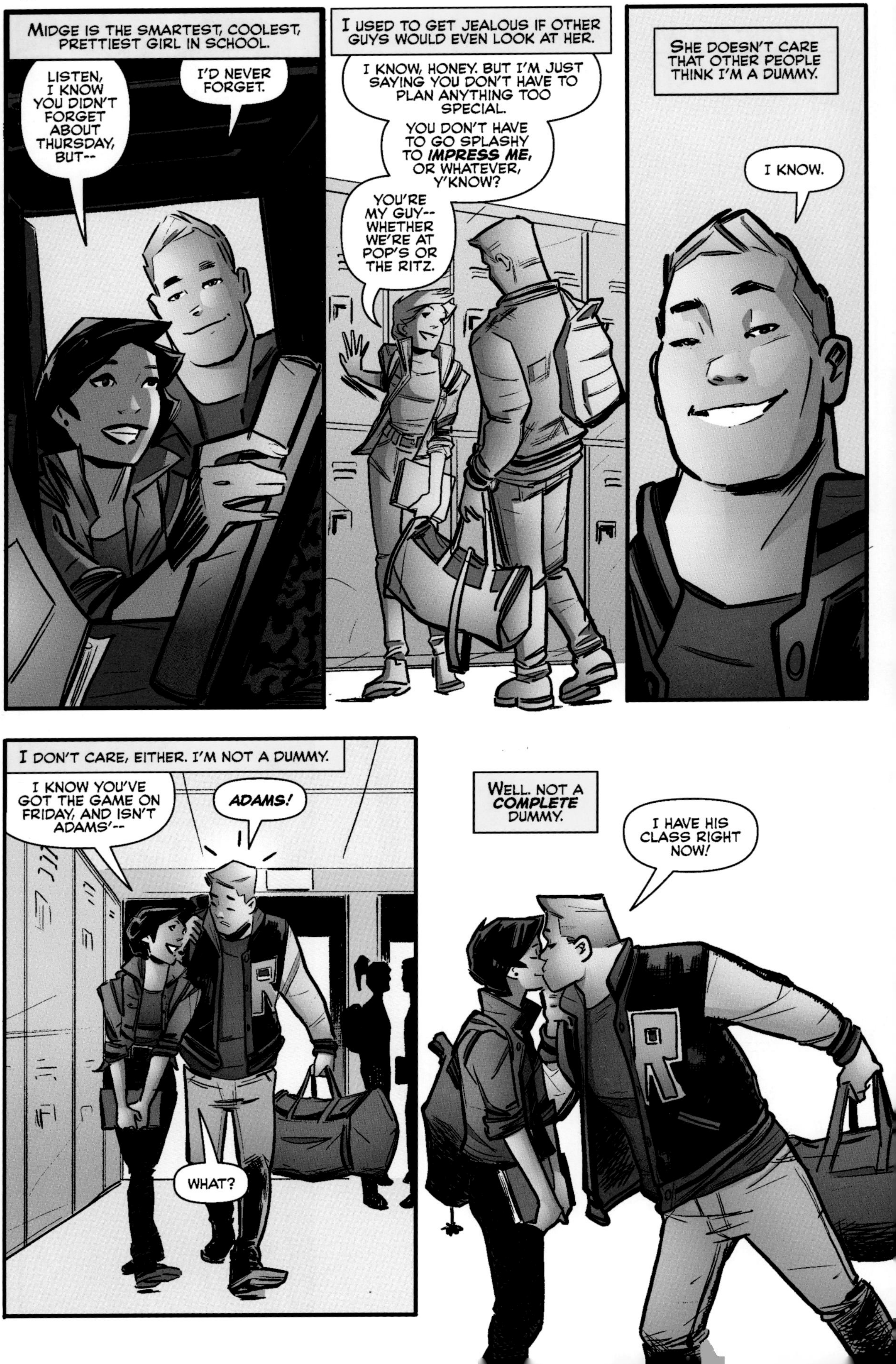
MIDGE IS THE SMARTEST, COOLEST, PRETTIEST GIRL IN SCHOOL.
LISTEN, I KNOW YOU DIDN'T FORGET ABOUT THURSDAY, BUT--
I'D NEVER FORGET.
I USED TO GET JEALOUS IF OTHER GUYS WOULD EVEN LOOK AT HER.
I KNOW, HONEY. BUT I'M JUST SAYING YOU DON'T HAVE TO PLAN ANYTHING TOO SPECIAL.
YOU DON'T HAVE TO GO SPLASHY TO *IMPRESS ME*, OR WHATEVER, Y'KNOW?
YOU'RE MY GUY-- WHETHER WE'RE AT POP'S OR THE RITZ.
SHE DOESN'T CARE THAT OTHER PEOPLE THINK I'M A DUMMY.
I KNOW.
I DON'T CARE, EITHER. I'M NOT A DUMMY.
I KNOW YOU'VE GOT THE GAME ON FRIDAY, AND ISN'T ADAMS'--
ADAMS!
WHAT?
WELL. NOT A *COMPLETE* DUMMY.
I HAVE HIS CLASS RIGHT NOW!

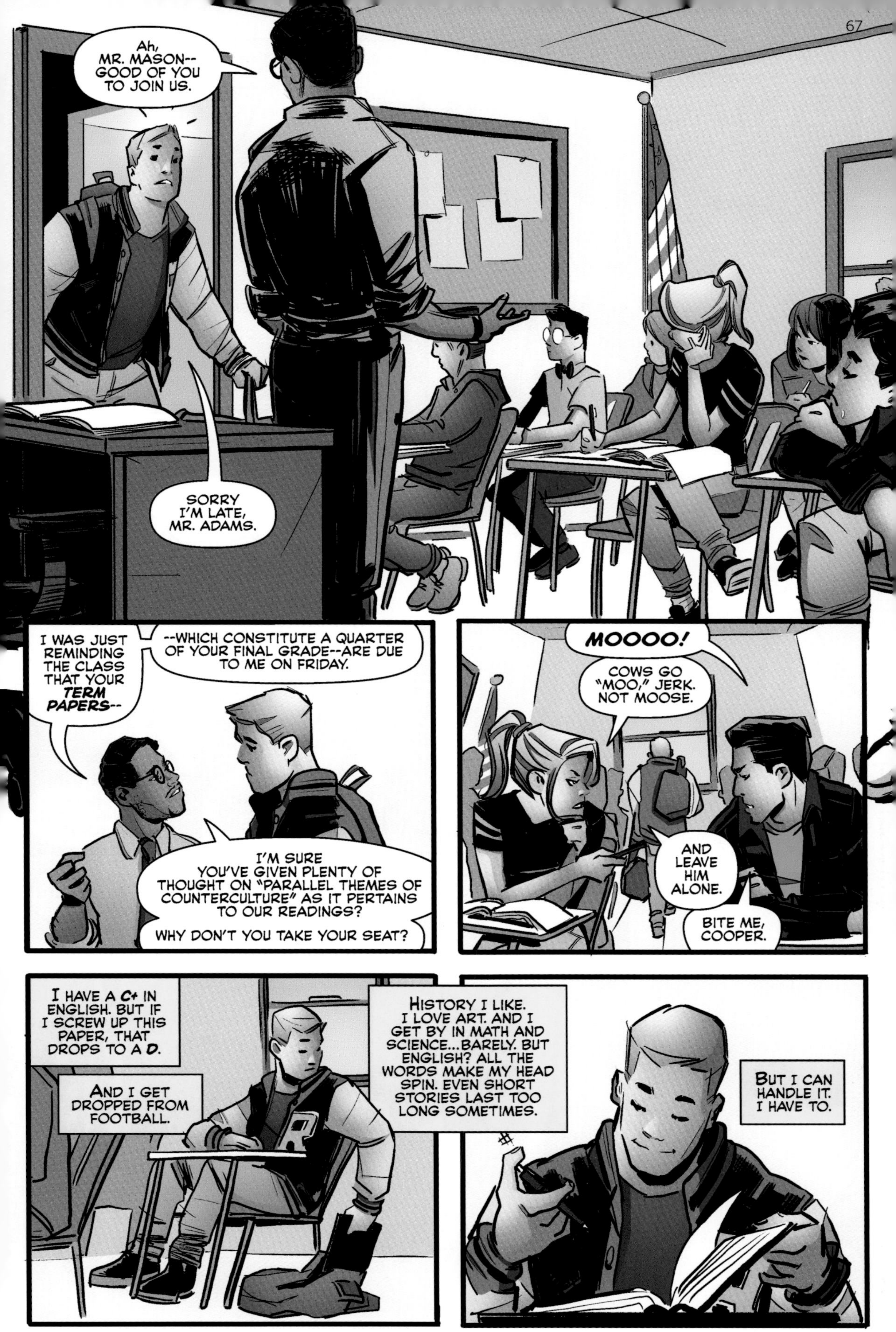

Ah, MR. MASON-- GOOD OF YOU TO JOIN US.
SORRY I'M LATE, MR. ADAMS.
I WAS JUST REMINDING THE CLASS THAT YOUR TERM PAPERS--
--WHICH CONSTITUTE A QUARTER OF YOUR FINAL GRADE--ARE DUE TO ME ON FRIDAY.
I'M SURE YOU'VE GIVEN PLENTY OF THOUGHT ON "PARALLEL THEMES OF COUNTERCULTURE" AS IT PERTAINS TO OUR READINGS?
WHY DON'T YOU TAKE YOUR SEAT?
MOOOO!
COWS GO "MOO," JERK. NOT MOOSE.
AND LEAVE HIM ALONE.
BITE ME, COOPER.
I HAVE A C+ IN ENGLISH. BUT IF I SCREW UP THIS PAPER, THAT DROPS TO A D.
AND I GET DROPPED FROM FOOTBALL.
HISTORY I LIKE. I LOVE ART. AND I GET BY IN MATH AND SCIENCE...BARELY. BUT ENGLISH? ALL THE WORDS MAKE MY HEAD SPIN. EVEN SHORT STORIES LAST TOO LONG SOMETIMES.
BUT I CAN HANDLE IT. I HAVE TO.

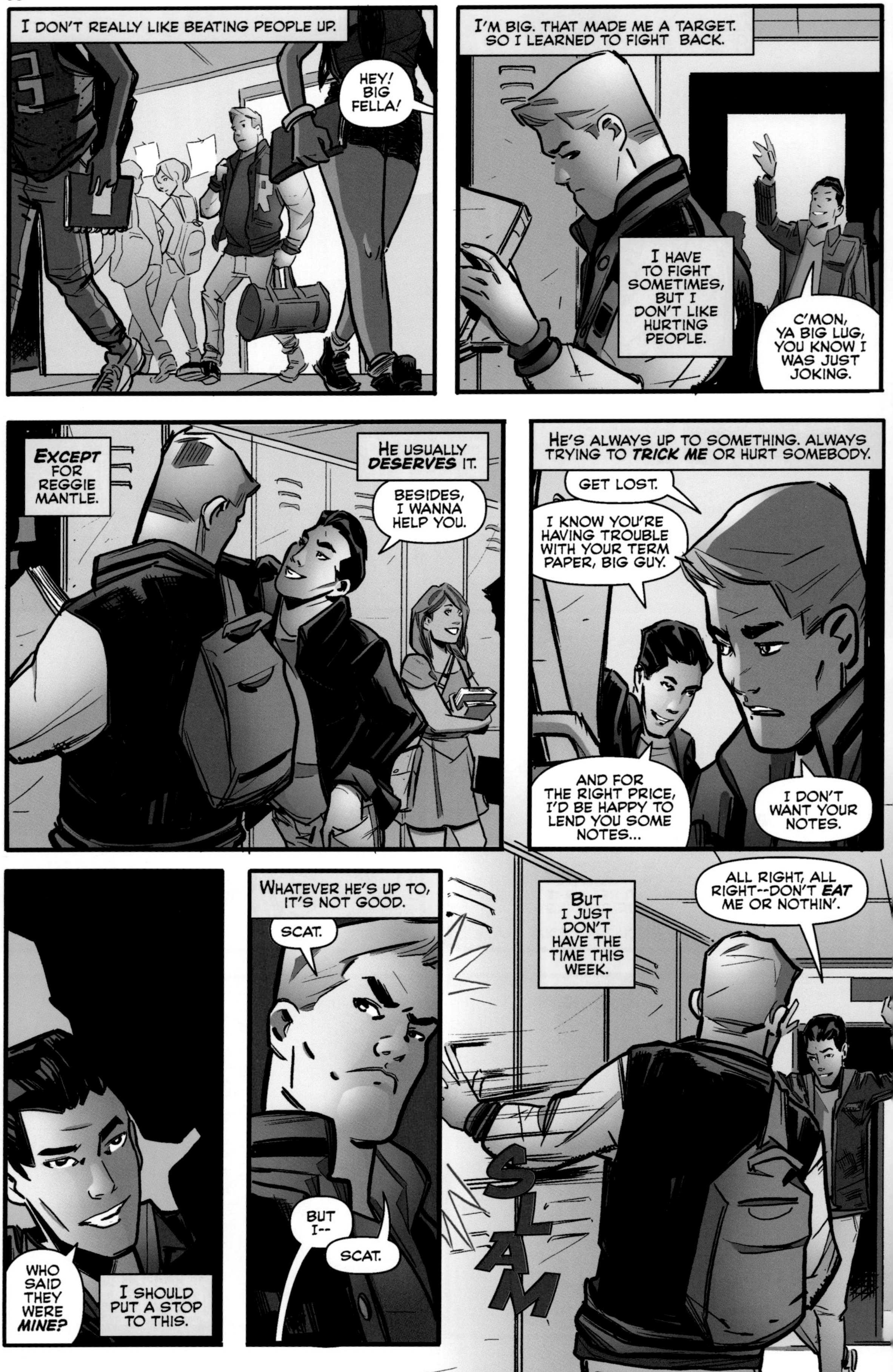
I DON'T REALLY LIKE BEATING PEOPLE UP.
HEY! BIG FELLA!
I'M BIG. THAT MADE ME A TARGET. SO I LEARNED TO FIGHT BACK.
I HAVE TO FIGHT SOMETIMES, BUT I DON'T LIKE HURTING PEOPLE.
C'MON, YA BIG LUG, YOU KNOW I WAS JUST JOKING.
EXCEPT FOR REGGIE MANTLE.
HE USUALLY DESERVES IT.
BESIDES, I WANNA HELP YOU.
HE'S ALWAYS UP TO SOMETHING. ALWAYS TRYING TO TRICK ME OR HURT SOMEBODY.
GET LOST.
I KNOW YOU'RE HAVING TROUBLE WITH YOUR TERM PAPER, BIG GUY.
AND FOR THE RIGHT PRICE, I'D BE HAPPY TO LEND YOU SOME NOTES...
I DON'T WANT YOUR NOTES.
WHO SAID THEY WERE MINE?
I SHOULD PUT A STOP TO THIS.
WHATEVER HE'S UP TO, IT'S NOT GOOD.
SCAT.
BUT I--
SCAT.
BUT I JUST DON'T HAVE THE TIME THIS WEEK.
ALL RIGHT, ALL RIGHT--DON'T EAT ME OR NOTHIN'.
SLAM

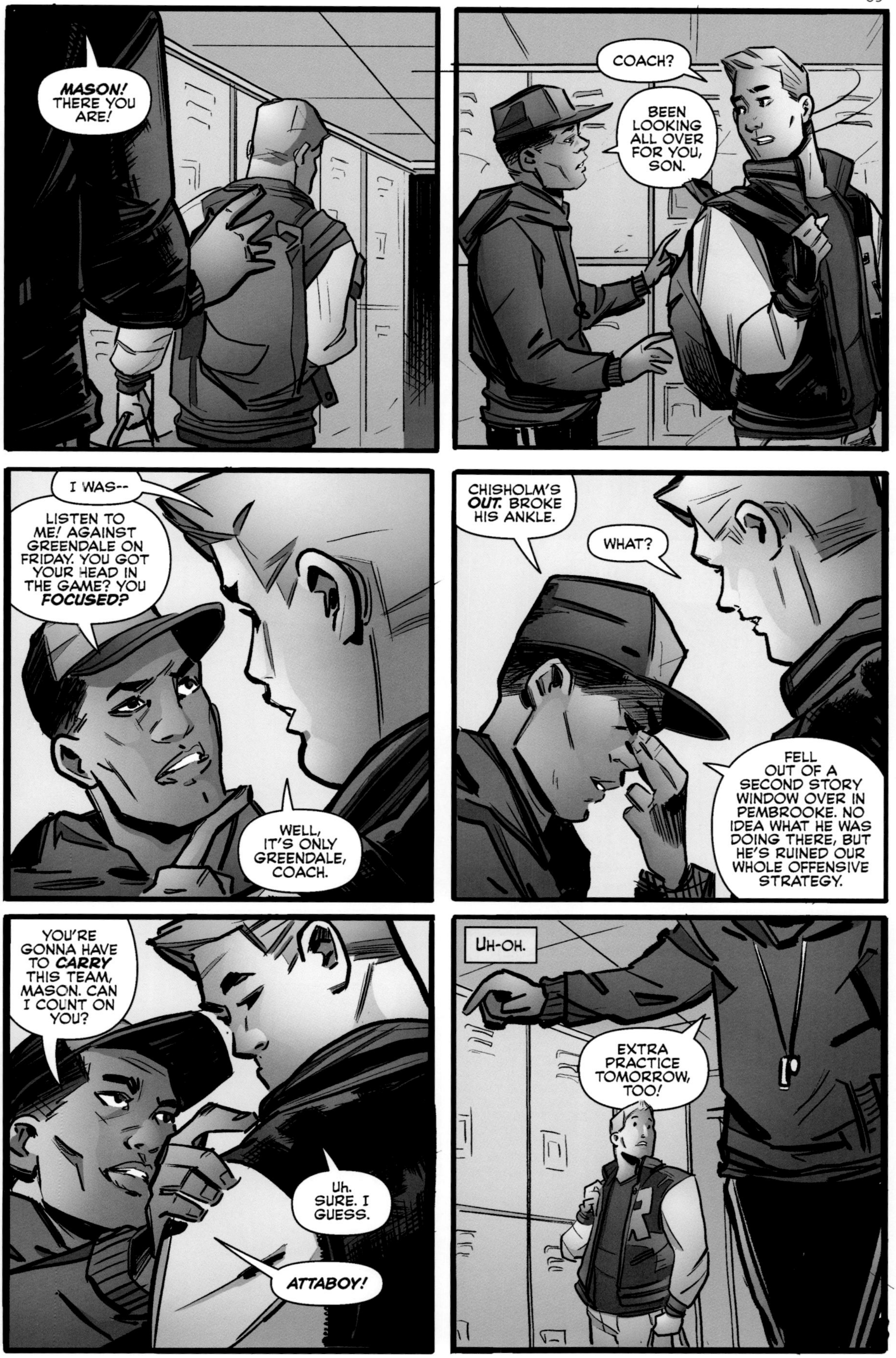
MASON! THERE YOU ARE!
COACH?
BEEN LOOKING ALL OVER FOR YOU, SON.
I WAS--
LISTEN TO ME! AGAINST GREENDALE ON FRIDAY. YOU GOT YOUR HEAD IN THE GAME? YOU FOCUSED?
WELL, IT'S ONLY GREENDALE, COACH.
CHISHOLM'S OUT. BROKE HIS ANKLE.
WHAT?
FELL OUT OF A SECOND STORY WINDOW OVER IN PEMBROOKE. NO IDEA WHAT HE WAS DOING THERE, BUT HE'S RUINED OUR WHOLE OFFENSIVE STRATEGY.
YOU'RE GONNA HAVE TO CARRY THIS TEAM, MASON. CAN I COUNT ON YOU?
Uh. SURE. I GUESS.
ATTABOY!
UH-OH.
EXTRA PRACTICE TOMORROW, TOO!

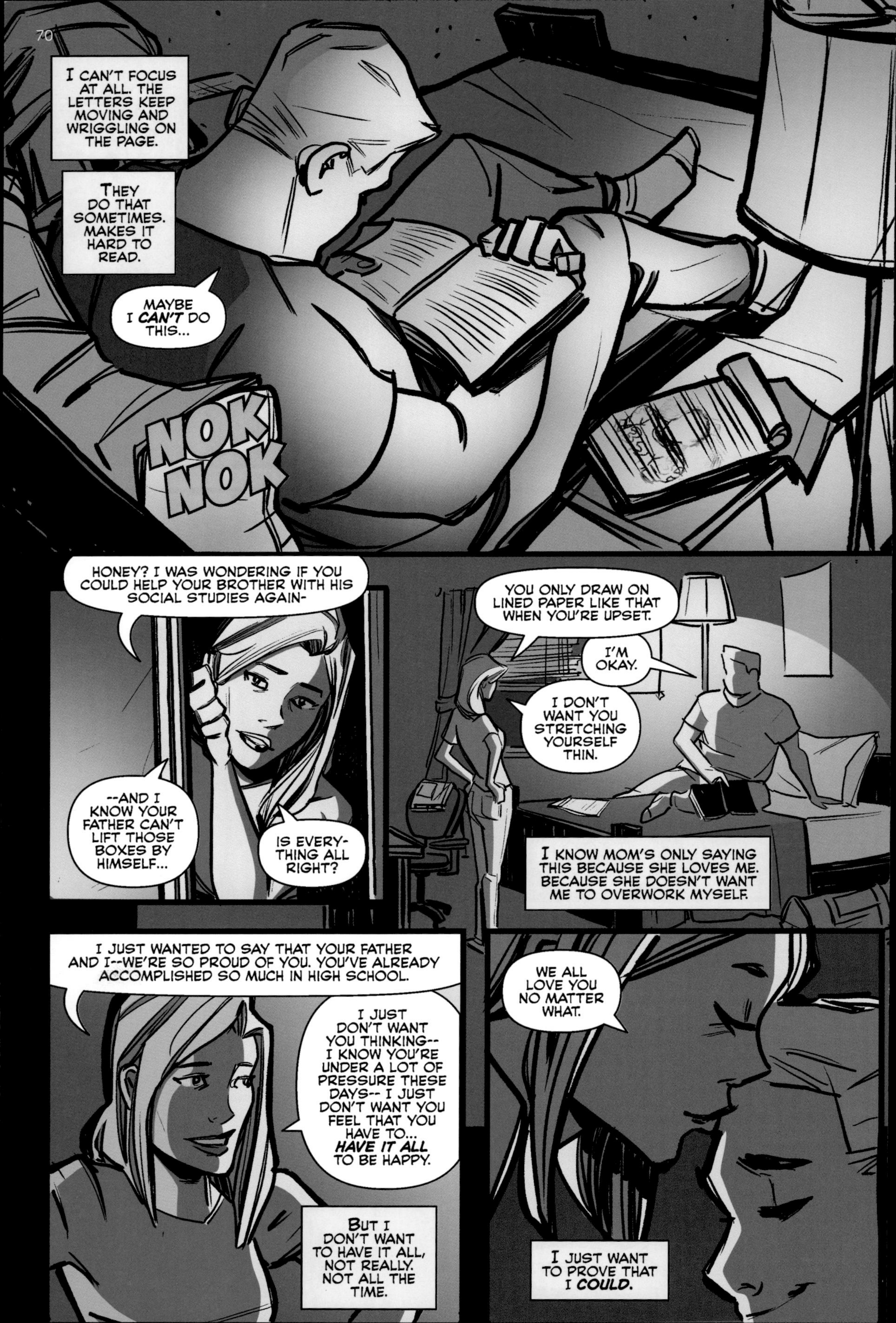
I CAN'T FOCUS AT ALL. THE LETTERS KEEP MOVING AND WRIGGLING ON THE PAGE.
THEY DO THAT SOMETIMES. MAKES IT HARD TO READ.
MAYBE I ***CAN'T*** DO THIS...
NOK NOK
HONEY? I WAS WONDERING IF YOU COULD HELP YOUR BROTHER WITH HIS SOCIAL STUDIES AGAIN-
--AND I KNOW YOUR FATHER CAN'T LIFT THOSE BOXES BY HIMSELF...
IS EVERY-THING ALL RIGHT?
YOU ONLY DRAW ON LINED PAPER LIKE THAT WHEN YOU'RE UPSET.
I'M OKAY.
I DON'T WANT YOU STRETCHING YOURSELF THIN.
I KNOW MOM'S ONLY SAYING THIS BECAUSE SHE LOVES ME. BECAUSE SHE DOESN'T WANT ME TO OVERWORK MYSELF.
I JUST WANTED TO SAY THAT YOUR FATHER AND I--WE'RE SO PROUD OF YOU. YOU'VE ALREADY ACCOMPLISHED SO MUCH IN HIGH SCHOOL.
I JUST DON'T WANT YOU THINKING-- I KNOW YOU'RE UNDER A LOT OF PRESSURE THESE DAYS-- I JUST DON'T WANT YOU FEEL THAT YOU HAVE TO... ***HAVE IT ALL*** TO BE HAPPY.
BUT I DON'T WANT TO HAVE IT ALL, NOT REALLY. NOT ALL THE TIME.
WE ALL LOVE YOU NO MATTER WHAT.
I JUST WANT TO PROVE THAT I ***COULD.***

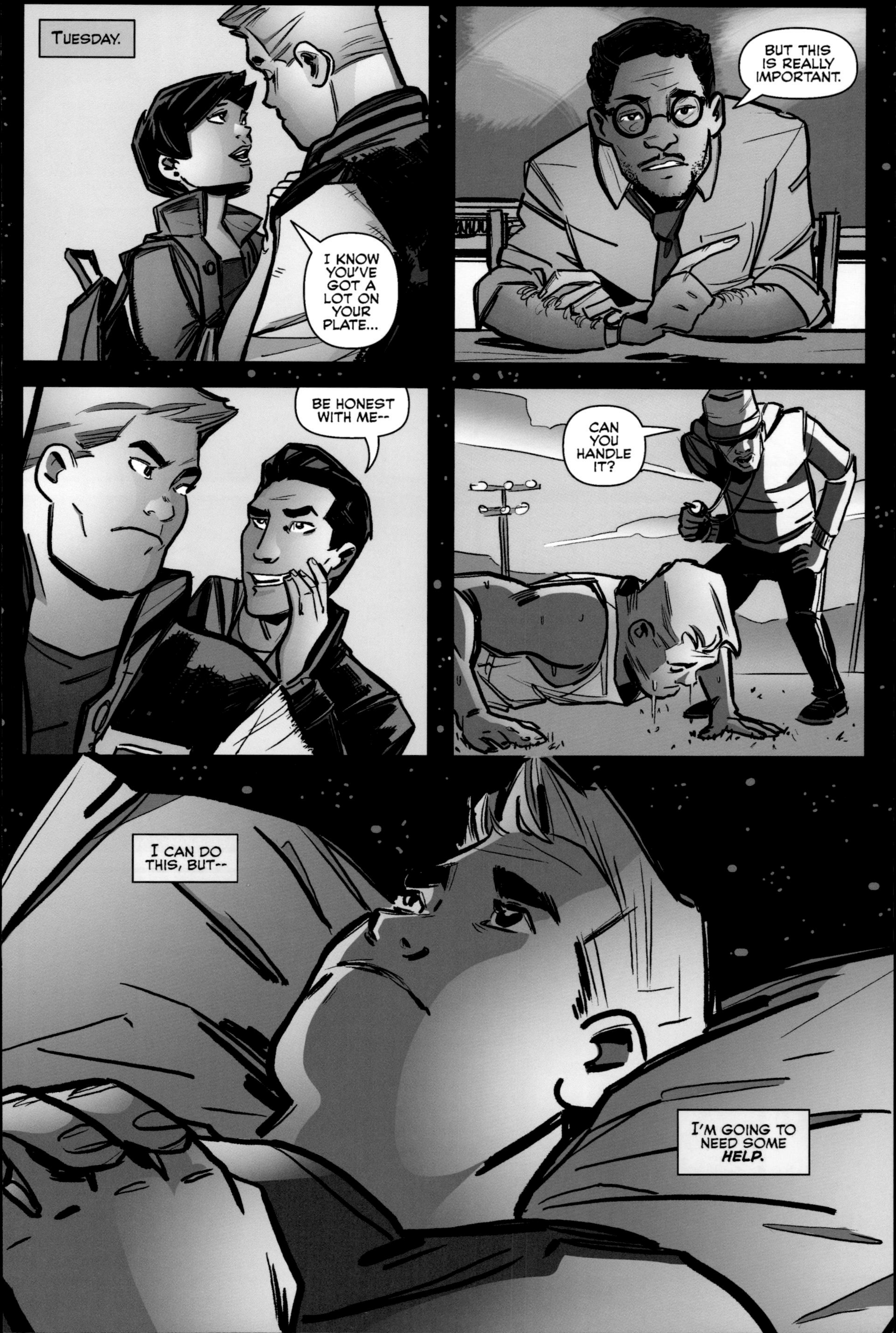
TUESDAY.
I KNOW YOU'VE GOT A LOT ON YOUR PLATE...
BUT THIS IS REALLY IMPORTANT.
BE HONEST WITH ME--
CAN YOU HANDLE IT?
I CAN DO THIS, BUT--
I'M GOING TO NEED SOME ***HELP.***

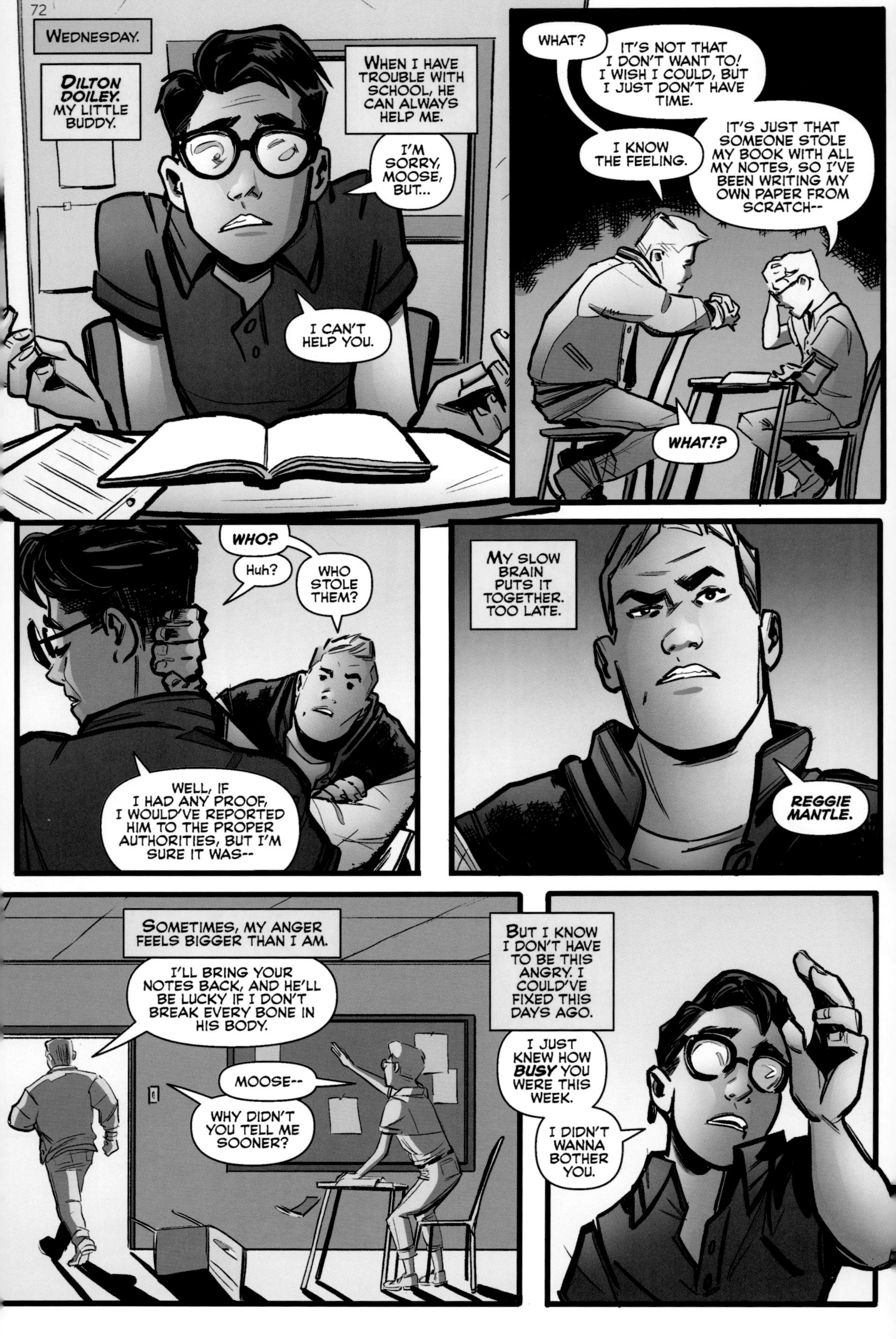

WEDNESDAY.
DILTON DOILEY. MY LITTLE BUDDY.
WHEN I HAVE TROUBLE WITH SCHOOL, HE CAN ALWAYS HELP ME.
I'M SORRY, MOOSE, BUT...
I CAN'T HELP YOU.
WHAT?
IT'S NOT THAT I DON'T WANT TO! I WISH I COULD, BUT I JUST DON'T HAVE TIME.
I KNOW THE FEELING.
IT'S JUST THAT SOMEONE STOLE MY BOOK WITH ALL MY NOTES, SO I'VE BEEN WRITING MY OWN PAPER FROM SCRATCH--
WHAT!?
WHO?
Huh?
WHO STOLE THEM?
WELL, IF I HAD ANY PROOF, I WOULD'VE REPORTED HIM TO THE PROPER AUTHORITIES, BUT I'M SURE IT WAS--
MY SLOW BRAIN PUTS IT TOGETHER. TOO LATE.
REGGIE MANTLE.
SOMETIMES, MY ANGER FEELS BIGGER THAN I AM.
I'LL BRING YOUR NOTES BACK, AND HE'LL BE LUCKY IF I DON'T BREAK EVERY BONE IN HIS BODY.
MOOSE--
WHY DIDN'T YOU TELL ME SOONER?
BUT I KNOW I DON'T HAVE TO BE THIS ANGRY. I COULD'VE FIXED THIS DAYS AGO.
I JUST KNEW HOW BUSY YOU WERE THIS WEEK.
I DIDN'T WANNA BOTHER YOU.

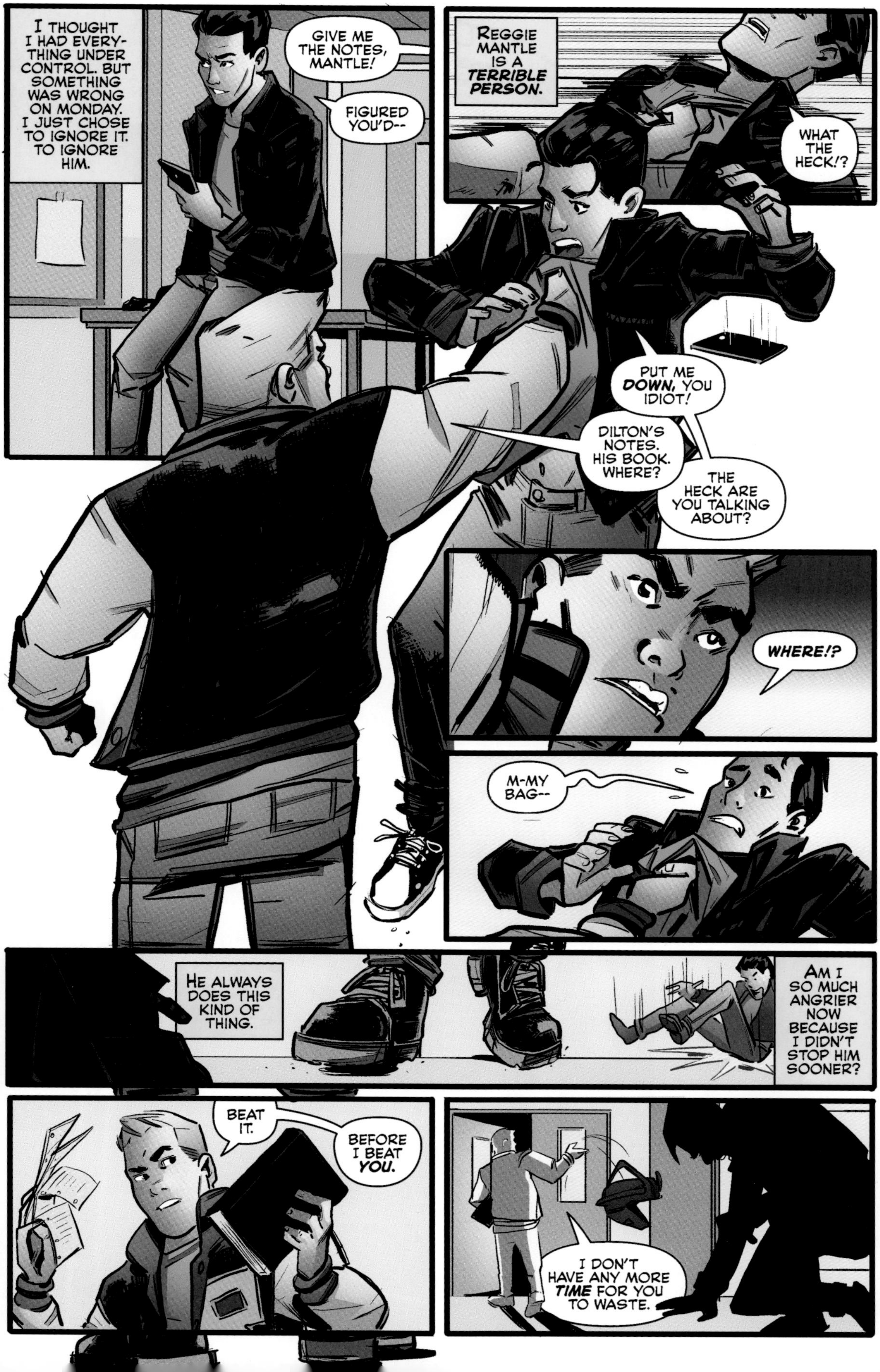
I THOUGHT I HAD EVERYTHING UNDER CONTROL. BUT SOMETHING WAS WRONG ON MONDAY. I JUST CHOSE TO IGNORE IT. TO IGNORE HIM.
GIVE ME THE NOTES, MANTLE!
FIGURED YOU'D--
REGGIE MANTLE IS A TERRIBLE PERSON.
WHAT THE HECK!?
PUT ME DOWN, YOU IDIOT!
DILTON'S NOTES. HIS BOOK. WHERE?
THE HECK ARE YOU TALKING ABOUT?
WHERE!?
M-MY BAG--
HE ALWAYS DOES THIS KIND OF THING.
AM I SO MUCH ANGRIER NOW BECAUSE I DIDN'T STOP HIM SOONER?
BEAT IT.
BEFORE I BEAT YOU.
I DON'T HAVE ANY MORE TIME FOR YOU TO WASTE.

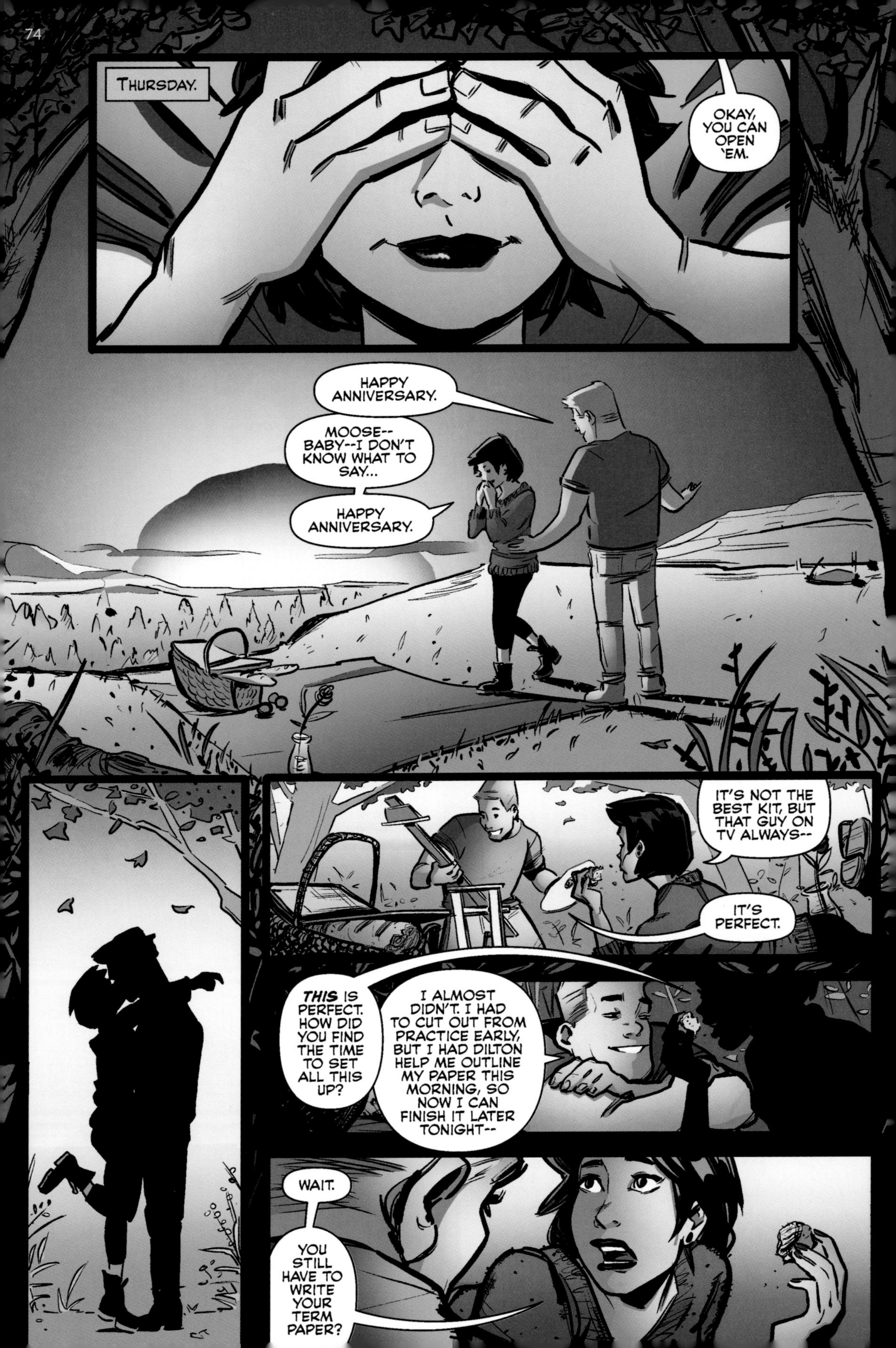
THURSDAY.
OKAY, YOU CAN OPEN 'EM.
HAPPY ANNIVERSARY.
MOOSE--BABY--I DON'T KNOW WHAT TO SAY...
HAPPY ANNIVERSARY.
IT'S NOT THE BEST KIT, BUT THAT GUY ON TV ALWAYS--
IT'S PERFECT.
THIS IS PERFECT. HOW DID YOU FIND THE TIME TO SET ALL THIS UP?
I ALMOST DIDN'T. I HAD TO CUT OUT FROM PRACTICE EARLY, BUT I HAD DILTON HELP ME OUTLINE MY PAPER THIS MORNING, SO NOW I CAN FINISH IT LATER TONIGHT--
WAIT.
YOU STILL HAVE TO WRITE YOUR TERM PAPER?

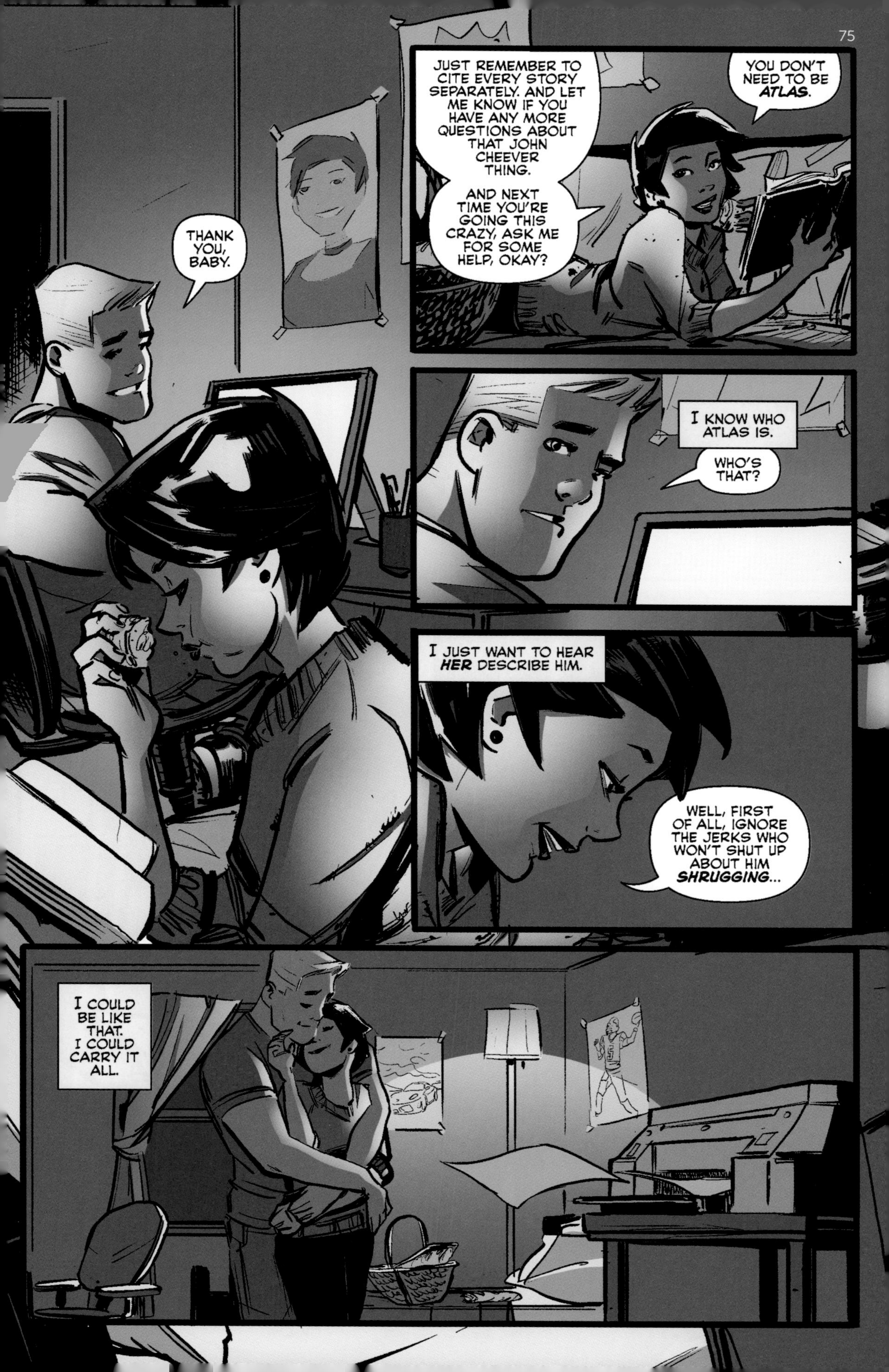
THANK YOU, BABY.
JUST REMEMBER TO CITE EVERY STORY SEPARATELY. AND LET ME KNOW IF YOU HAVE ANY MORE QUESTIONS ABOUT THAT JOHN CHEEVER THING.
AND NEXT TIME YOU'RE GOING THIS CRAZY, ASK ME FOR SOME HELP, OKAY?
YOU DON'T NEED TO BE ***ATLAS***.
I KNOW WHO ATLAS IS.
WHO'S THAT?
I JUST WANT TO HEAR ***HER*** DESCRIBE HIM.
WELL, FIRST OF ALL, IGNORE THE JERKS WHO WON'T SHUT UP ABOUT HIM ***SHRUGGING***...
I COULD BE LIKE THAT. I COULD CARRY IT ALL.

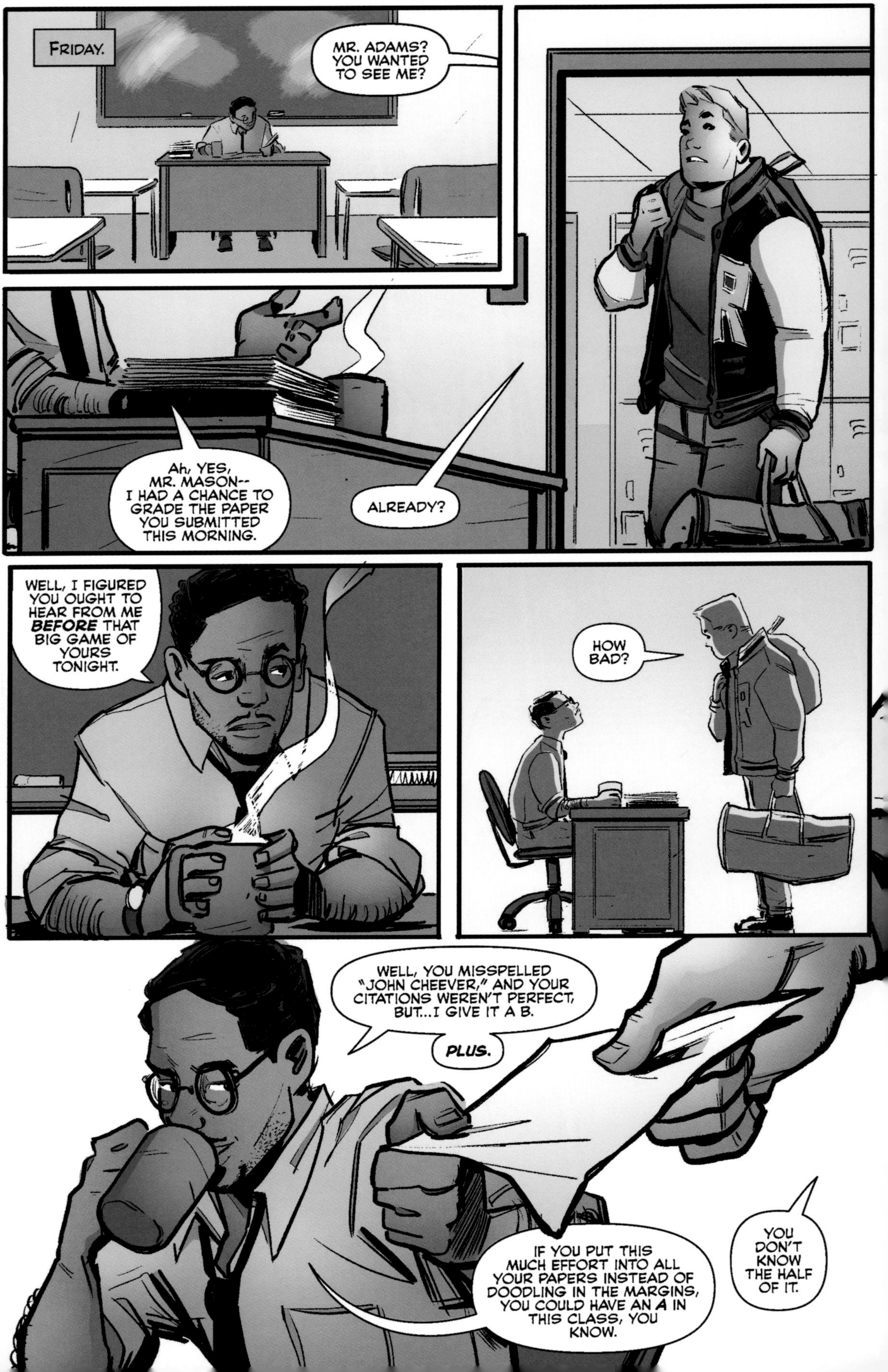
FRIDAY.
MR. ADAMS? YOU WANTED TO SEE ME?
Ah, YES, MR. MASON-- I HAD A CHANCE TO GRADE THE PAPER YOU SUBMITTED THIS MORNING.
ALREADY?
WELL, I FIGURED YOU OUGHT TO HEAR FROM ME *BEFORE* THAT BIG GAME OF YOURS TONIGHT.
HOW BAD?
WELL, YOU MISSPELLED "JOHN CHEEVER," AND YOUR CITATIONS WEREN'T PERFECT, BUT...I GIVE IT A B.
PLUS.
IF YOU PUT THIS MUCH EFFORT INTO ALL YOUR PAPERS INSTEAD OF DOODLING IN THE MARGINS, YOU COULD HAVE AN *A* IN THIS CLASS, YOU KNOW.
YOU DON'T KNOW THE HALF OF IT.

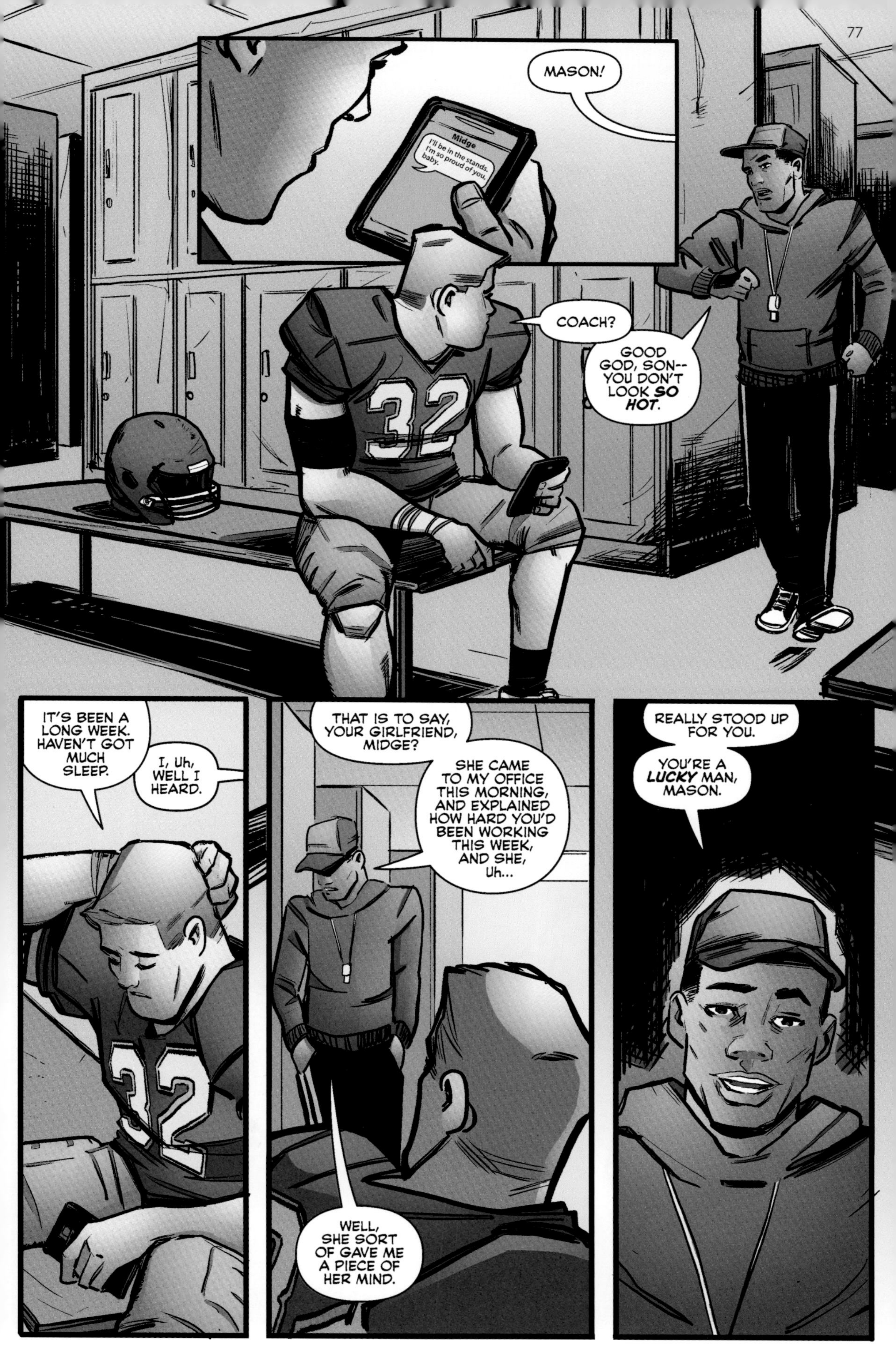
Midge
I'll be in the stands. I'm so proud of you, baby.
MASON!
COACH?
GOOD GOD, SON-- YOU DON'T LOOK **SO HOT**.
IT'S BEEN A LONG WEEK. HAVEN'T GOT MUCH SLEEP.
I, UH, WELL I HEARD.
THAT IS TO SAY, YOUR GIRLFRIEND, MIDGE?
SHE CAME TO MY OFFICE THIS MORNING, AND EXPLAINED HOW HARD YOU'D BEEN WORKING THIS WEEK, AND SHE, UH...
WELL, SHE SORT OF GAVE ME A PIECE OF HER MIND.
REALLY STOOD UP FOR YOU.
YOU'RE A **LUCKY** MAN, MASON.

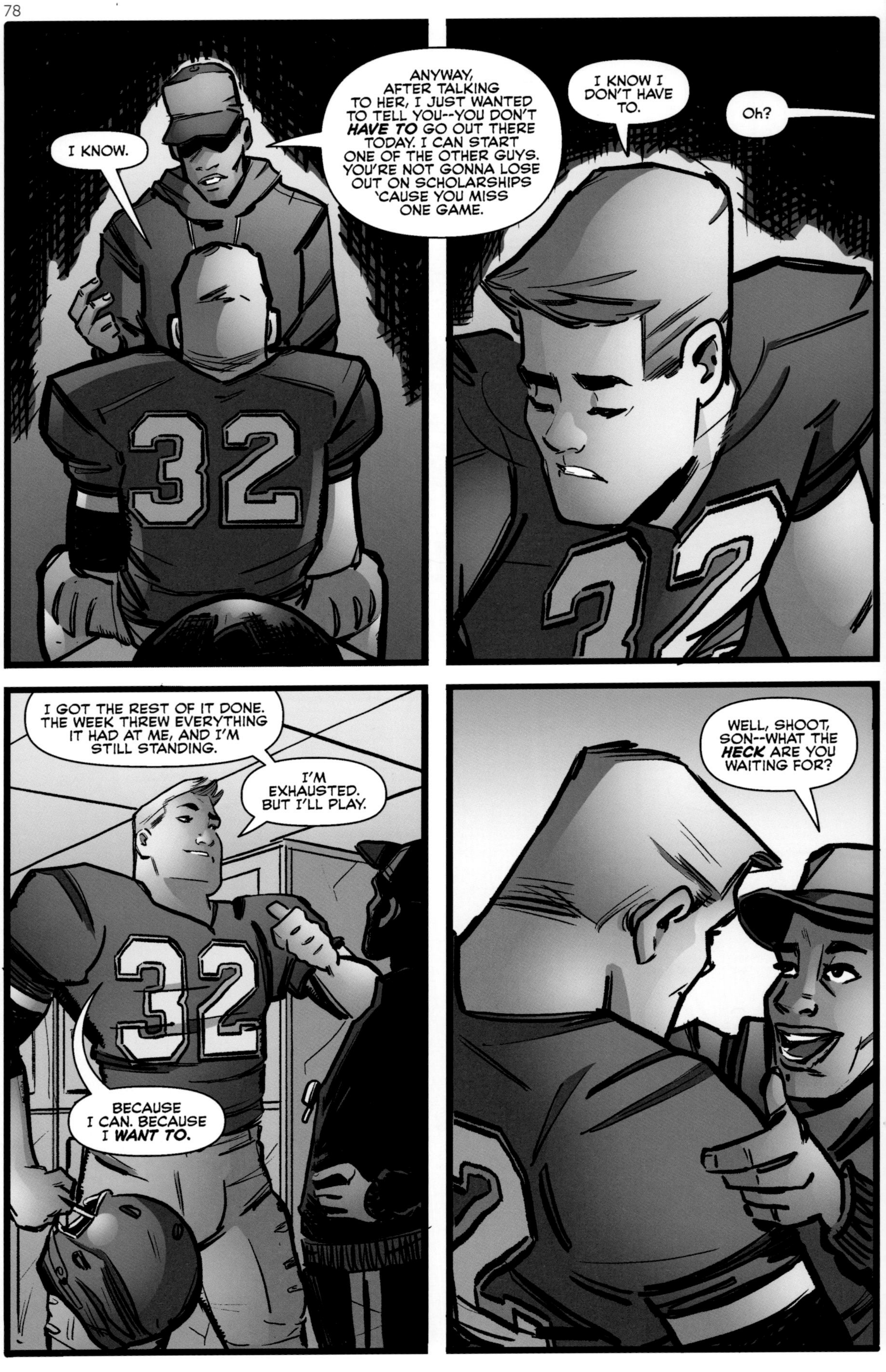
I KNOW.
ANYWAY, AFTER TALKING TO HER, I JUST WANTED TO TELL YOU--YOU DON'T **HAVE TO** GO OUT THERE TODAY. I CAN START ONE OF THE OTHER GUYS. YOU'RE NOT GONNA LOSE OUT ON SCHOLARSHIPS 'CAUSE YOU MISS ONE GAME.
I KNOW I DON'T HAVE TO.
Oh?
I GOT THE REST OF IT DONE. THE WEEK THREW EVERYTHING IT HAD AT ME, AND I'M STILL STANDING.
I'M EXHAUSTED. BUT I'LL PLAY.
BECAUSE I CAN. BECAUSE I **WANT TO.**
WELL, SHOOT, SON--WHAT THE **HECK** ARE YOU WAITING FOR?

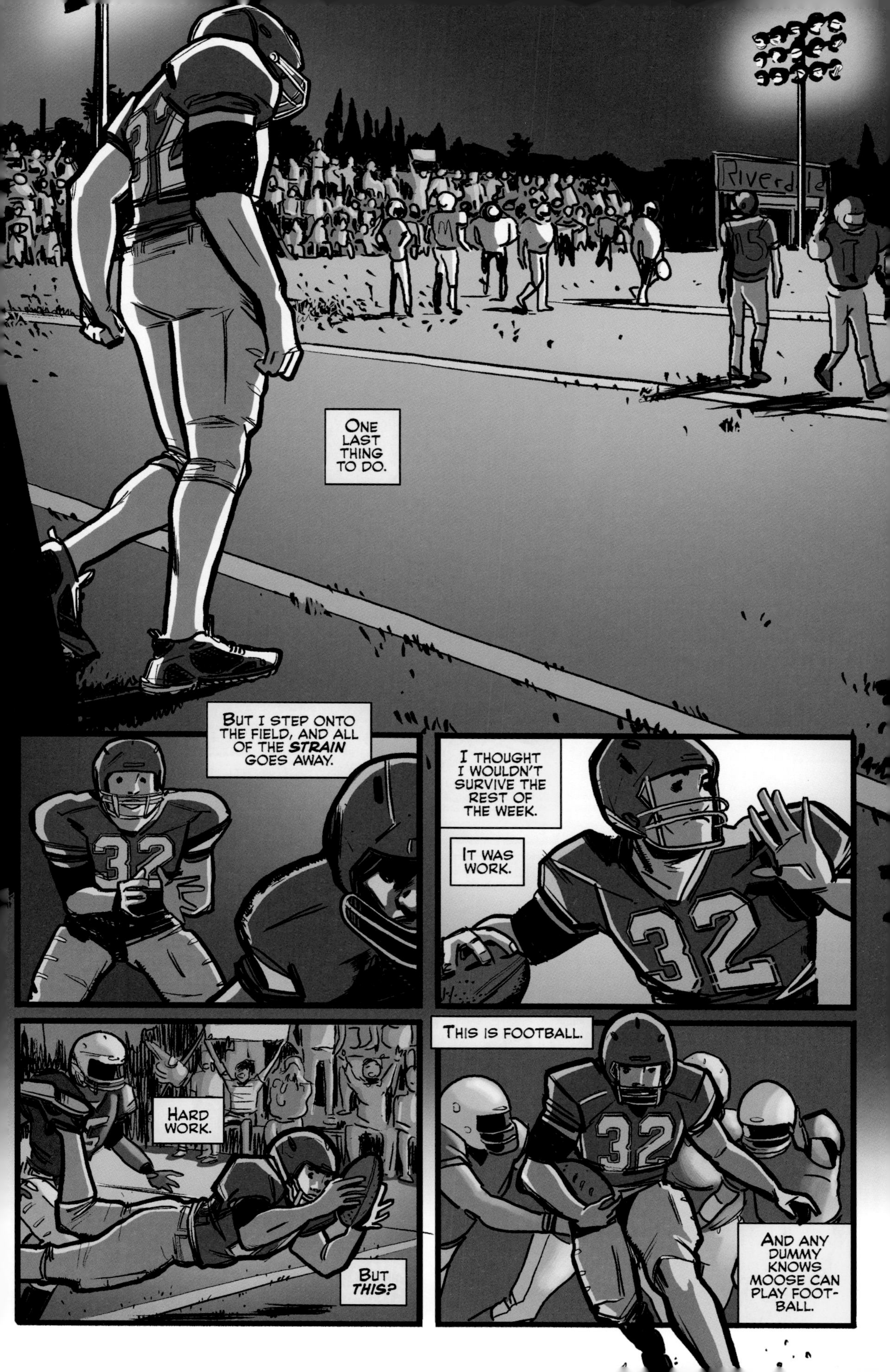
Riverdale
ONE LAST THING TO DO.
BUT I STEP ONTO THE FIELD, AND ALL OF THE STRAIN GOES AWAY.
I THOUGHT I WOULDN'T SURVIVE THE REST OF THE WEEK.
IT WAS WORK.
HARD WORK.
BUT THIS?
THIS IS FOOTBALL.
AND ANY DUMMY KNOWS MOOSE CAN PLAY FOOTBALL.

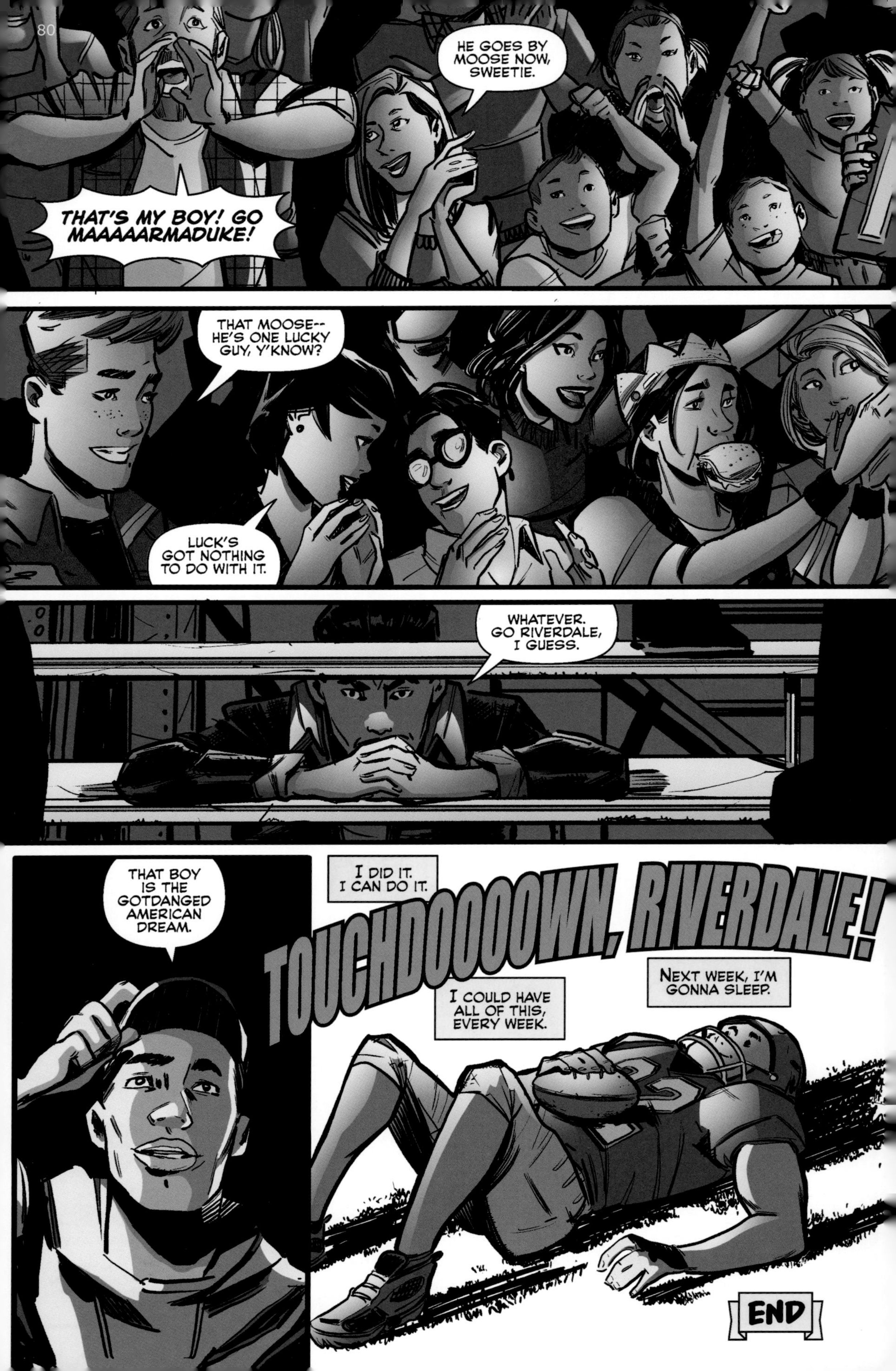
THAT'S MY BOY! GO MAAAAARMADUKE!
HE GOES BY MOOSE NOW, SWEETIE.
THAT MOOSE-- HE'S ONE LUCKY GUY, Y'KNOW?
LUCK'S GOT NOTHING TO DO WITH IT.
WHATEVER. GO RIVERDALE, I GUESS.
THAT BOY IS THE GOTDANGED AMERICAN DREAM.
I DID IT. I CAN DO IT.
TOUCHDOOOOWN, RIVERDALE!
I COULD HAVE ALL OF THIS, EVERY WEEK.
NEXT WEEK, I'M GONNA SLEEP.
END

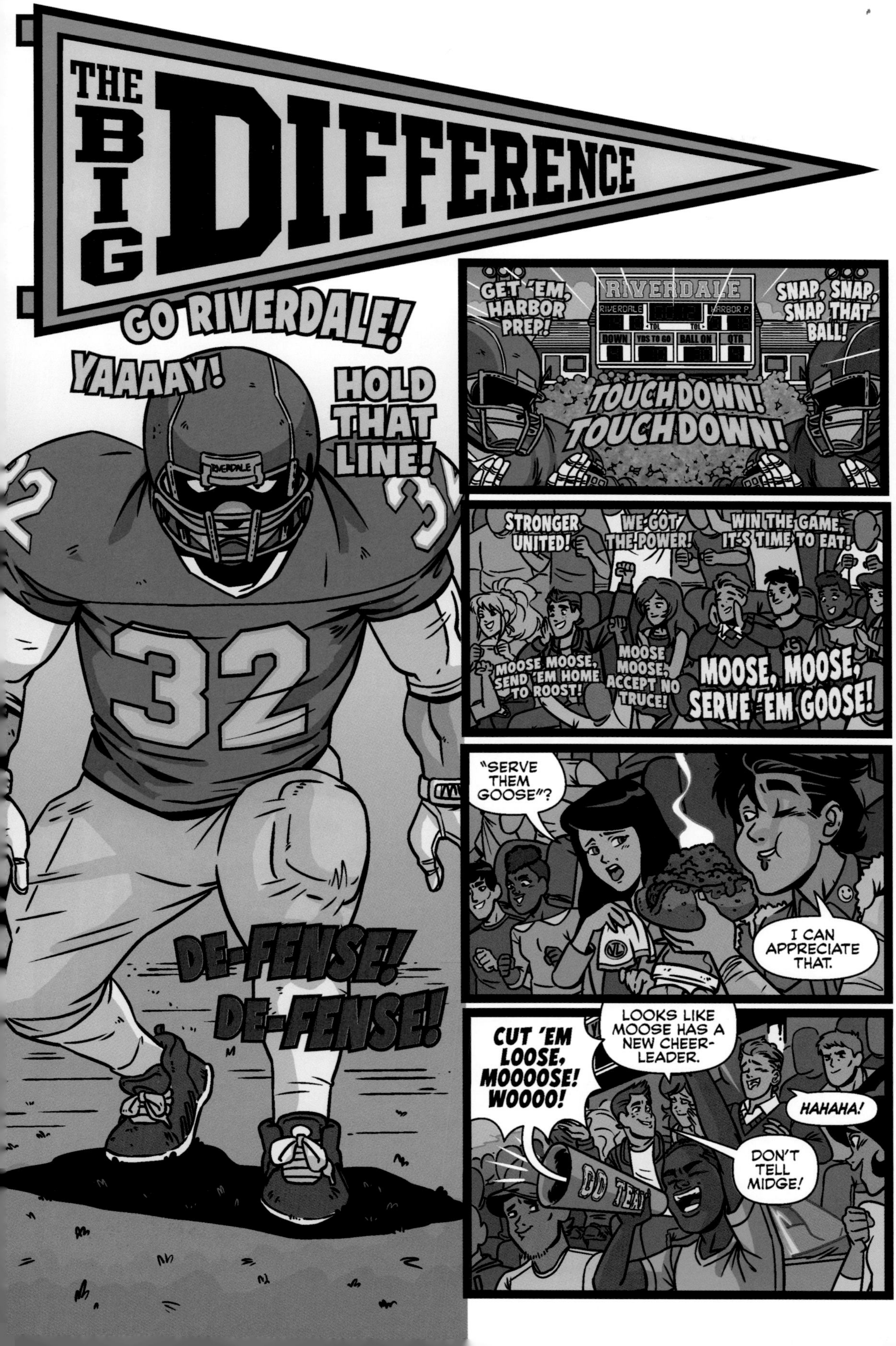
THE BIG DIFFERENCE
GO RIVERDALE!
YAAAAY!
HOLD THAT LINE!
RIVERDALE
DE-FENSE! DE-FENSE!
GET 'EM, HARBOR PREP!
RIVERDALE
RIVERDALE HARBOR P.
DOWN YDS TO GO BALL ON QTR
SNAP, SNAP, SNAP THAT BALL!
TOUCHDOWN! TOUCHDOWN!
STRONGER UNITED!
WE GOT THE POWER!
WIN THE GAME, IT'S TIME TO EAT!
MOOSE MOOSE, SEND 'EM HOME TO ROOST!
MOOSE MOOSE, ACCEPT NO TRUCE!
MOOSE, MOOSE, SERVE 'EM GOOSE!
"SERVE THEM GOOSE"?
I CAN APPRECIATE THAT.
CUT 'EM LOOSE, MOOOOSE! WOOOO!
LOOKS LIKE MOOSE HAS A NEW CHEER-LEADER.
HAHAHA!
DON'T TELL MIDGE!

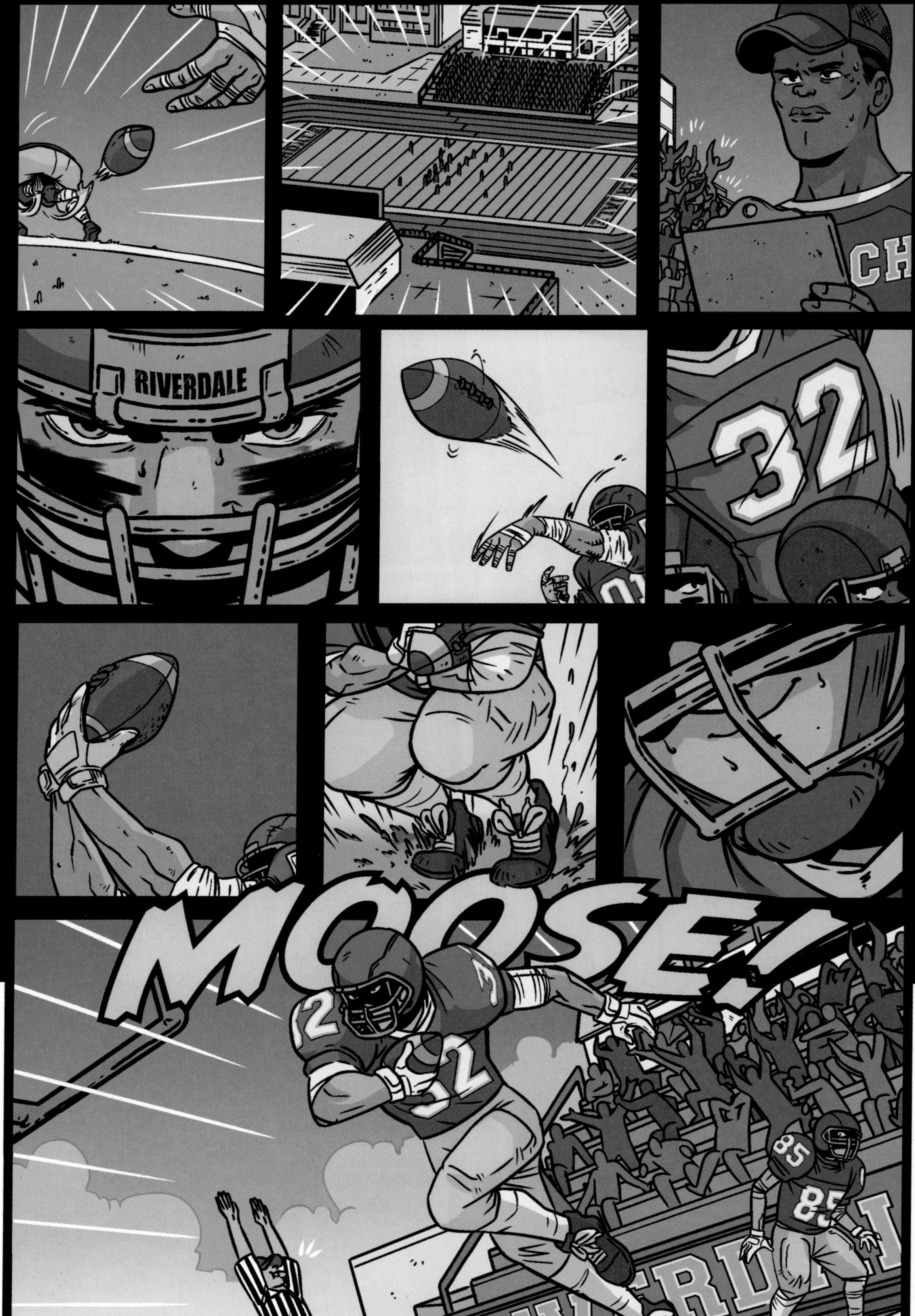
RIVERDALE
MOOSE!

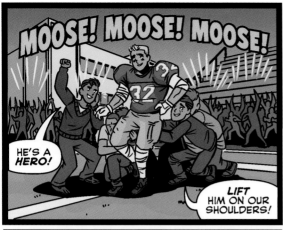

MOOSE! MOOSE! MOOSE!

HE'S A *HERO!*

LIFT HIM ON OUR SHOULDERS!

HEY, ARCHIE, MAYBE YOU SHOULD LET MOOSE CARRY HIMSELF?

MOOSE, MOOSE, HEY MOOSE! CAN I, LIKE, CARRY YOUR GEAR OR... OR SOMETHING?

GOOD IDEA, MIDGE.

SURE.

AWESOME!

THANKS.

KLATTLLL

HEY, FRESHIE, LEMME GIVE YOU A HAND.

NO, THANKS. I'VE GOT THIS.

WHATEVS.

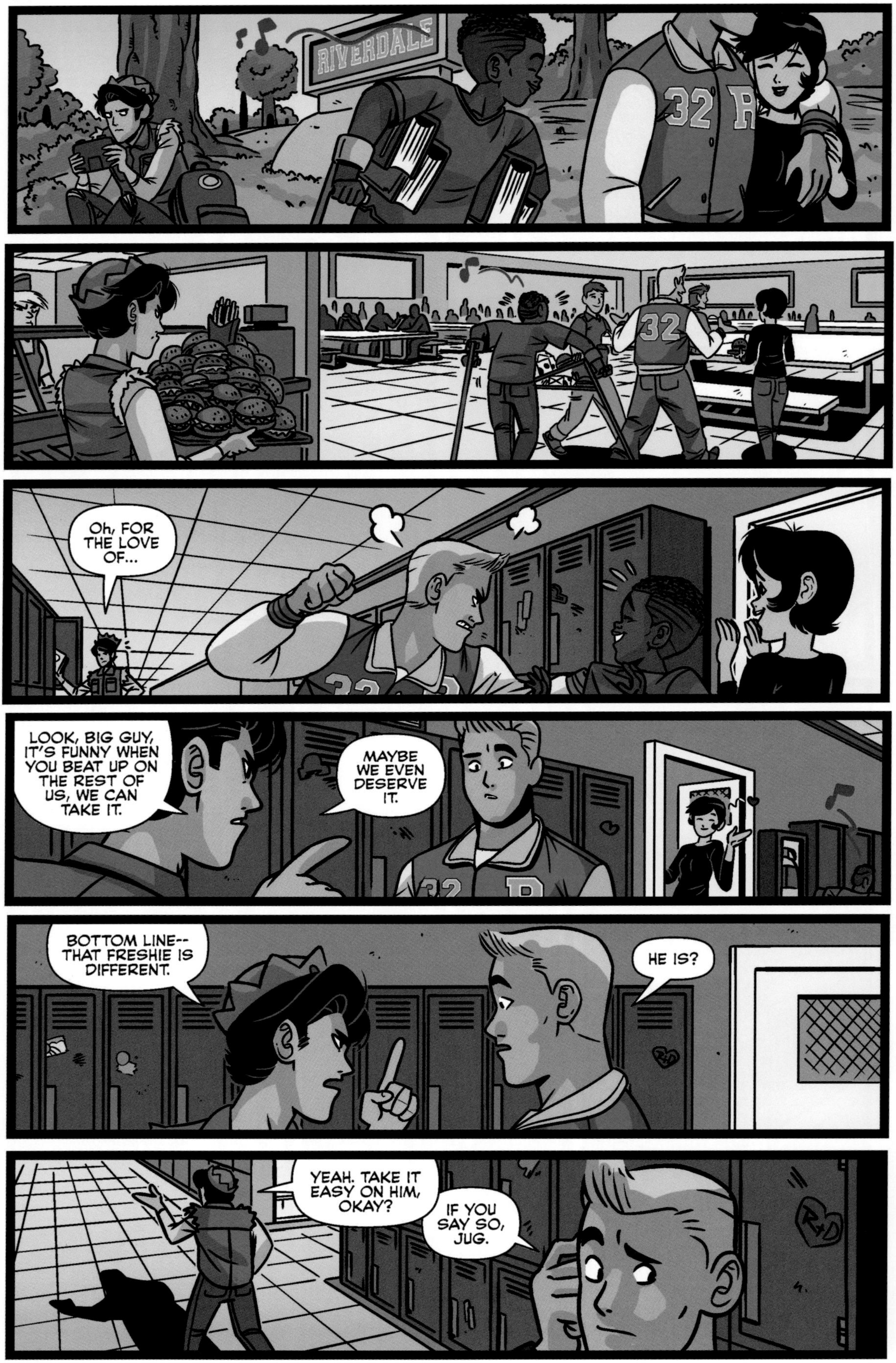
RIVERDALE
32
R
32
Oh, FOR THE LOVE OF...
LOOK, BIG GUY, IT'S FUNNY WHEN YOU BEAT UP ON THE REST OF US, WE CAN TAKE IT.
MAYBE WE EVEN DESERVE IT.
BOTTOM LINE-- THAT FRESHIE IS DIFFERENT.
HE IS?
YEAH. TAKE IT EASY ON HIM, OKAY?
IF YOU SAY SO, JUG.

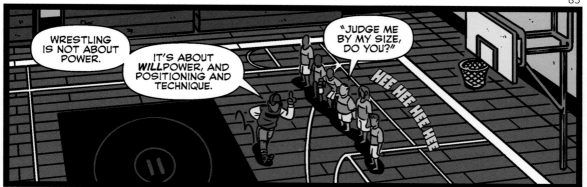

WRESTLING IS NOT ABOUT POWER.

IT'S ABOUT *WILL*POWER, AND POSITIONING AND TECHNIQUE.

"JUDGE ME BY MY SIZE, DO YOU?"

HEE HEE HEE HEE

I HEAR A *SKEPTIC* AMONGST US. I GET ONE OF YOU EVERY YEAR. ALTHOUGH THE *YODA* IMPERSONATION IS USUALLY MORE SPOT-ON.

P0WN3D!

WELL, I'LL PROVE TO YOU THAT OLD COACH AIN'T JUST TALKING SMACK. I'VE INVITED A *SPECIAL GUEST* TO HELP US WITH A DEMON-STRATION.

≑GASP!≑

I PRESUME HE NEEDS NO INTRODUCTION...

HI. I'M MOOSE MASON.

...OOOR HE CAN INTRODUCE HIMSELF, THAT WORKS, TOO.

ARE YOU READY TO RUUUUMBLE?

THAT WAS YOUR CUE TO VOLUNTEER. ANYONE?

Oh, Oh, Oh! ME, COACH CLAYTON! ME, ME! Oh, Oh, Oh, PICK ME!

ANYONE? *ANYONE?*

OKAY, MR. GATES, YOU'RE UP.

YES.

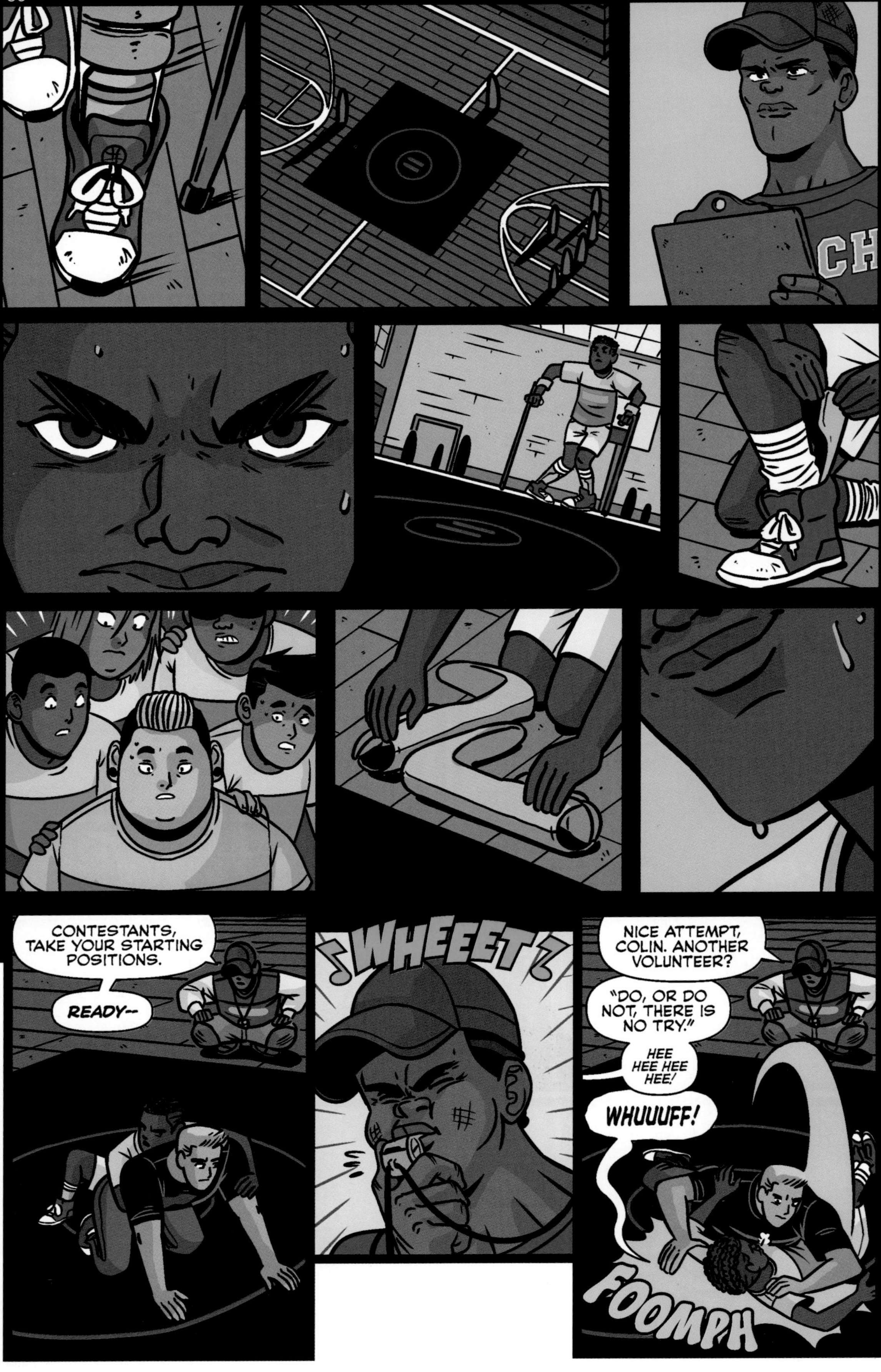
CH
CONTESTANTS, TAKE YOUR STARTING POSITIONS.
READY--
WHEEEET
NICE ATTEMPT, COLIN. ANOTHER VOLUNTEER?
"DO, OR DO NOT, THERE IS NO TRY."
HEE HEE HEE HEE!
WHUUUFF!
FOOMPH

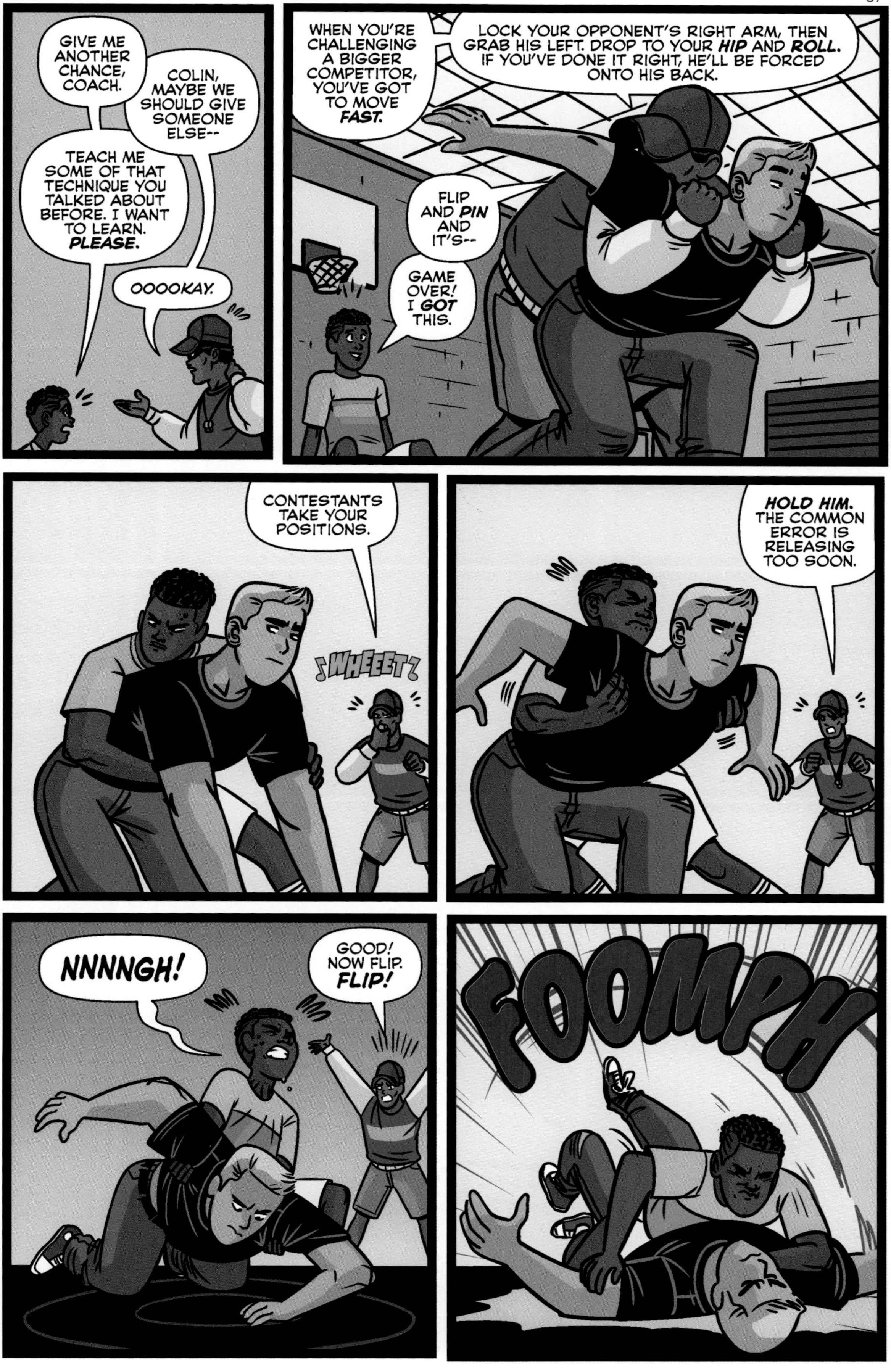
GIVE ME ANOTHER CHANCE, COACH.
COLIN, MAYBE WE SHOULD GIVE SOMEONE ELSE--
TEACH ME SOME OF THAT TECHNIQUE YOU TALKED ABOUT BEFORE. I WANT TO LEARN. PLEASE.
OOOOKAY.
WHEN YOU'RE CHALLENGING A BIGGER COMPETITOR, YOU'VE GOT TO MOVE FAST.
LOCK YOUR OPPONENT'S RIGHT ARM, THEN GRAB HIS LEFT. DROP TO YOUR HIP AND ROLL. IF YOU'VE DONE IT RIGHT, HE'LL BE FORCED ONTO HIS BACK.
FLIP AND PIN AND IT'S--
GAME OVER! I GOT THIS.
CONTESTANTS TAKE YOUR POSITIONS.
WHEEET
HOLD HIM. THE COMMON ERROR IS RELEASING TOO SOON.
NNNNGH!
GOOD! NOW FLIP. FLIP!
FOOMPH

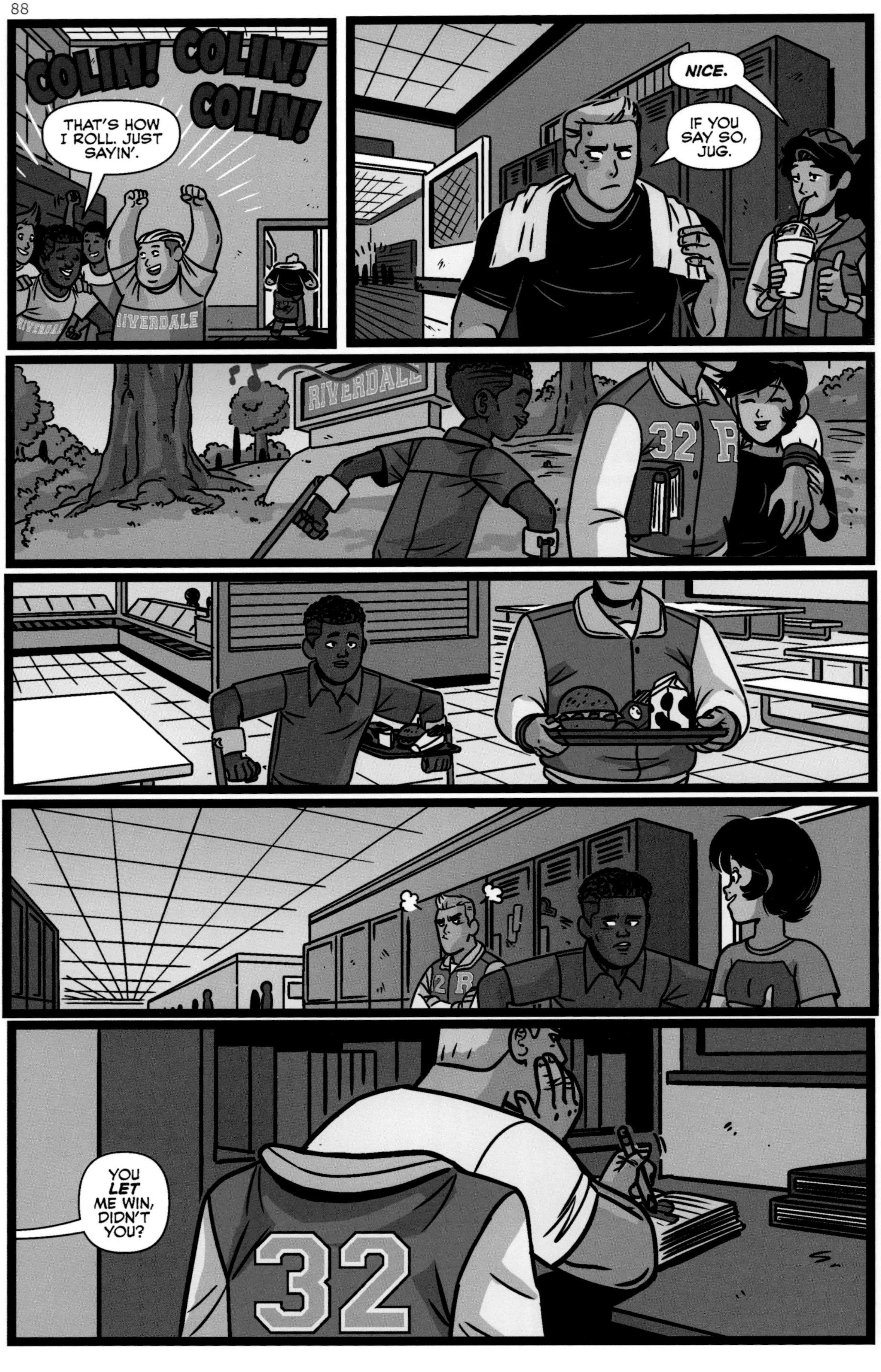
COLIN! COLIN! COLIN!
THAT'S HOW I ROLL. JUST SAYIN'.
RIVERDALE
RIVERDALE
NICE.
IF YOU SAY SO, JUG.
RIVERDALE
YOU *LET* ME WIN, DIDN'T YOU?

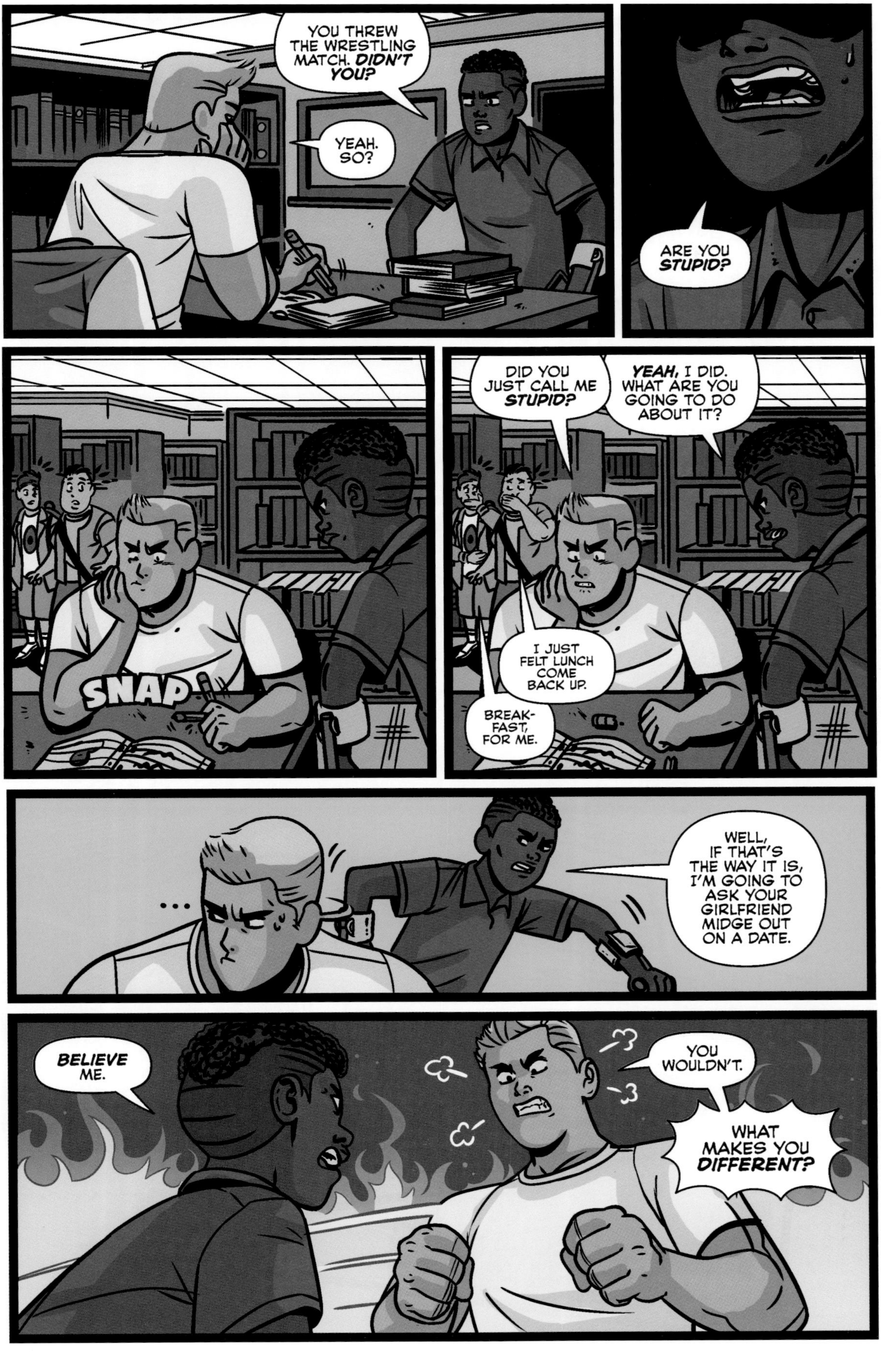
YOU THREW THE WRESTLING MATCH. ***DIDN'T YOU?***
YEAH. SO?
ARE YOU ***STUPID?***
SNAP
DID YOU JUST CALL ME ***STUPID?***
YEAH, I DID. WHAT ARE YOU GOING TO DO ABOUT IT?
I JUST FELT LUNCH COME BACK UP.
BREAK-FAST, FOR ME.
...
WELL, IF THAT'S THE WAY IT IS, I'M GOING TO ASK YOUR GIRLFRIEND MIDGE OUT ON A DATE.
BELIEVE ME.
YOU WOULDN'T.
WHAT MAKES YOU ***DIFFERENT?***

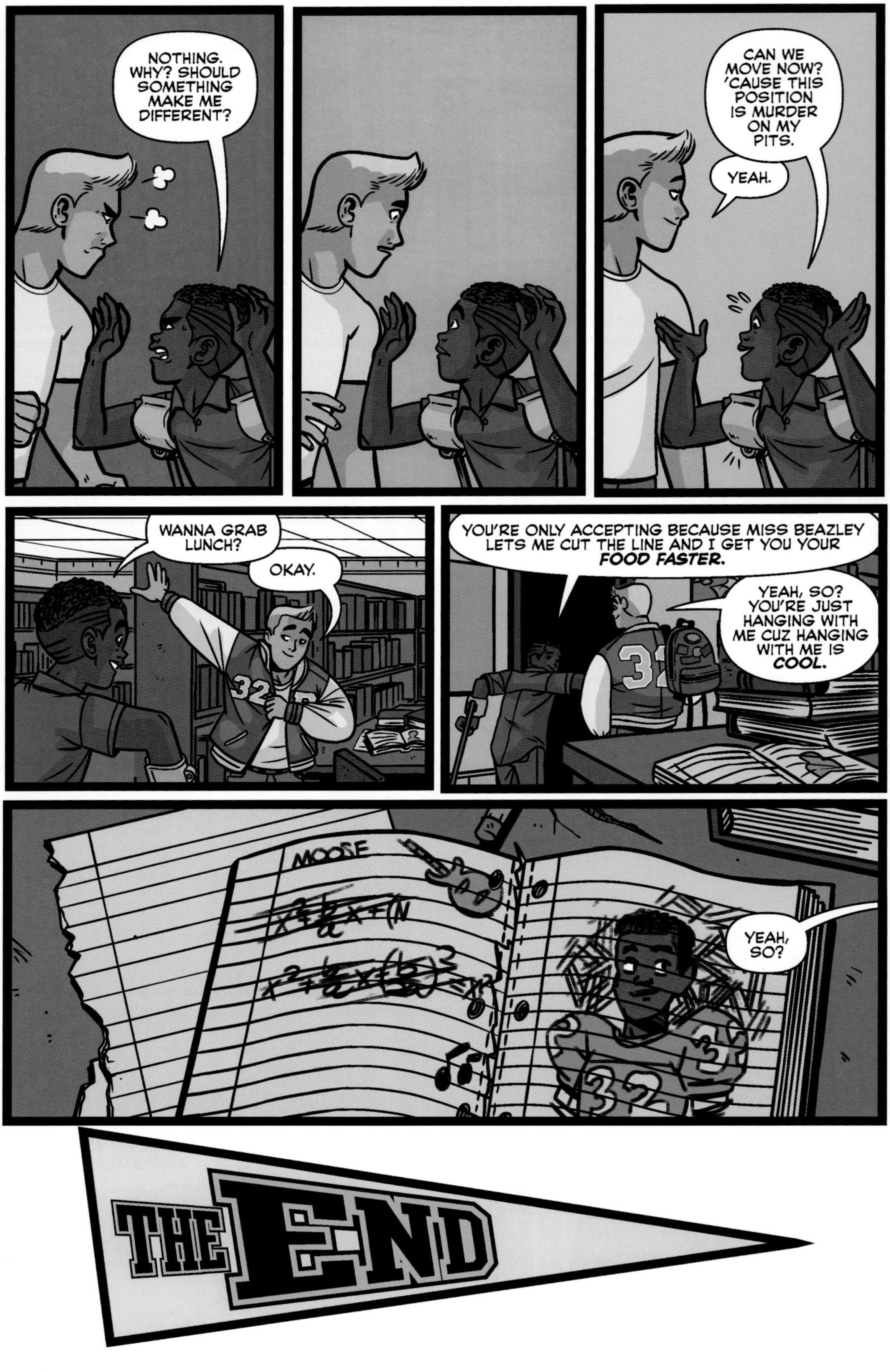
NOTHING. WHY? SHOULD SOMETHING MAKE ME DIFFERENT?
CAN WE MOVE NOW? 'CAUSE THIS POSITION IS MURDER ON MY PITS.
YEAH.
WANNA GRAB LUNCH?
OKAY.
YOU'RE ONLY ACCEPTING BECAUSE MISS BEAZLEY LETS ME CUT THE LINE AND I GET YOU YOUR FOOD FASTER.
YEAH, SO? YOU'RE JUST HANGING WITH ME CUZ HANGING WITH ME IS COOL.
MOOSE
YEAH, SO?
THE END

COVER GALLERY

BIG MOOSE

1: Thomas Pitilli

2: Cory Smith

3: Wilfredo Torres

1

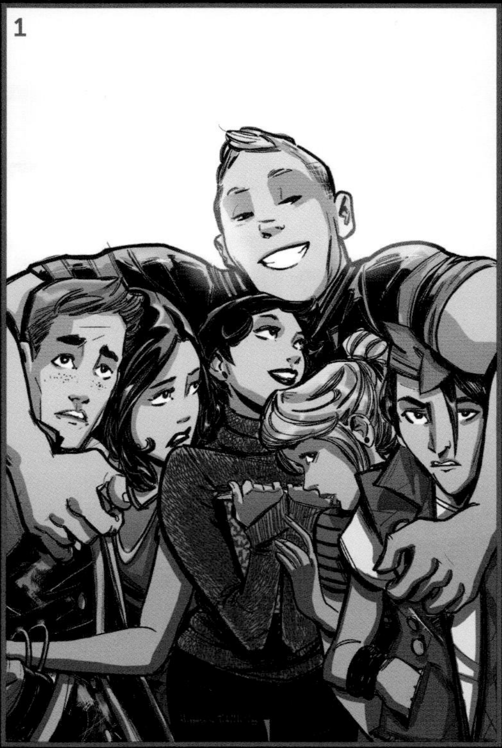

2

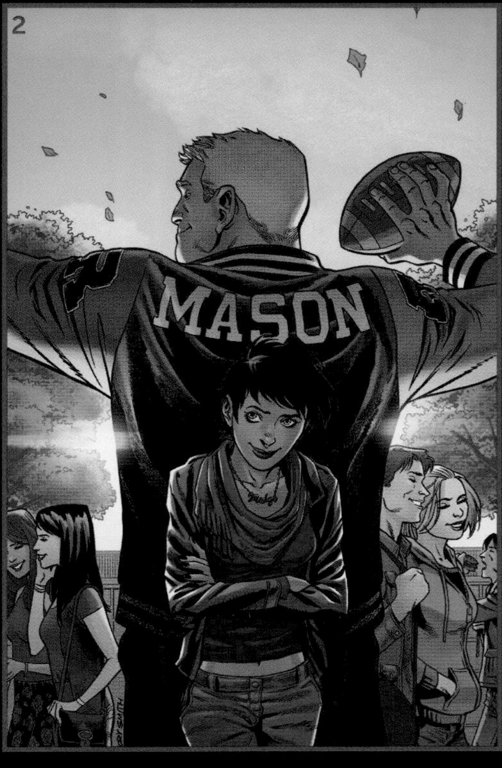
MASON

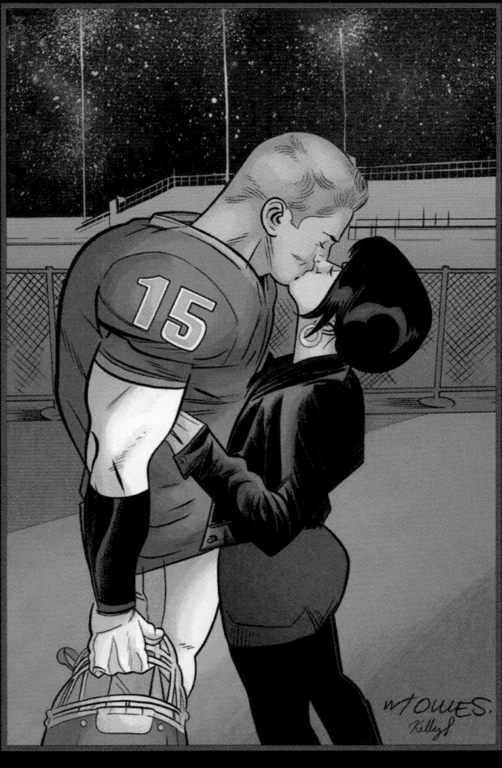
15

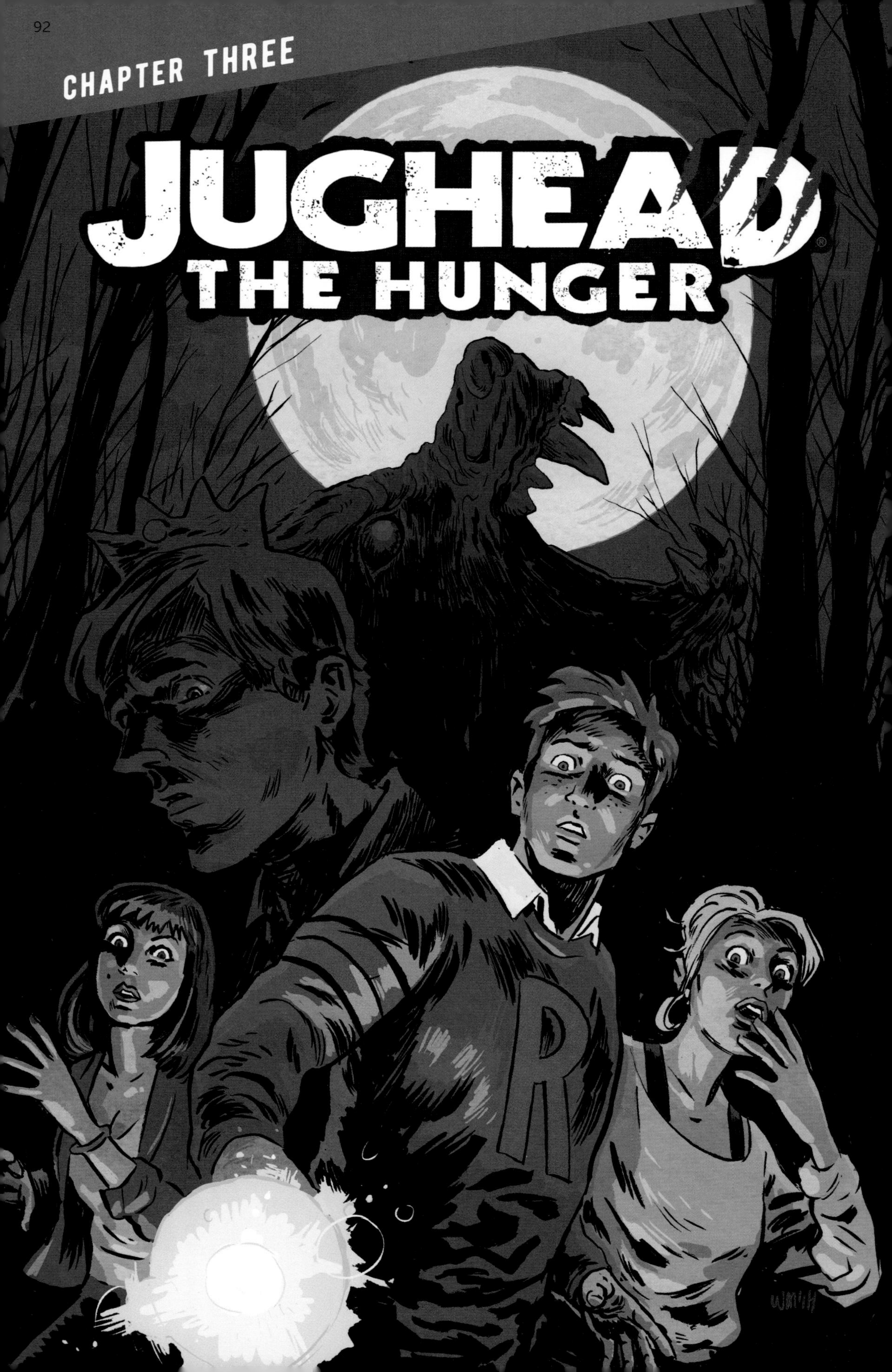
CHAPTER THREE
JUGHEAD®
THE HUNGER

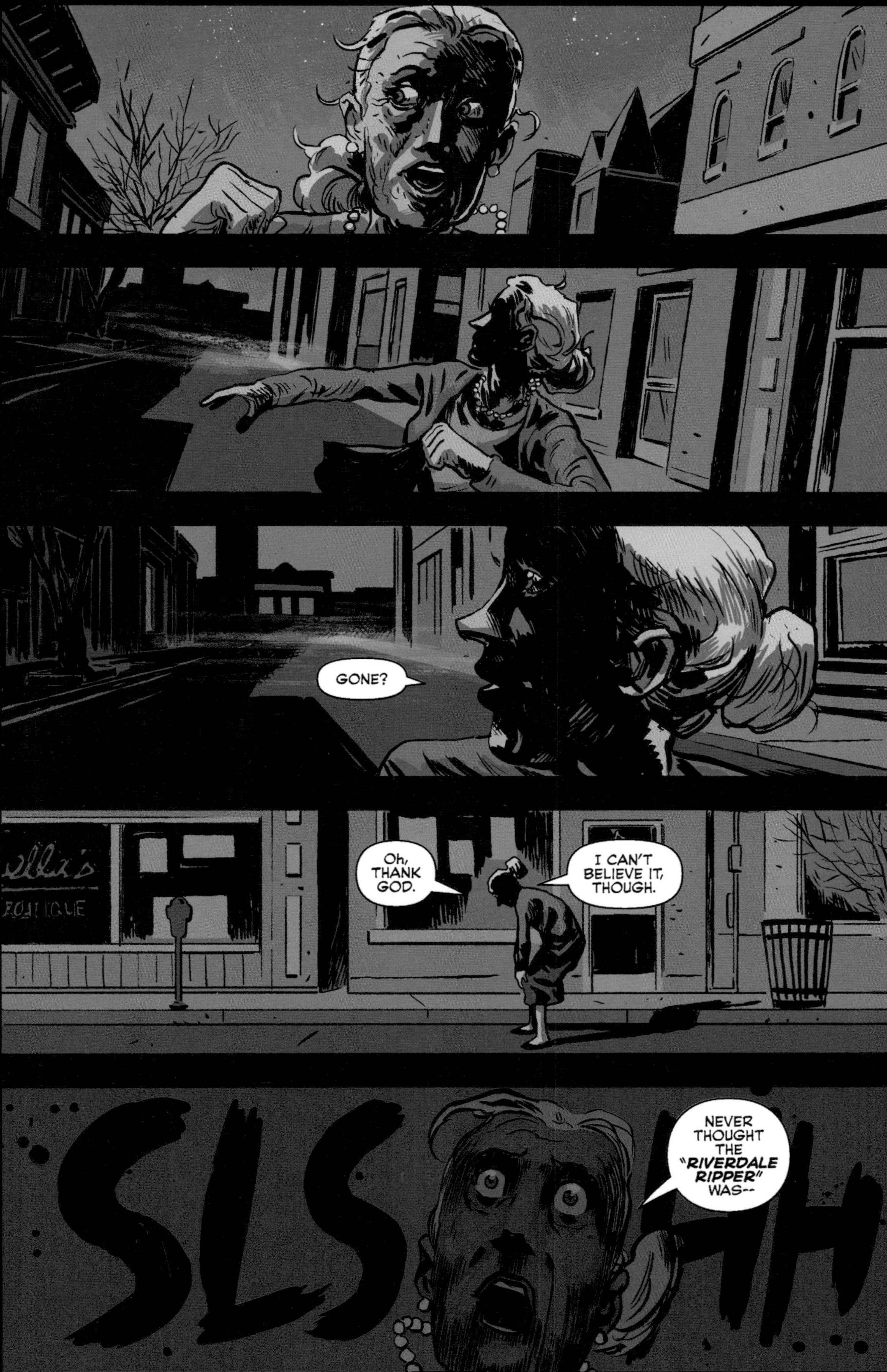
GONE?
Oh, THANK GOD.
I CAN'T BELIEVE IT, THOUGH.
NEVER THOUGHT THE "RIVERDALE RIPPER" WAS--

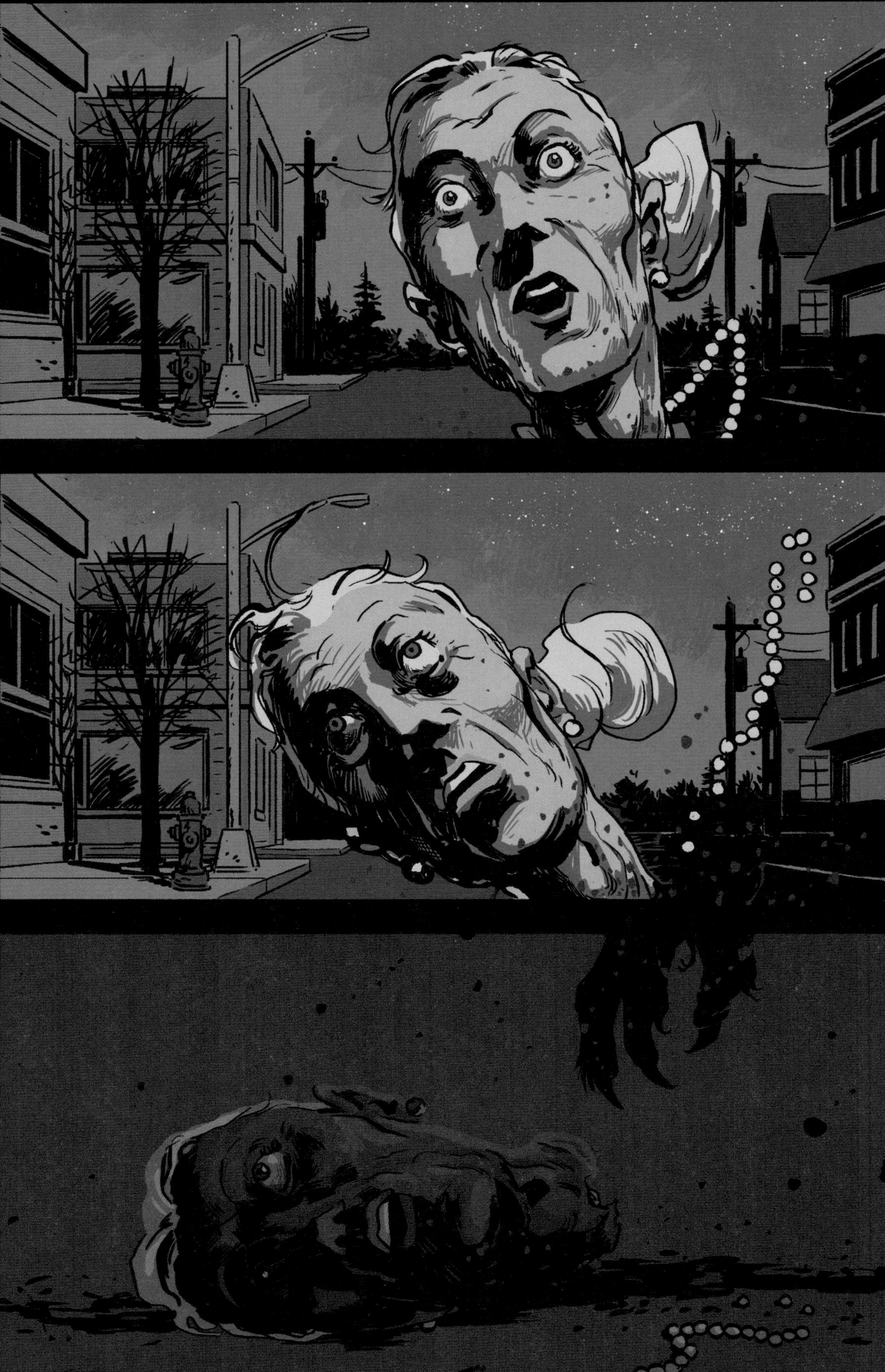

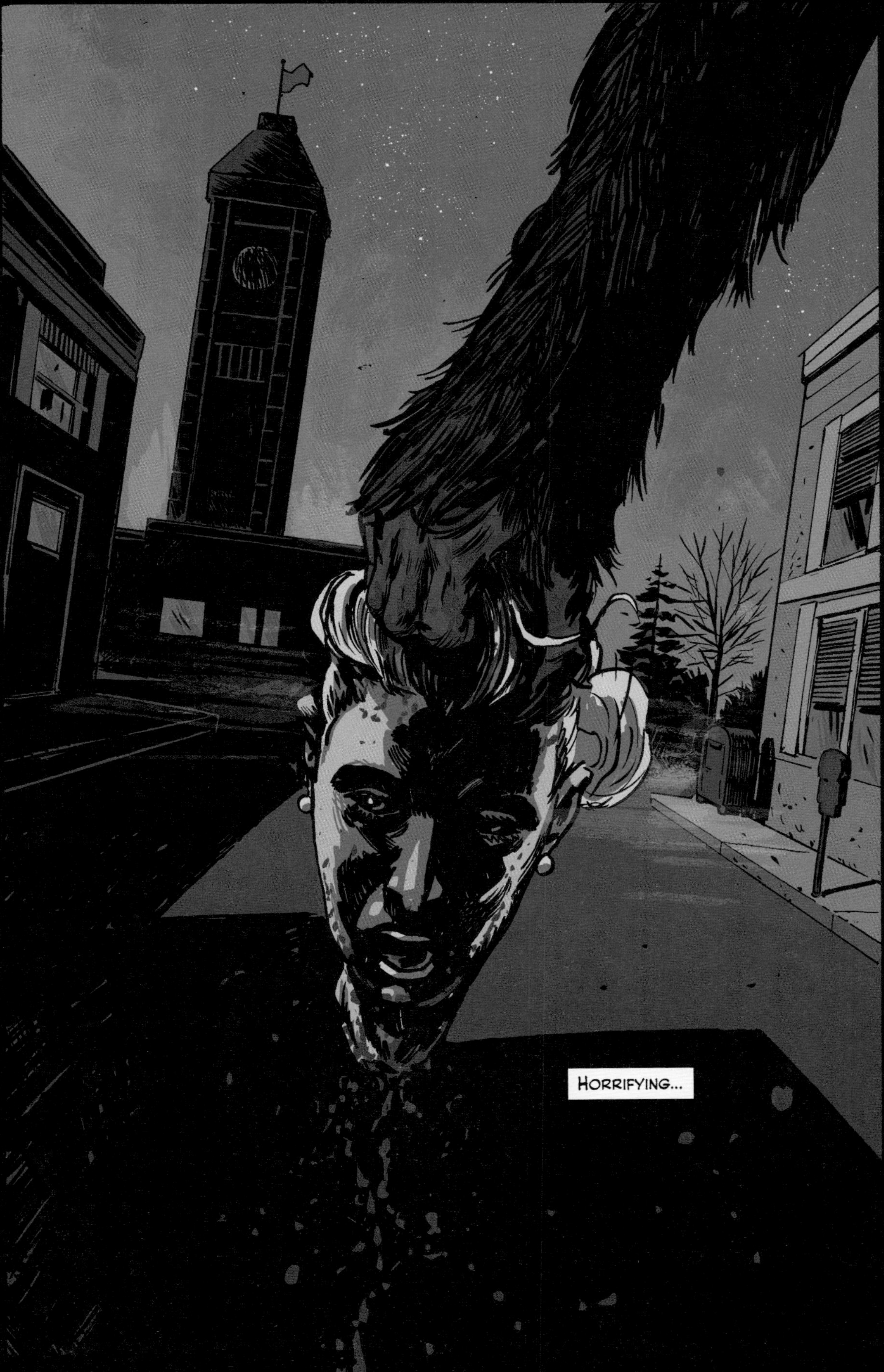
HORRIFYING...

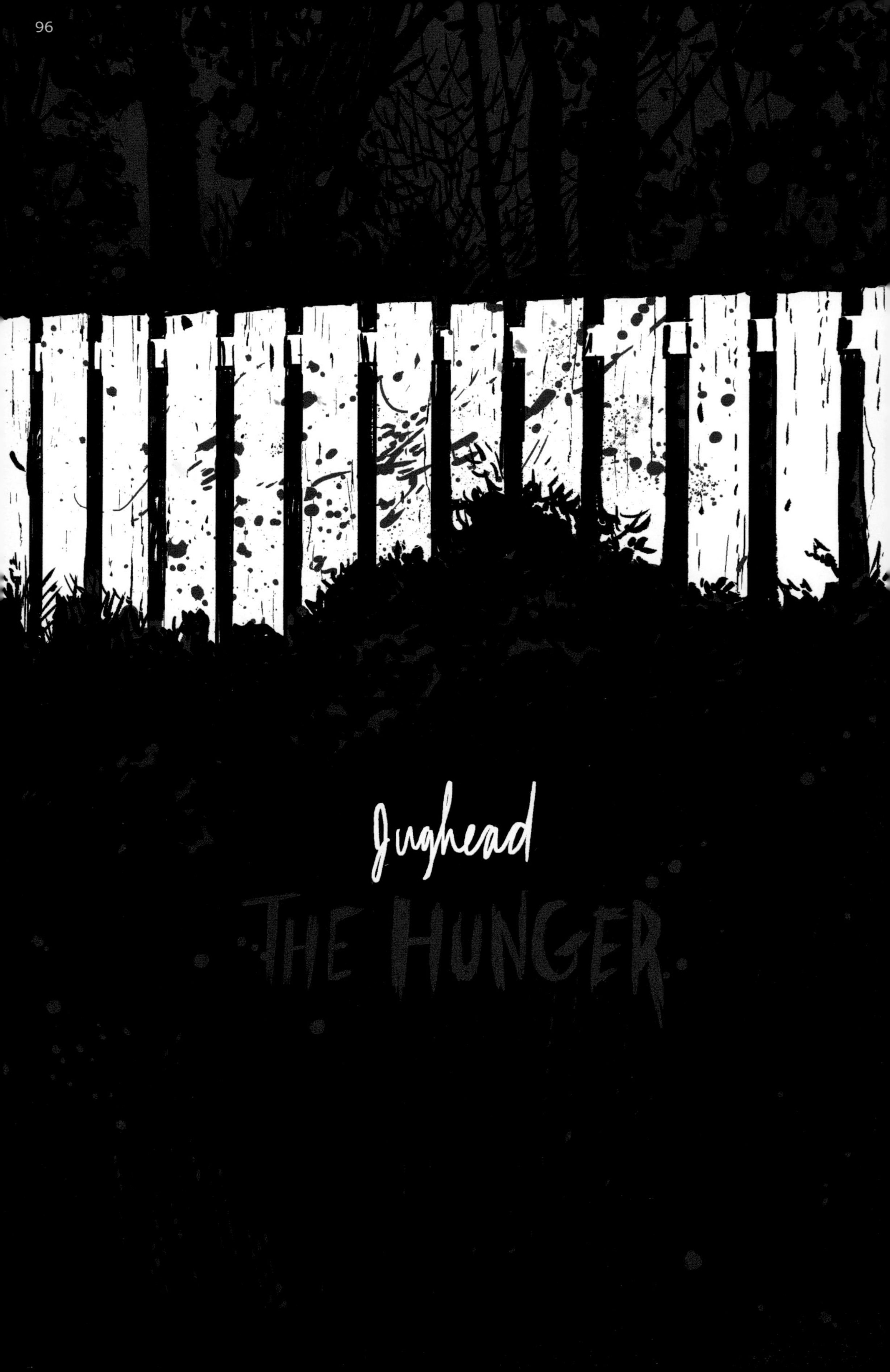
Jughead
THE HUNGER

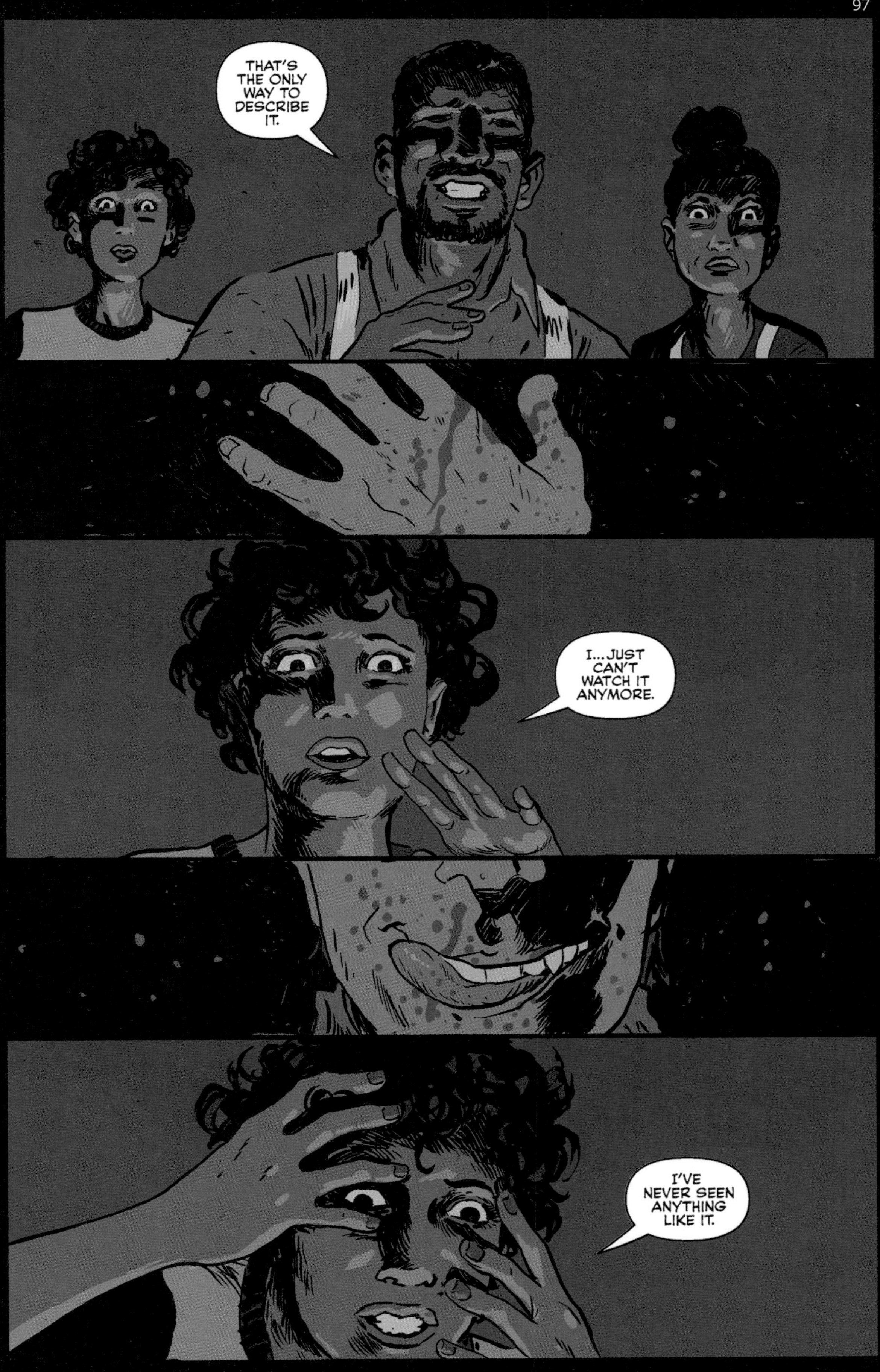
THAT'S THE ONLY WAY TO DESCRIBE IT.
I...JUST CAN'T WATCH IT ANYMORE.
I'VE NEVER SEEN ANYTHING LIKE IT.

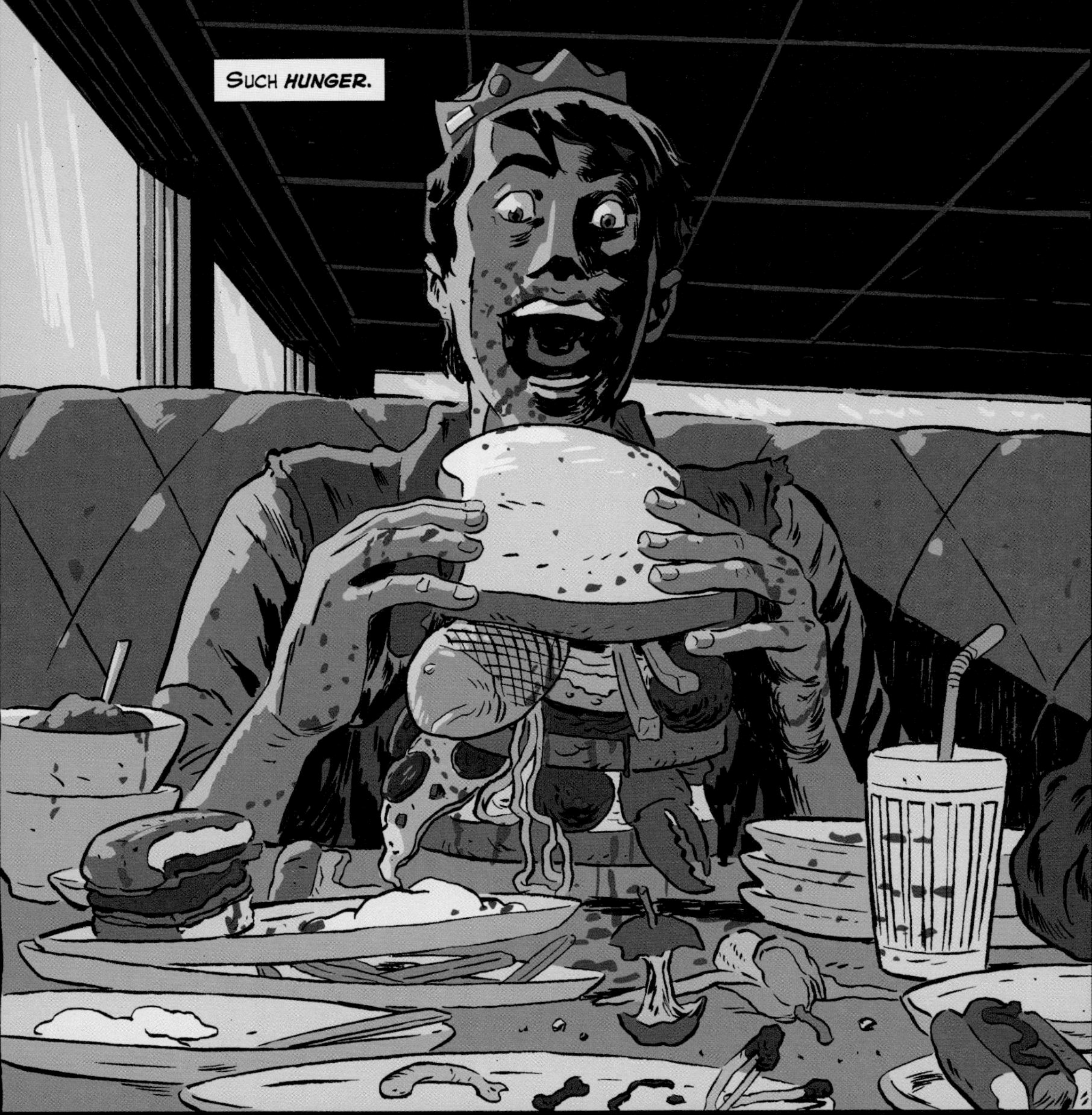
SUCH **HUNGER.**

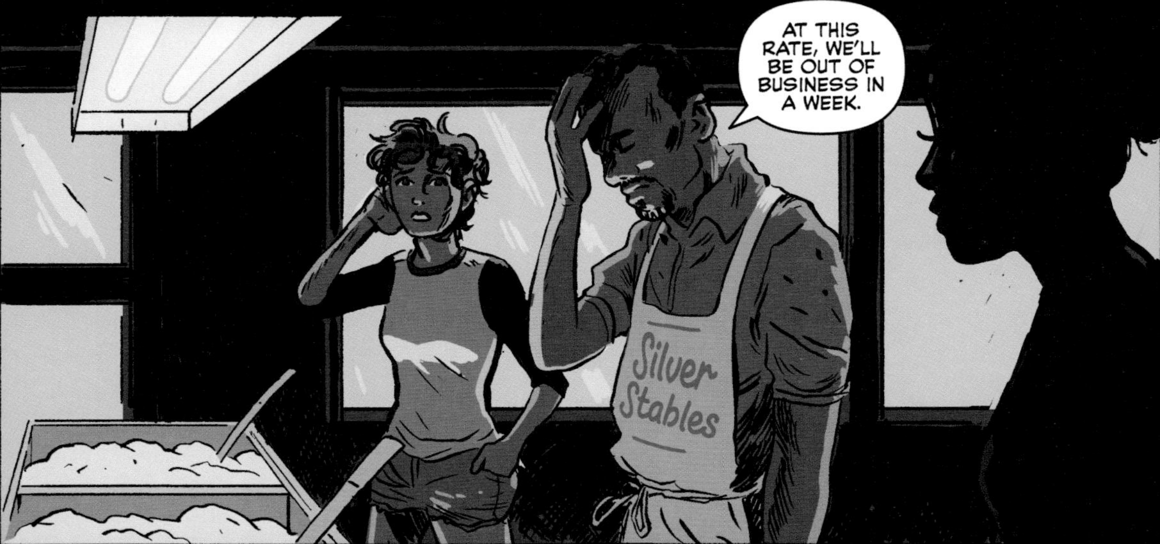
AT THIS RATE, WE'LL BE OUT OF BUSINESS IN A WEEK.
Silver Stables

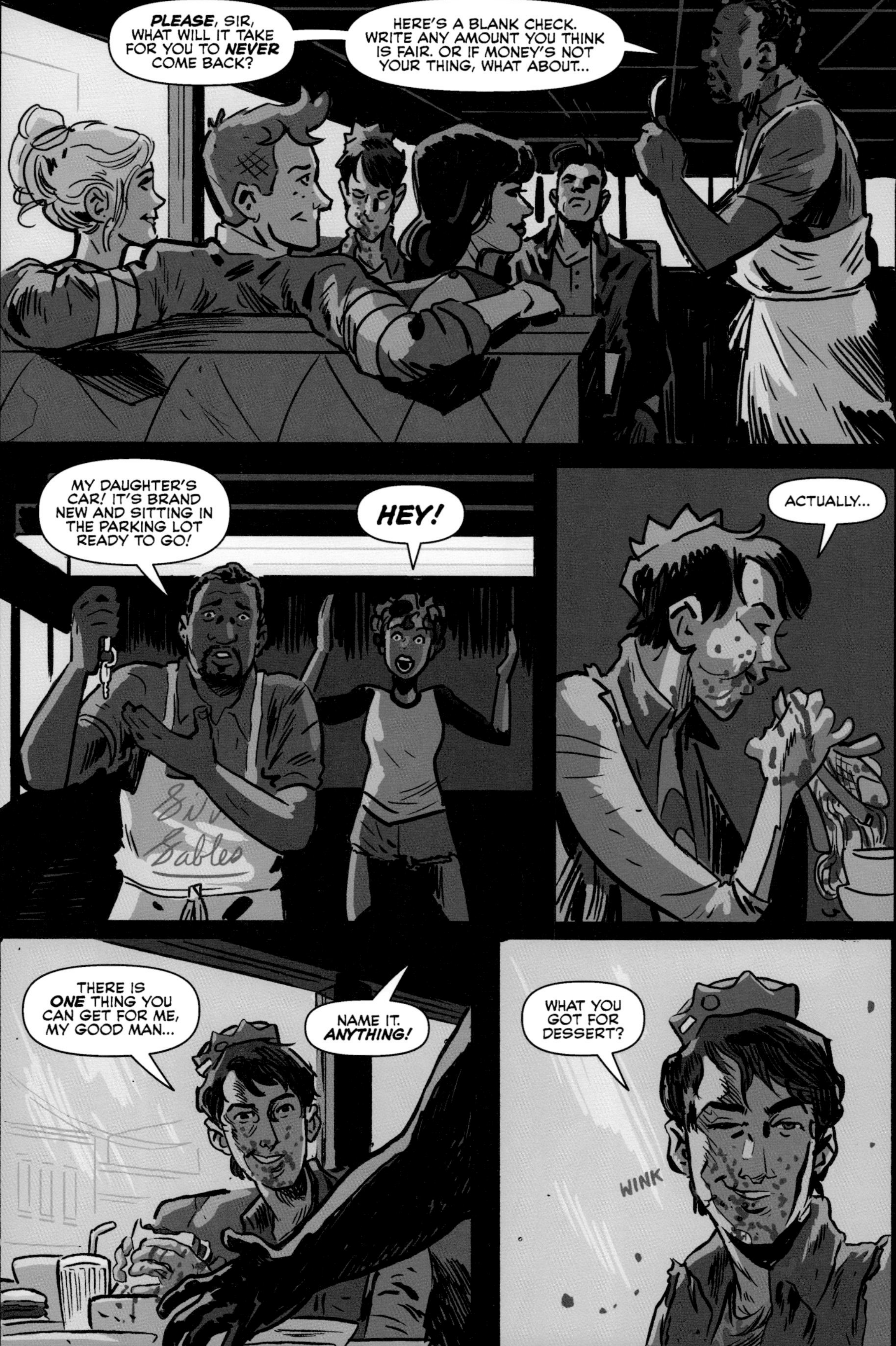
PLEASE, SIR, WHAT WILL IT TAKE FOR YOU TO NEVER COME BACK?
HERE'S A BLANK CHECK. WRITE ANY AMOUNT YOU THINK IS FAIR. OR IF MONEY'S NOT YOUR THING, WHAT ABOUT...
MY DAUGHTER'S CAR! IT'S BRAND NEW AND SITTING IN THE PARKING LOT READY TO GO!
HEY!
ACTUALLY...
THERE IS ONE THING YOU CAN GET FOR ME, MY GOOD MAN...
NAME IT. ANYTHING!
WHAT YOU GOT FOR DESSERT?
WINK

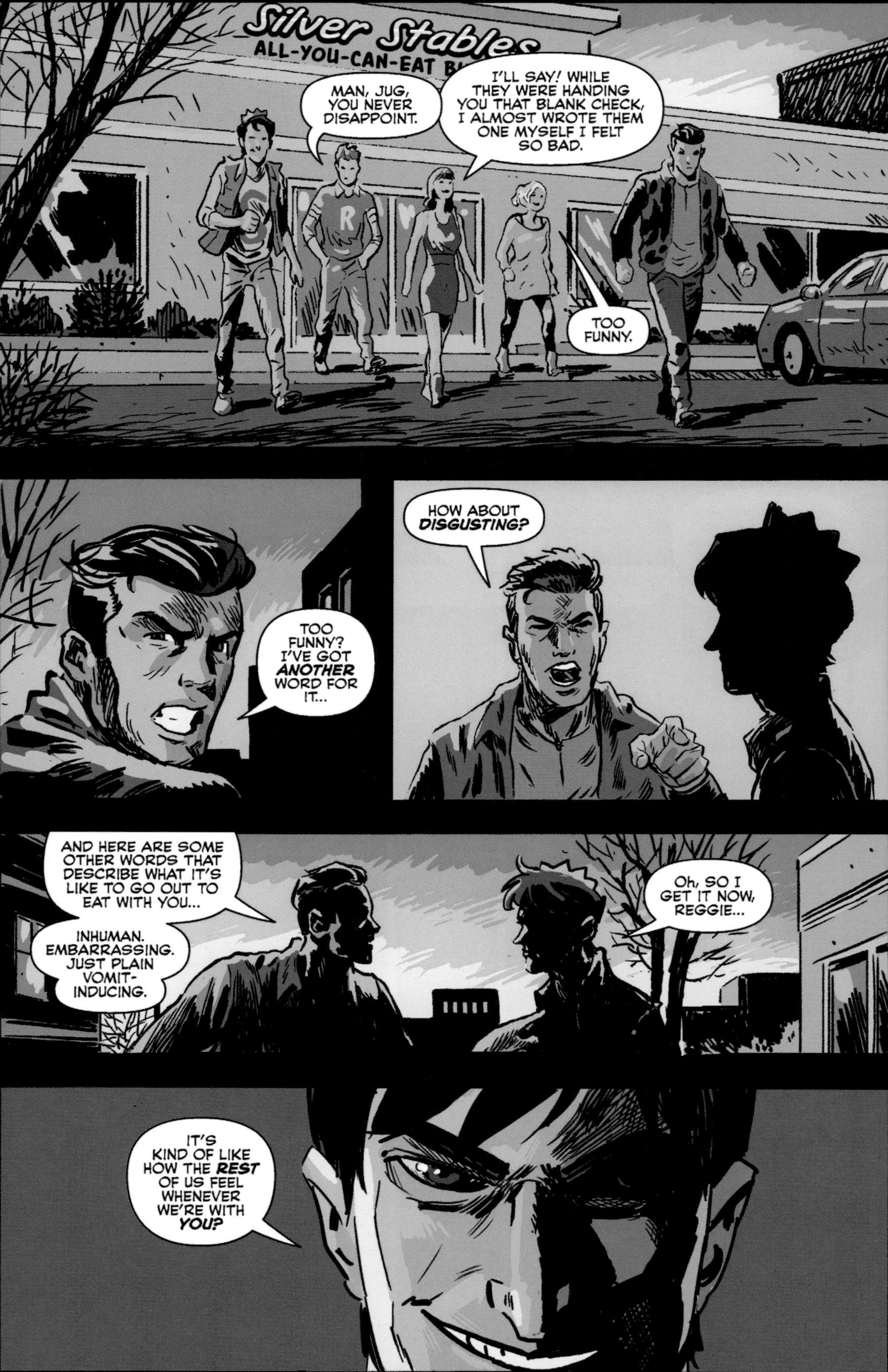
Silver Stables
ALL-YOU-CAN-EAT B
MAN, JUG, YOU NEVER DISAPPOINT.
I'LL SAY! WHILE THEY WERE HANDING YOU THAT BLANK CHECK, I ALMOST WROTE THEM ONE MYSELF I FELT SO BAD.
TOO FUNNY.
TOO FUNNY? I'VE GOT ANOTHER WORD FOR IT...
HOW ABOUT DISGUSTING?
AND HERE ARE SOME OTHER WORDS THAT DESCRIBE WHAT IT'S LIKE TO GO OUT TO EAT WITH YOU...
INHUMAN. EMBARRASSING. JUST PLAIN VOMIT-INDUCING.
Oh, SO I GET IT NOW, REGGIE...
IT'S KIND OF LIKE HOW THE REST OF US FEEL WHENEVER WE'RE WITH YOU?

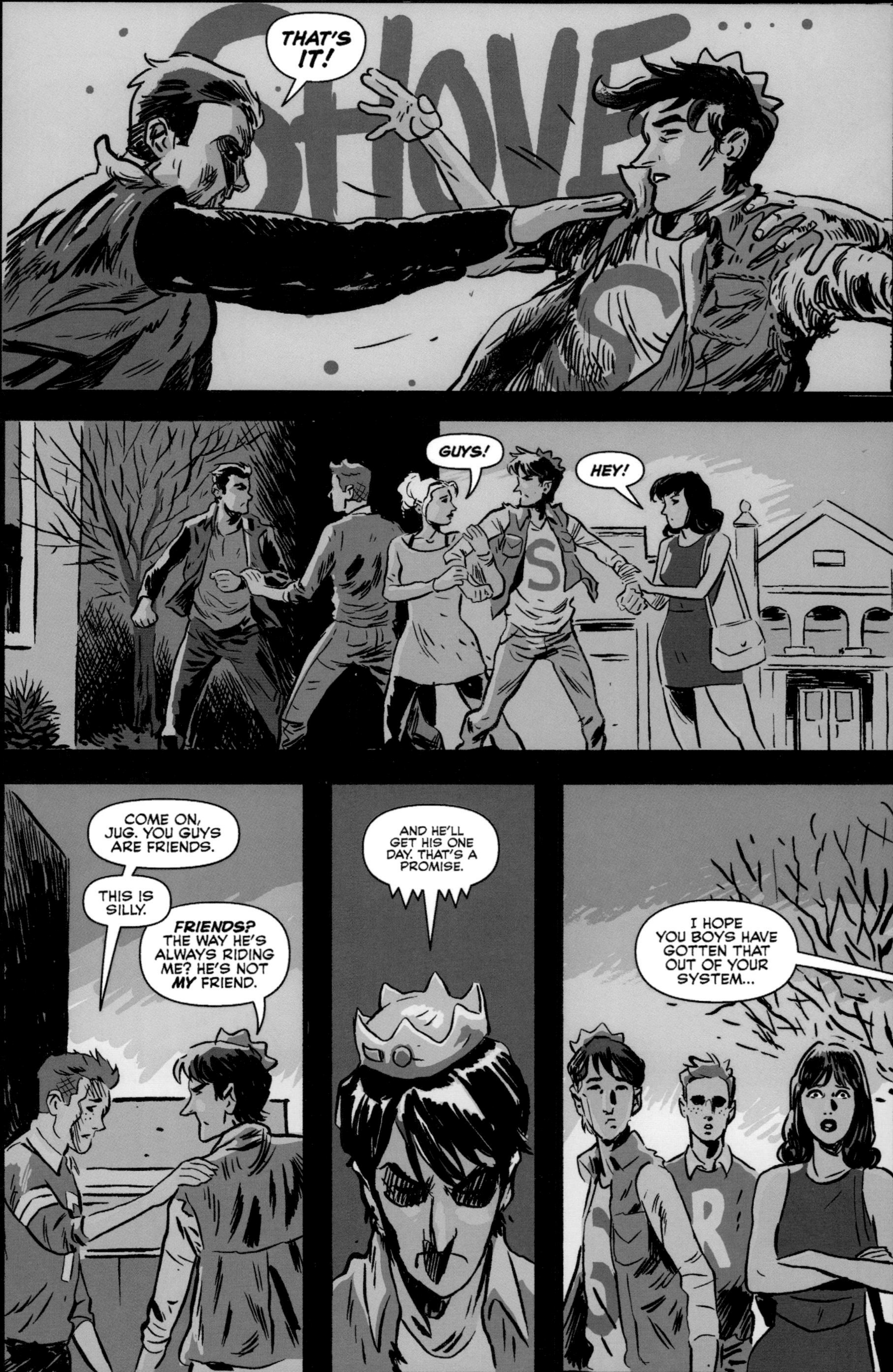
THAT'S IT!
SHOVE
GUYS!
HEY!
COME ON, JUG. YOU GUYS ARE FRIENDS.
THIS IS SILLY.
FRIENDS? THE WAY HE'S ALWAYS RIDING ME? HE'S NOT MY FRIEND.
AND HE'LL GET HIS ONE DAY. THAT'S A PROMISE.
I HOPE YOU BOYS HAVE GOTTEN THAT OUT OF YOUR SYSTEM...

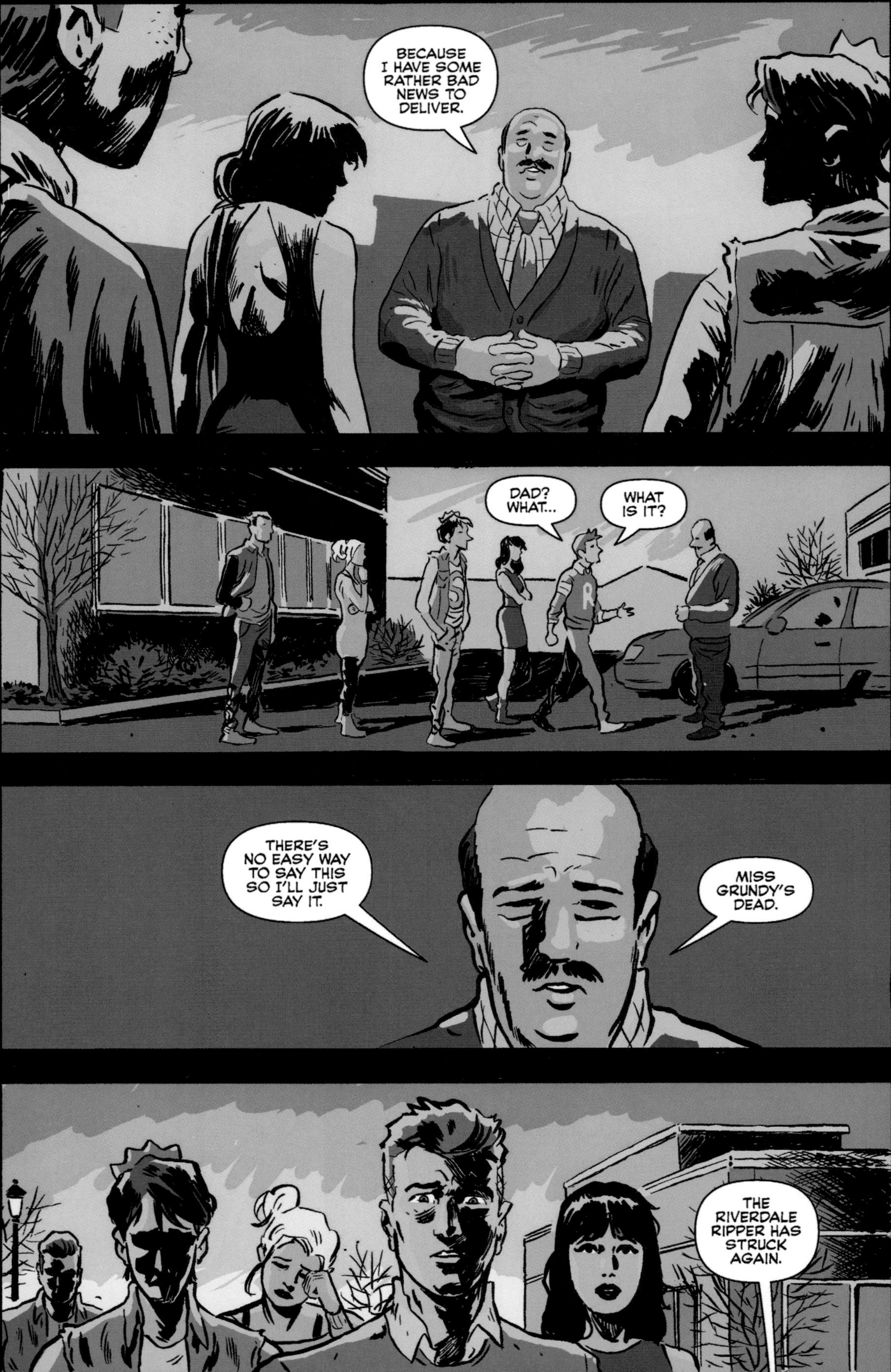
BECAUSE I HAVE SOME RATHER BAD NEWS TO DELIVER.
DAD? WHAT...
WHAT IS IT?
THERE'S NO EASY WAY TO SAY THIS SO I'LL JUST SAY IT.
MISS GRUNDY'S DEAD.
THE RIVERDALE RIPPER HAS STRUCK AGAIN.

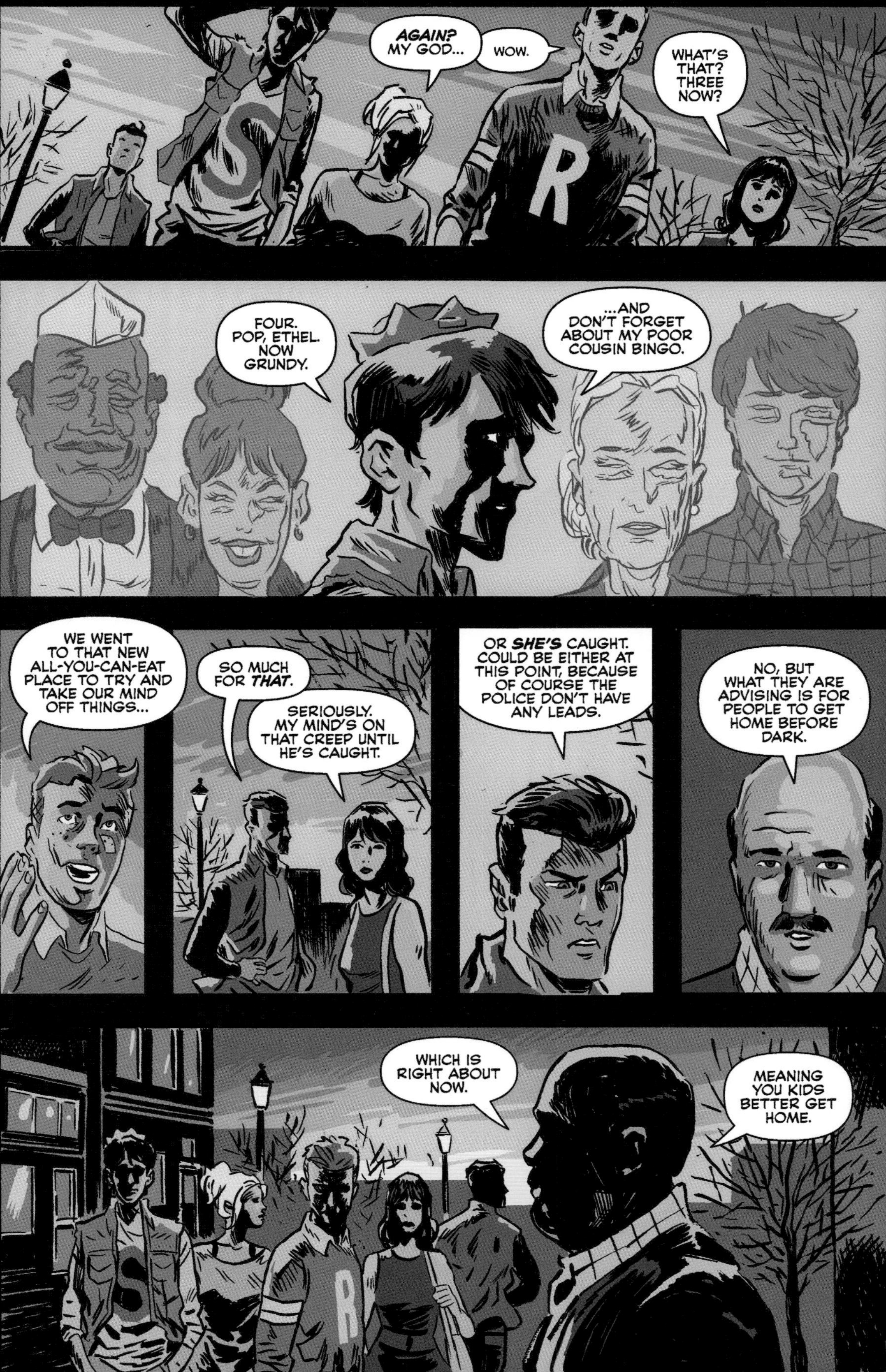
AGAIN? MY GOD...
WOW.
WHAT'S THAT? THREE NOW?
FOUR. POP, ETHEL. NOW GRUNDY.
...AND DON'T FORGET ABOUT MY POOR COUSIN BINGO.
WE WENT TO THAT NEW ALL-YOU-CAN-EAT PLACE TO TRY AND TAKE OUR MIND OFF THINGS...
SO MUCH FOR THAT.
SERIOUSLY. MY MIND'S ON THAT CREEP UNTIL HE'S CAUGHT.
OR SHE'S CAUGHT. COULD BE EITHER AT THIS POINT, BECAUSE OF COURSE THE POLICE DON'T HAVE ANY LEADS.
NO, BUT WHAT THEY ARE ADVISING IS FOR PEOPLE TO GET HOME BEFORE DARK.
WHICH IS RIGHT ABOUT NOW.
MEANING YOU KIDS BETTER GET HOME.

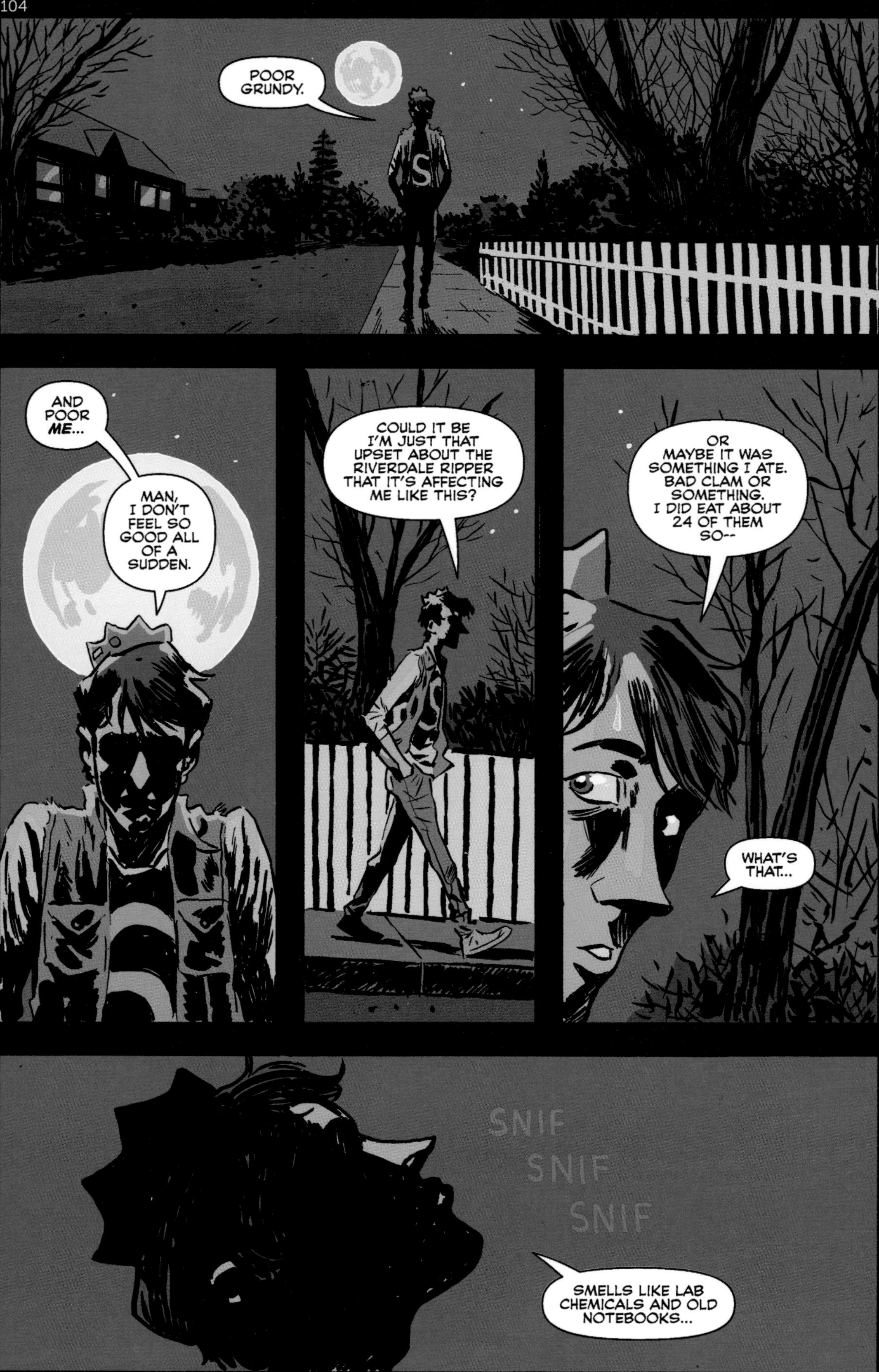
POOR GRUNDY.
AND POOR *ME*...
MAN, I DON'T FEEL SO GOOD ALL OF A SUDDEN.
COULD IT BE I'M JUST THAT UPSET ABOUT THE RIVERDALE RIPPER THAT IT'S AFFECTING ME LIKE THIS?
OR MAYBE IT WAS SOMETHING I ATE. BAD CLAM OR SOMETHING. I DID EAT ABOUT 24 OF THEM SO--
WHAT'S THAT...
SNIF
SNIF
SNIF
SMELLS LIKE LAB CHEMICALS AND OLD NOTEBOOKS...

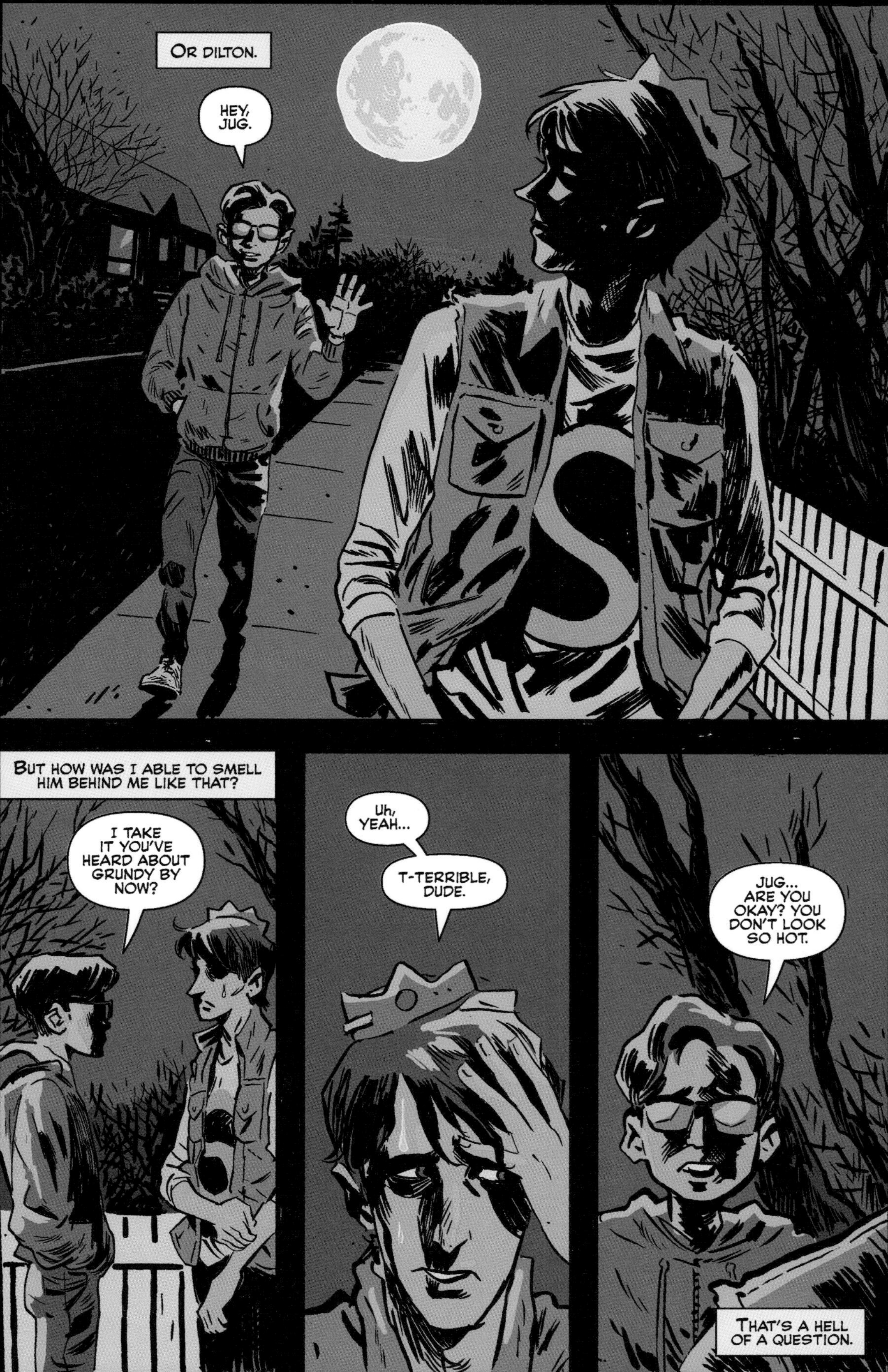
Or dilton.
HEY, JUG.
But how was I able to smell him behind me like that?
I TAKE IT YOU'VE HEARD ABOUT GRUNDY BY NOW?
Uh, YEAH...
T-TERRIBLE, DUDE.
JUG... ARE YOU OKAY? YOU DON'T LOOK SO HOT.
That's a hell of a question.

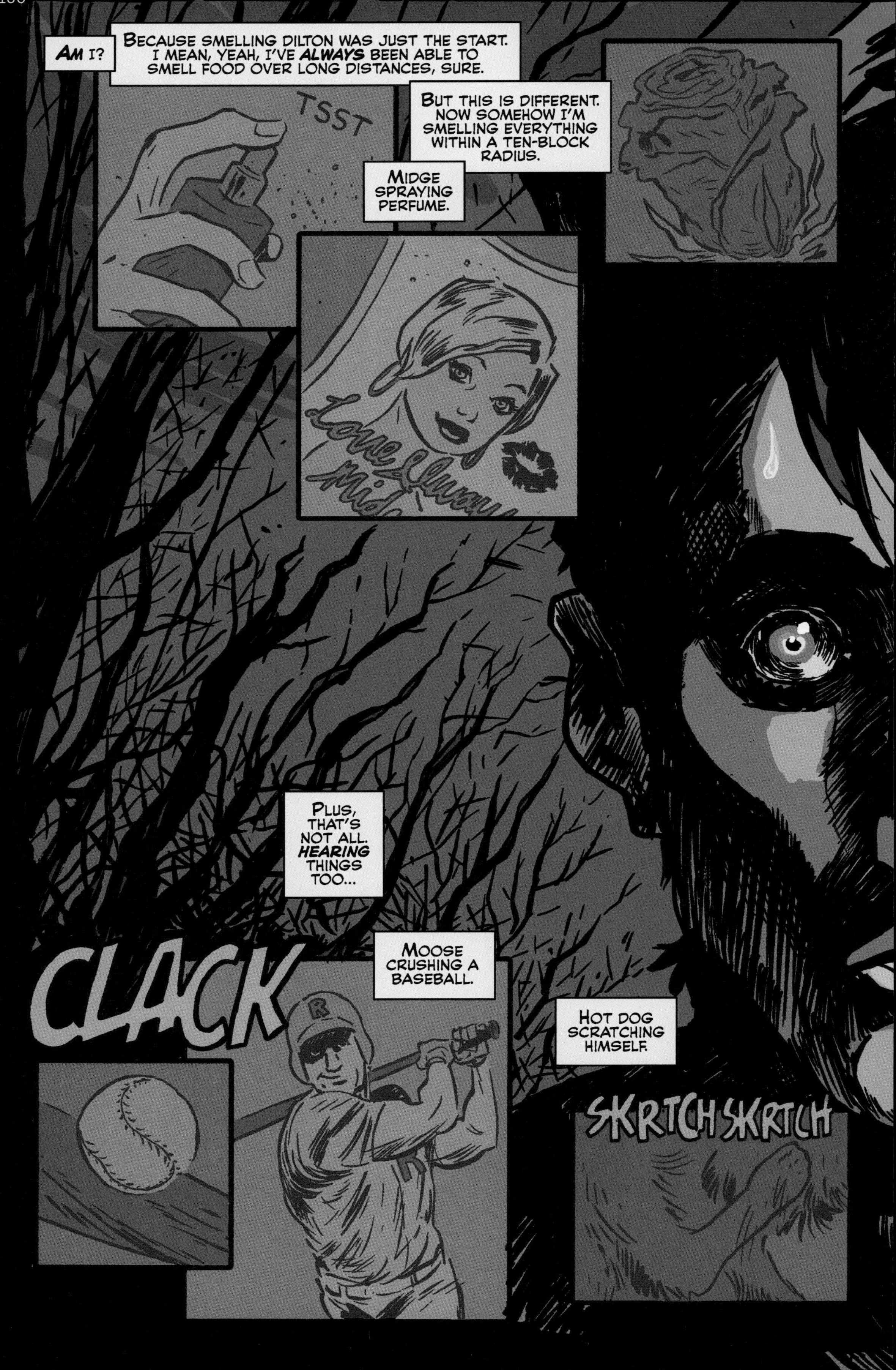
AM I?
BECAUSE SMELLING DILTON WAS JUST THE START. I MEAN, YEAH, I'VE ALWAYS BEEN ABLE TO SMELL FOOD OVER LONG DISTANCES, SURE.
TSST
BUT THIS IS DIFFERENT. NOW SOMEHOW I'M SMELLING EVERYTHING WITHIN A TEN-BLOCK RADIUS.
MIDGE SPRAYING PERFUME.
PLUS, THAT'S NOT ALL. HEARING THINGS TOO...
CLACK
MOOSE CRUSHING A BASEBALL.
HOT DOG SCRATCHING HIMSELF.
SKRTCH SKRTCH

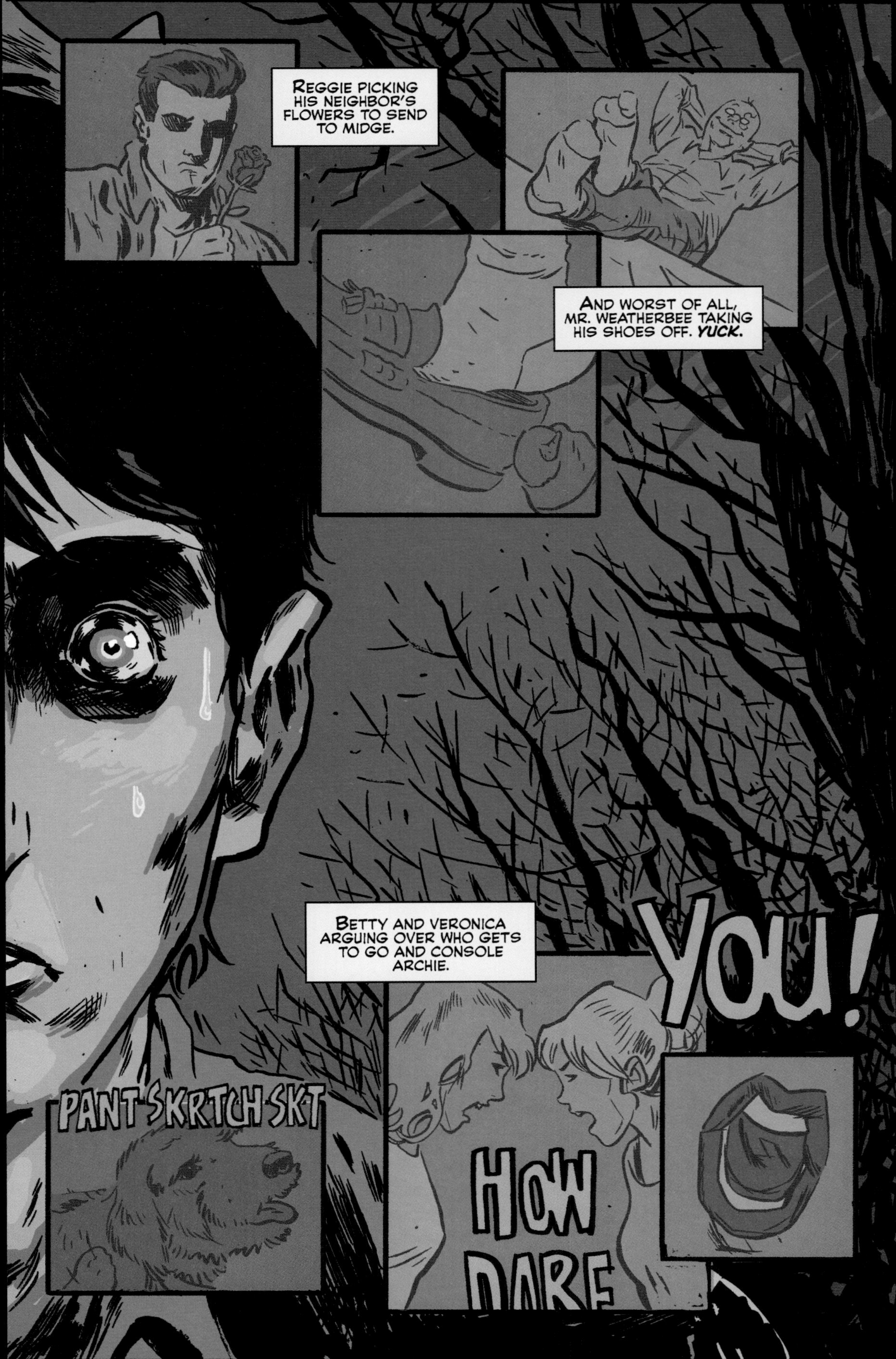

REGGIE PICKING HIS NEIGHBOR'S FLOWERS TO SEND TO MIDGE.
AND WORST OF ALL, MR. WEATHERBEE TAKING HIS SHOES OFF. ***YUCK.***
BETTY AND VERONICA ARGUING OVER WHO GETS TO GO AND CONSOLE ARCHIE.
PANT SKRTCH SKT
HOW DARE
YOU!

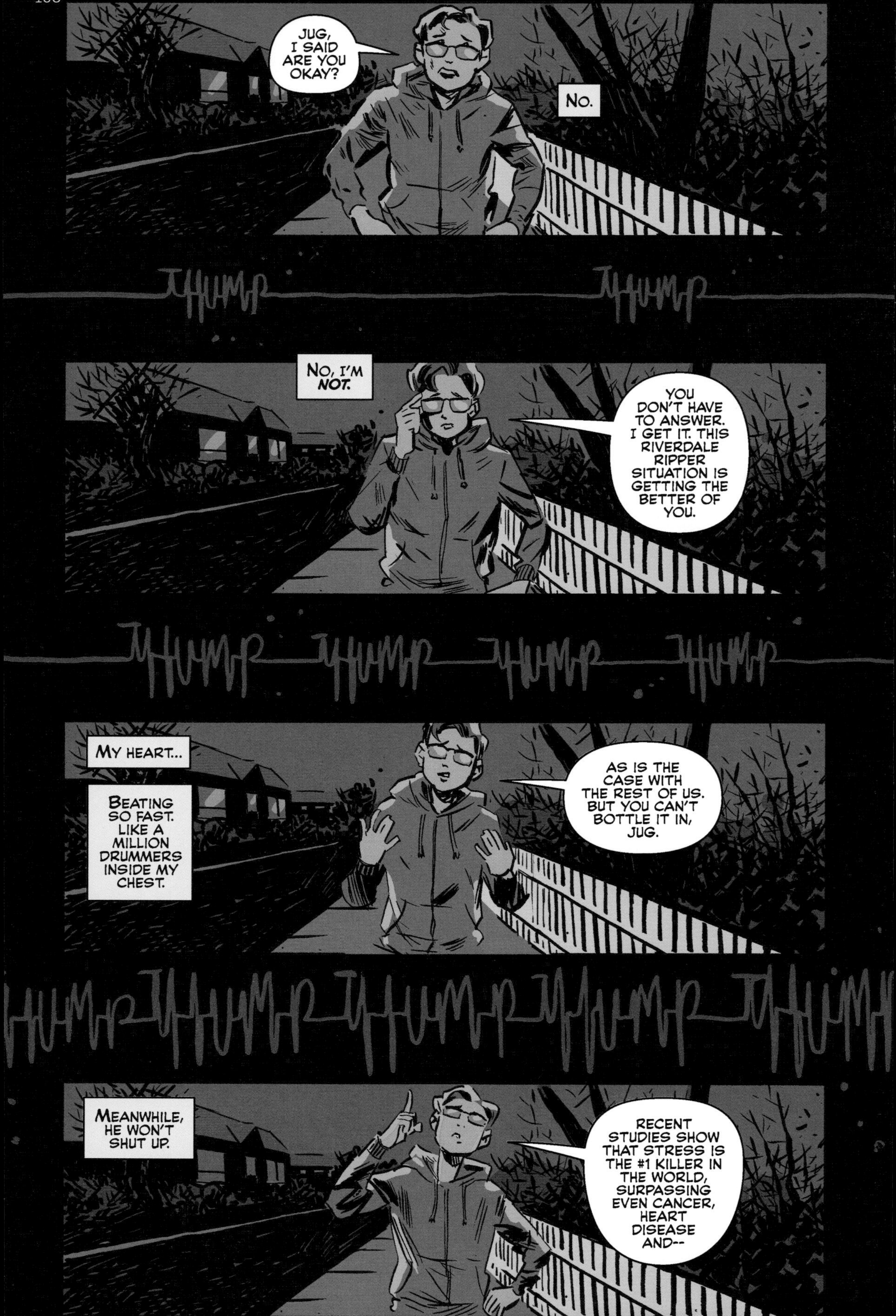
JUG, I SAID ARE YOU OKAY?
No.
THUMP THUMP
No, I'M NOT.
YOU DON'T HAVE TO ANSWER. I GET IT. THIS RIVERDALE RIPPER SITUATION IS GETTING THE BETTER OF YOU.
THUMP THUMP THUMP THUMP
My heart...
Beating so fast. Like a million drummers inside my chest.
AS IS THE CASE WITH THE REST OF US. BUT YOU CAN'T BOTTLE IT IN, JUG.
THUMP THUMP THUMP THUMP THUMP
Meanwhile, he won't shut up.
RECENT STUDIES SHOW THAT STRESS IS THE #1 KILLER IN THE WORLD, SURPASSING EVEN CANCER, HEART DISEASE AND--

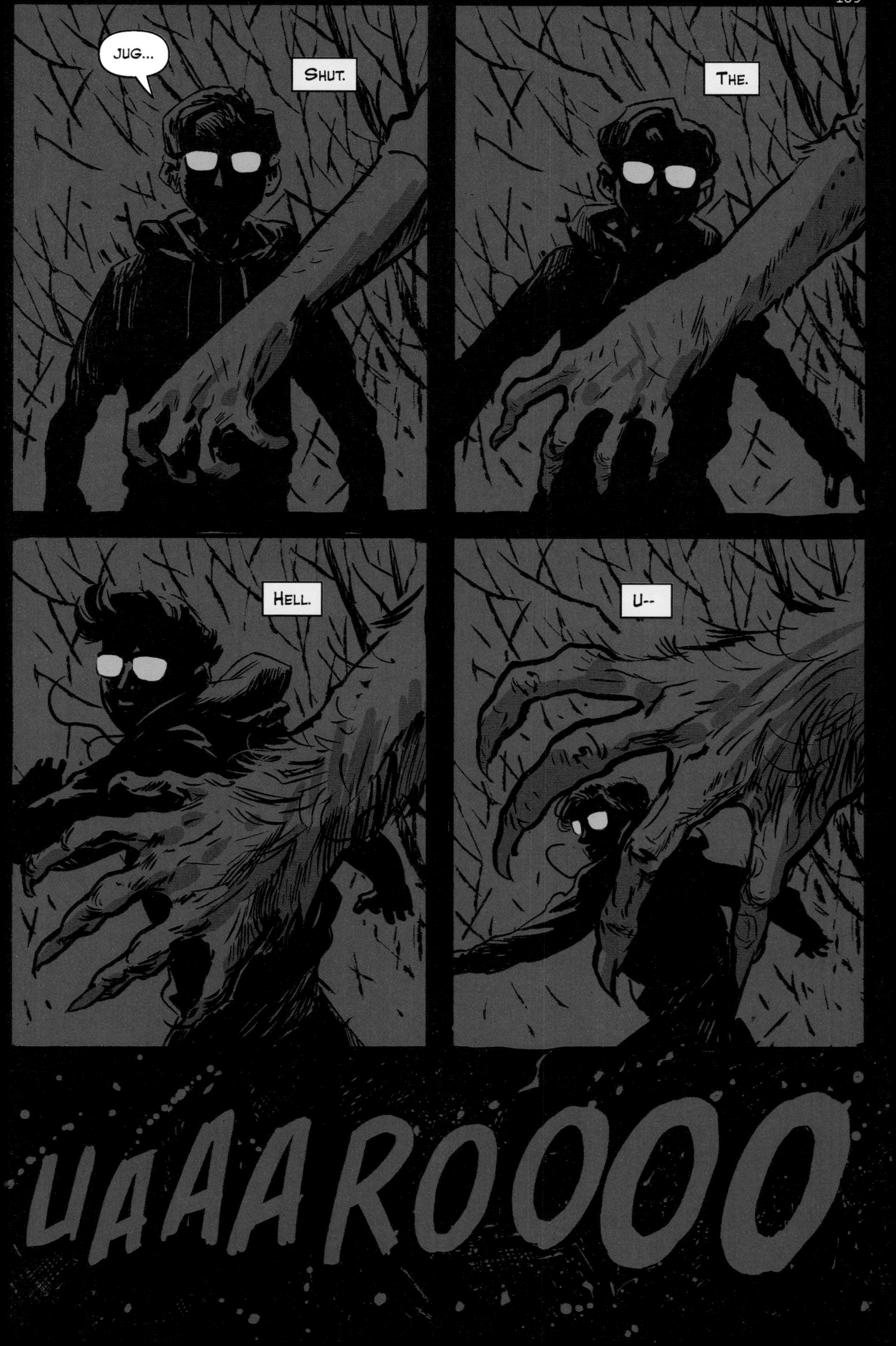
JUG...
SHUT.
THE.
HELL.
U--
UAAAROOOO

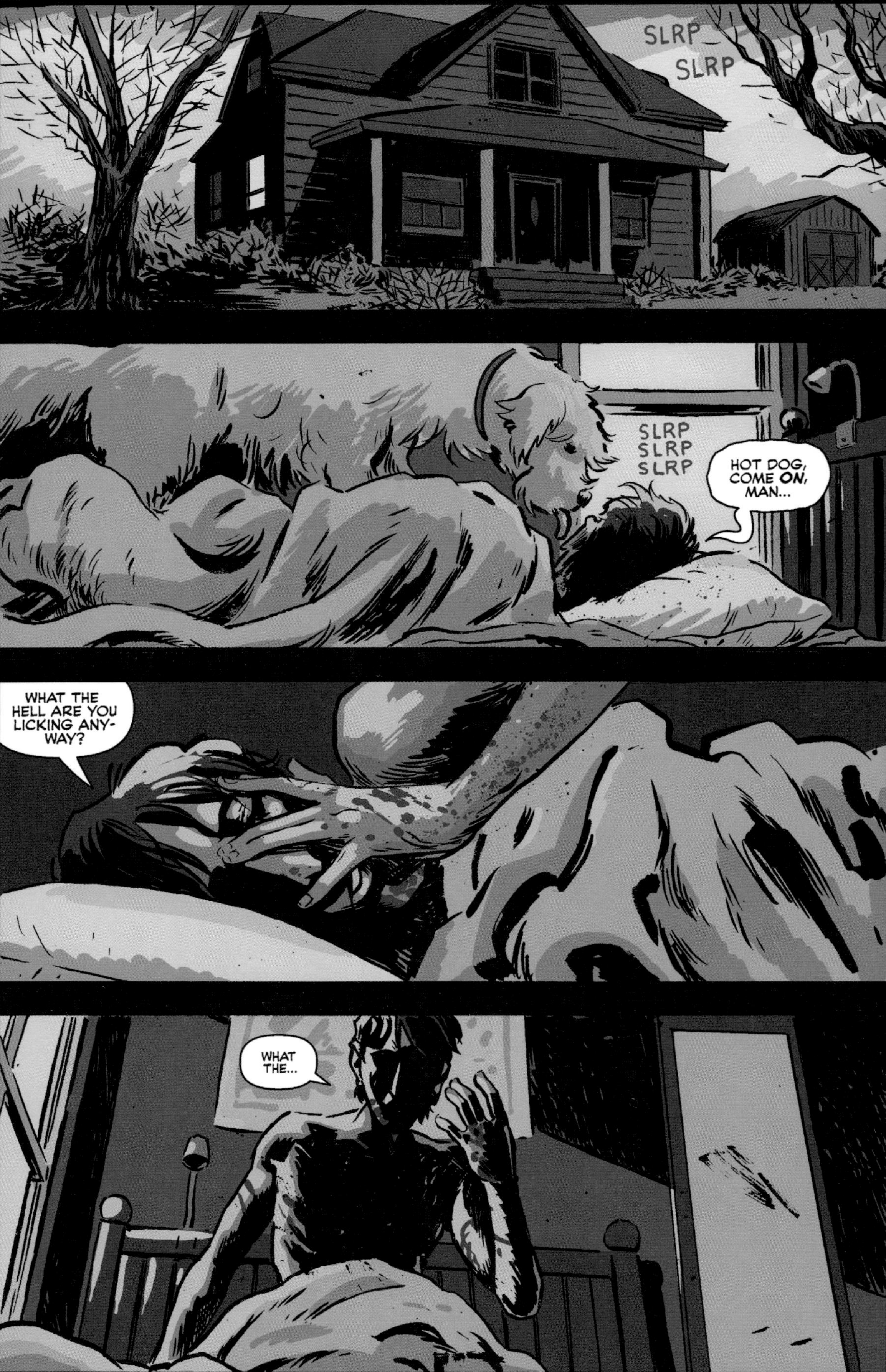
SLRP
SLRP
SLRP
SLRP
SLRP
HOT DOG, COME **ON**, MAN...
WHAT THE HELL ARE YOU LICKING ANY-WAY?
WHAT THE...

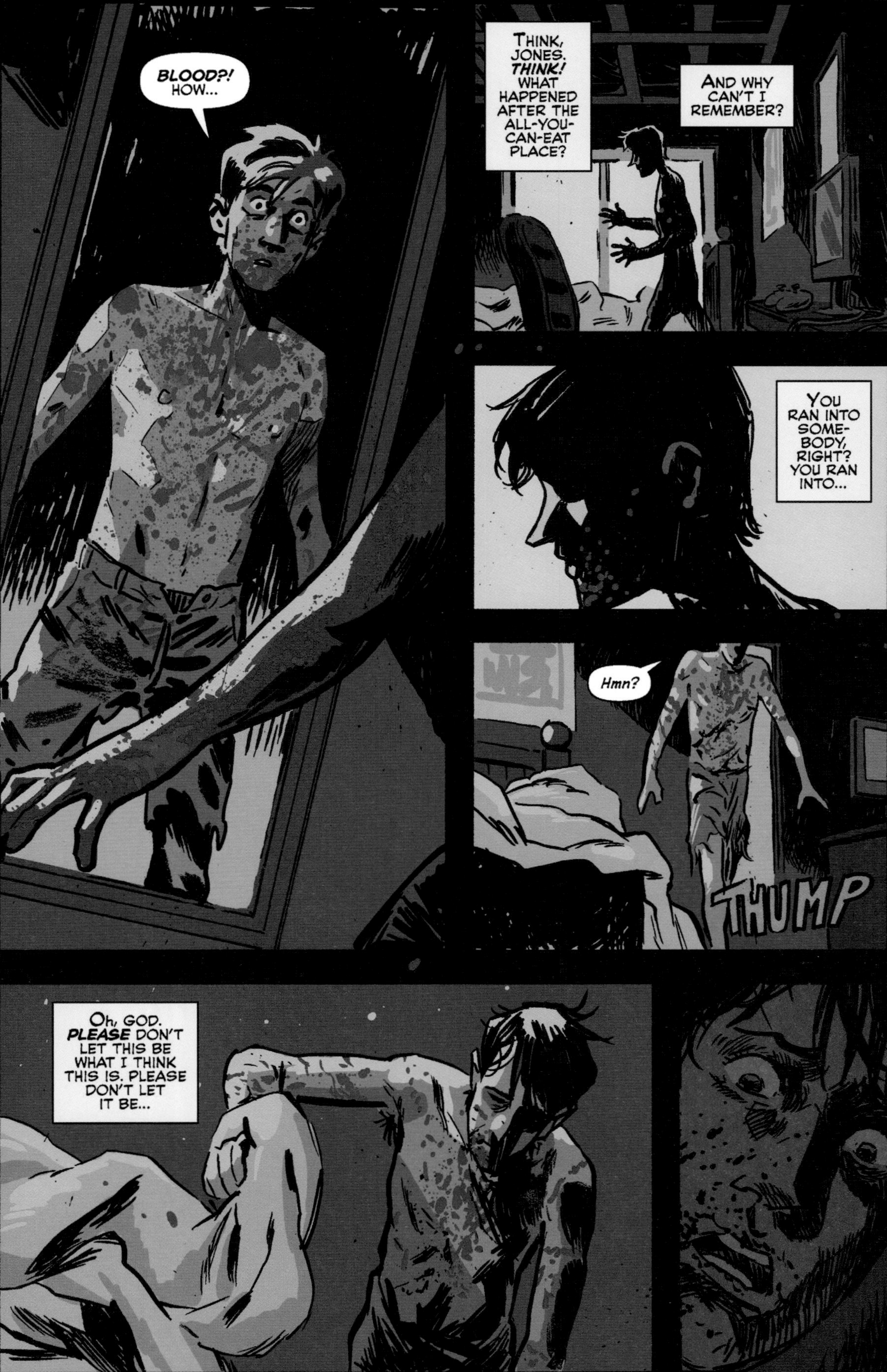
BLOOD?! HOW...
THINK, JONES. THINK! WHAT HAPPENED AFTER THE ALL-YOU-CAN-EAT PLACE?
AND WHY CAN'T I REMEMBER?
YOU RAN INTO SOME-BODY, RIGHT? YOU RAN INTO...
Hmn?
THUMP
OH, GOD. PLEASE DON'T LET THIS BE WHAT I THINK THIS IS. PLEASE DON'T LET IT BE...

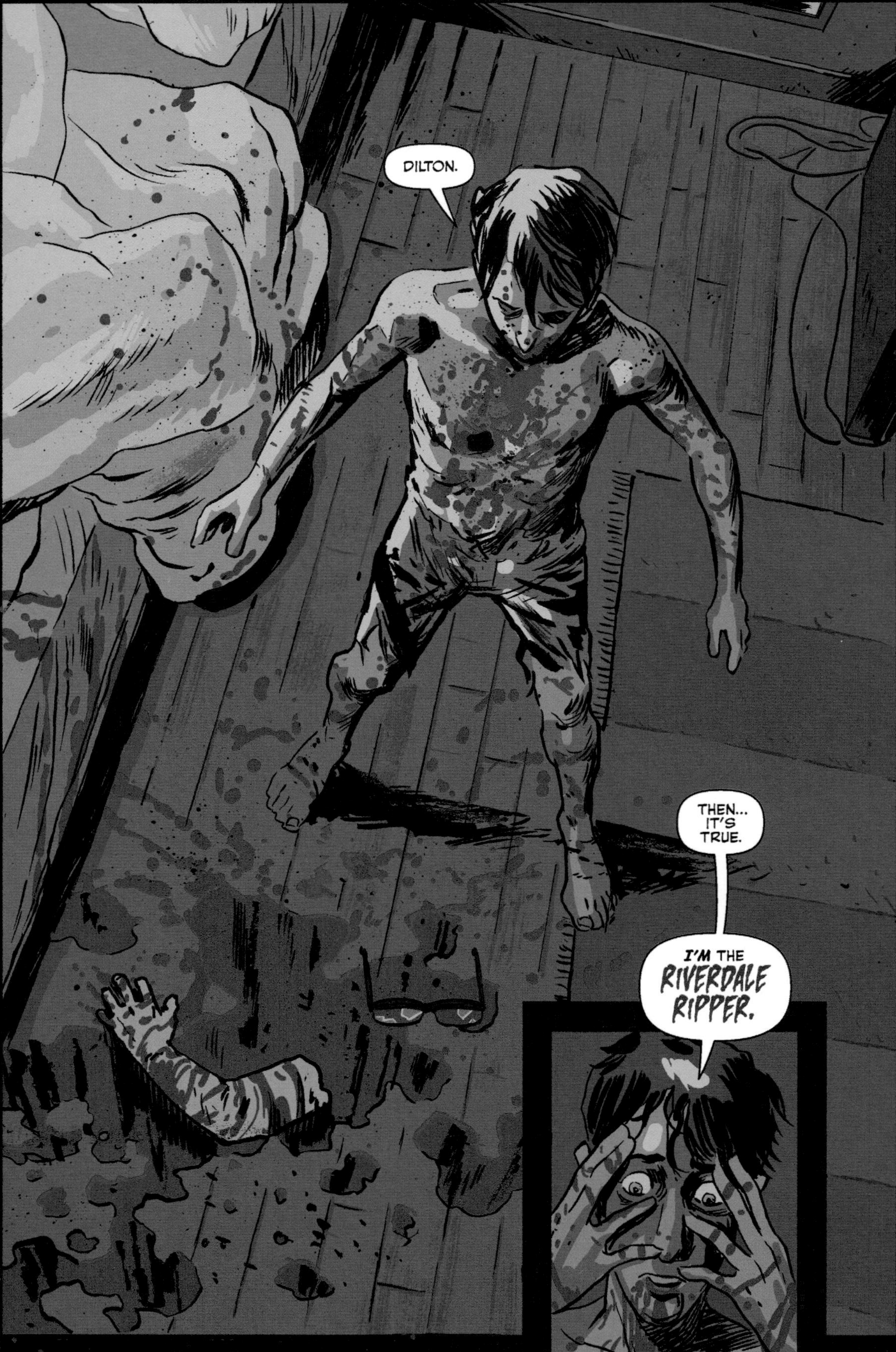
DILTON.
THEN... IT'S TRUE.
I'M THE RIVERDALE RIPPER.

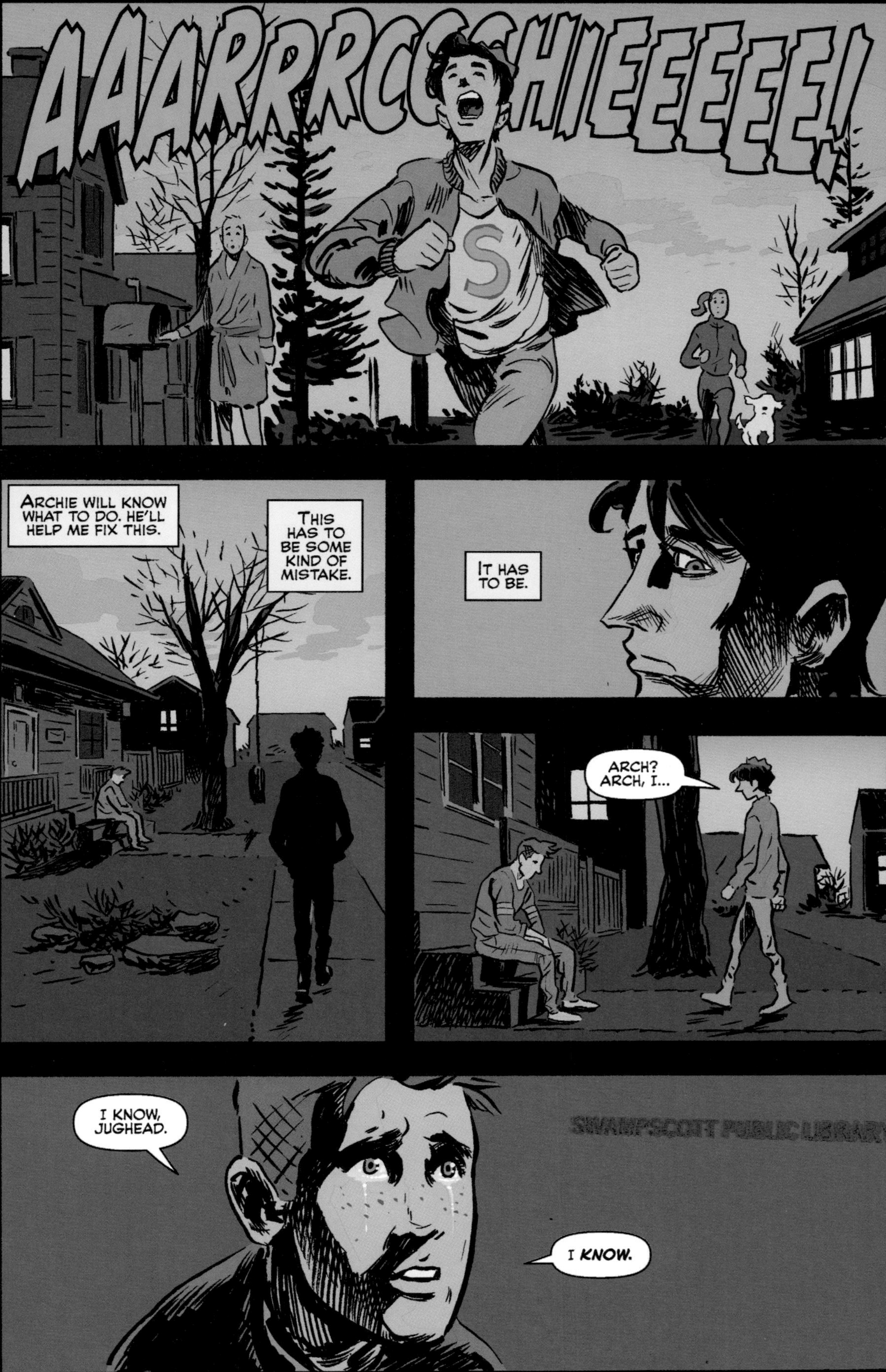
AAARRRCCCHIEEEEEE!
ARCHIE WILL KNOW WHAT TO DO. HE'LL HELP ME FIX THIS.
THIS HAS TO BE SOME KIND OF MISTAKE.
IT HAS TO BE.
ARCH? ARCH, I...
I KNOW, JUGHEAD.
I *KNOW.*

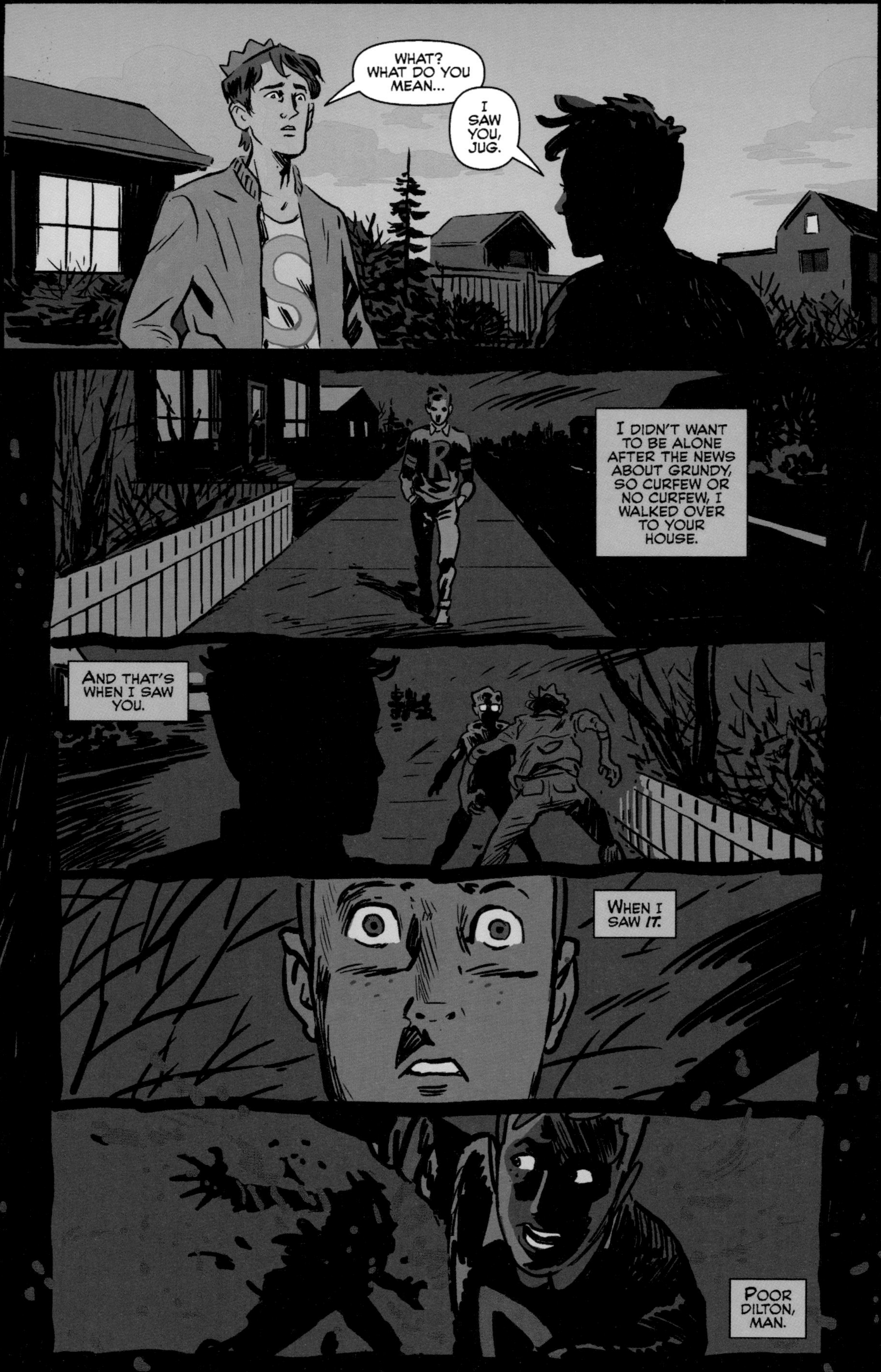
WHAT? WHAT DO YOU MEAN...
I SAW YOU, JUG.
I DIDN'T WANT TO BE ALONE AFTER THE NEWS ABOUT GRUNDY, SO CURFEW OR NO CURFEW, I WALKED OVER TO YOUR HOUSE.
AND THAT'S WHEN I SAW YOU.
WHEN I SAW *IT*.
POOR DILTON, MAN.

I MEAN, MY GOD...

WHAT **ARE** YOU?

I...I DON'T KNOW.

HELL, ALL I KNOW IS I'M HAVING THE HARDEST TIME PROCESSING ANY OF THIS.

PROCESSING WHAT?

Oh.

UH...HEY, BETTY.

YEAH, HEY.

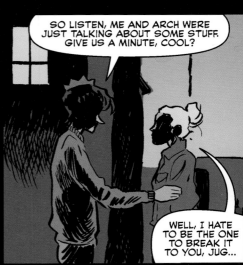

SO LISTEN, ME AND ARCH WERE JUST TALKING ABOUT SOME STUFF. GIVE US A MINUTE, COOL?

WELL, I HATE TO BE THE ONE TO BREAK IT TO YOU, JUG...

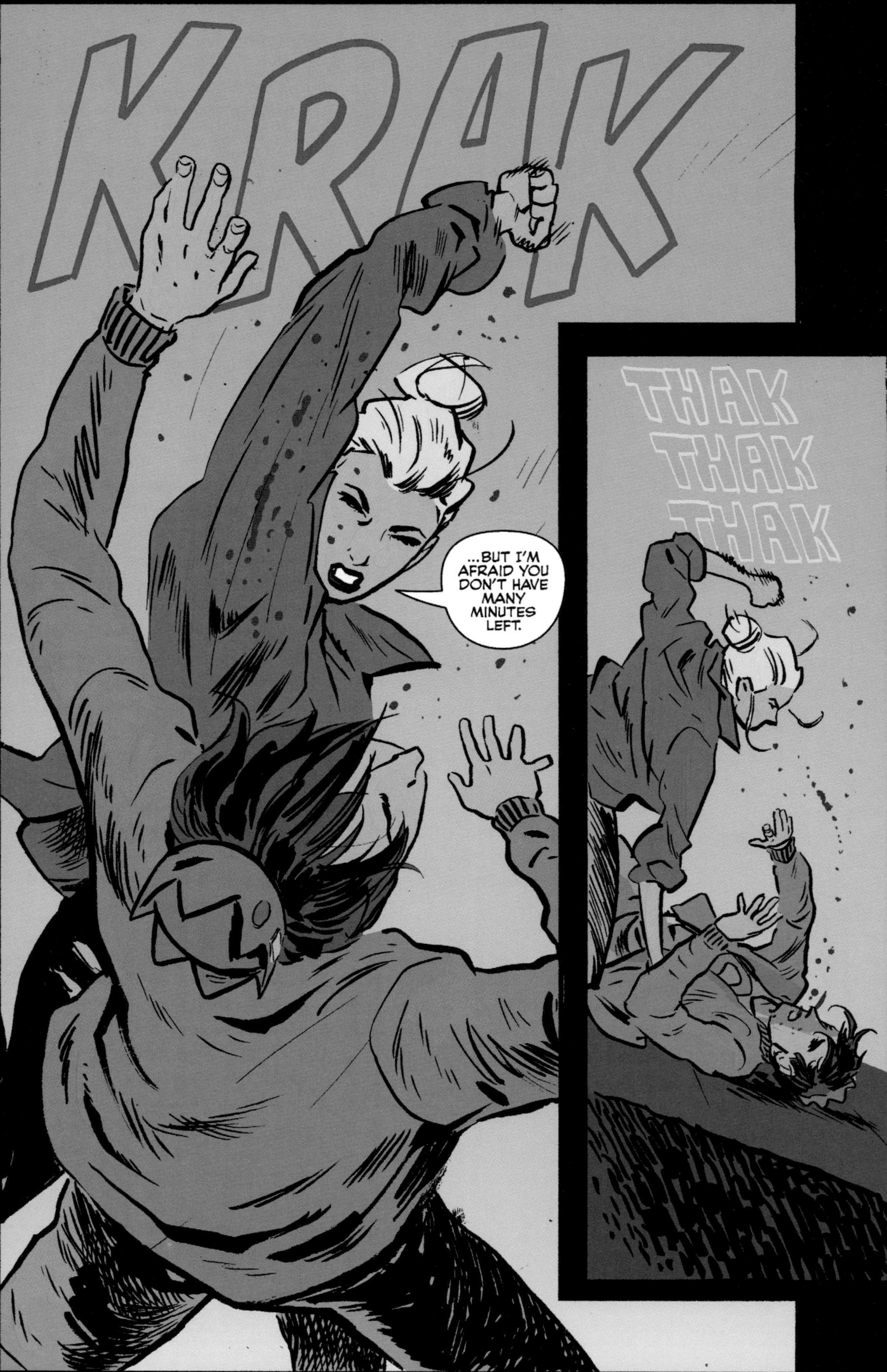
KRAK
...BUT I'M AFRAID YOU DON'T HAVE MANY MINUTES LEFT.
THAK
THAK
THAK

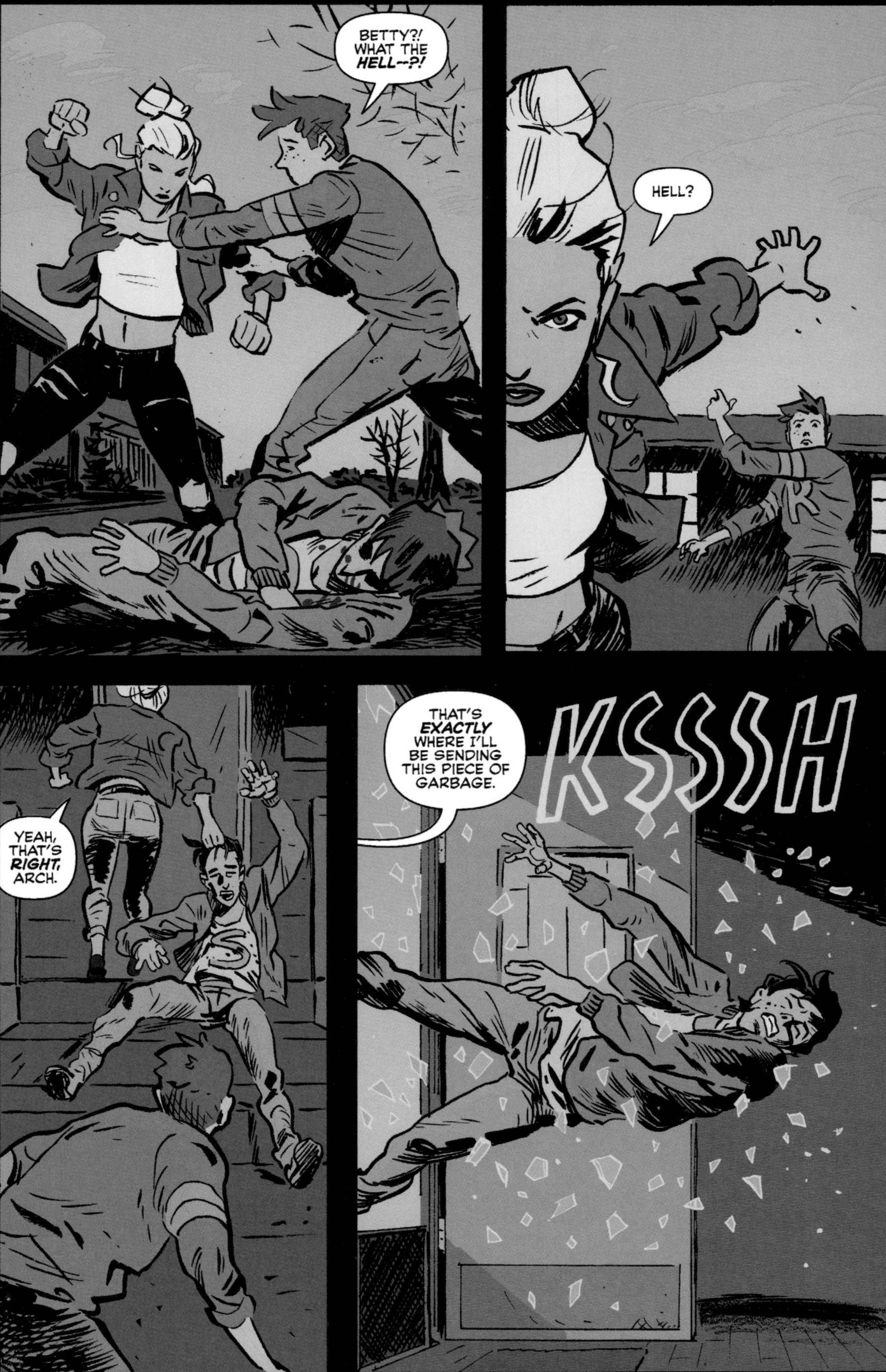
BETTY?! WHAT THE HELL--?!
HELL?
YEAH, THAT'S RIGHT, ARCH.
THAT'S EXACTLY WHERE I'LL BE SENDING THIS PIECE OF GARBAGE.
KSSSH

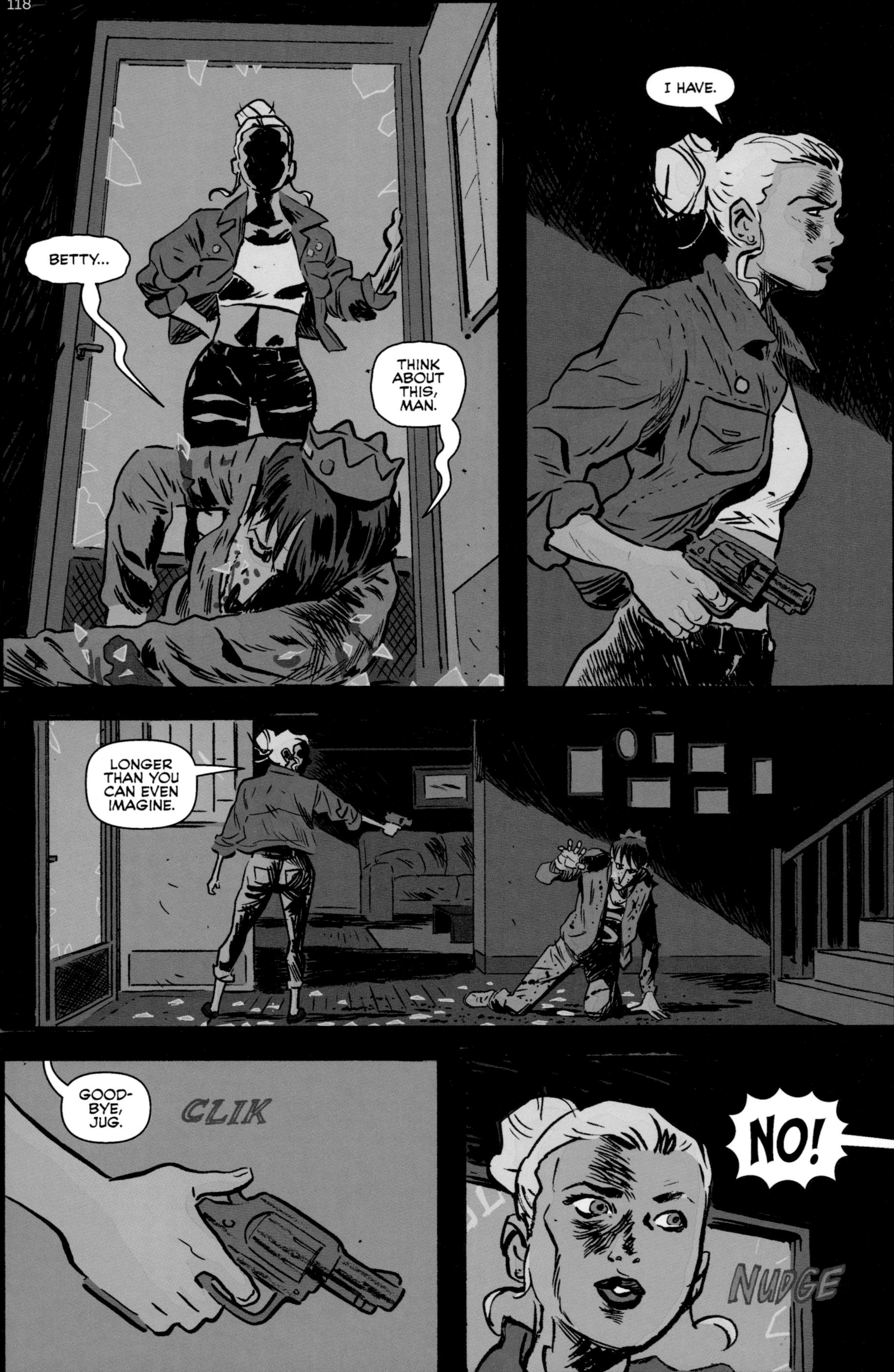
BETTY...
THINK ABOUT THIS, MAN.
I HAVE.
LONGER THAN YOU CAN EVEN IMAGINE.
GOOD-BYE, JUG.
CLIK
NO!
NUDGE

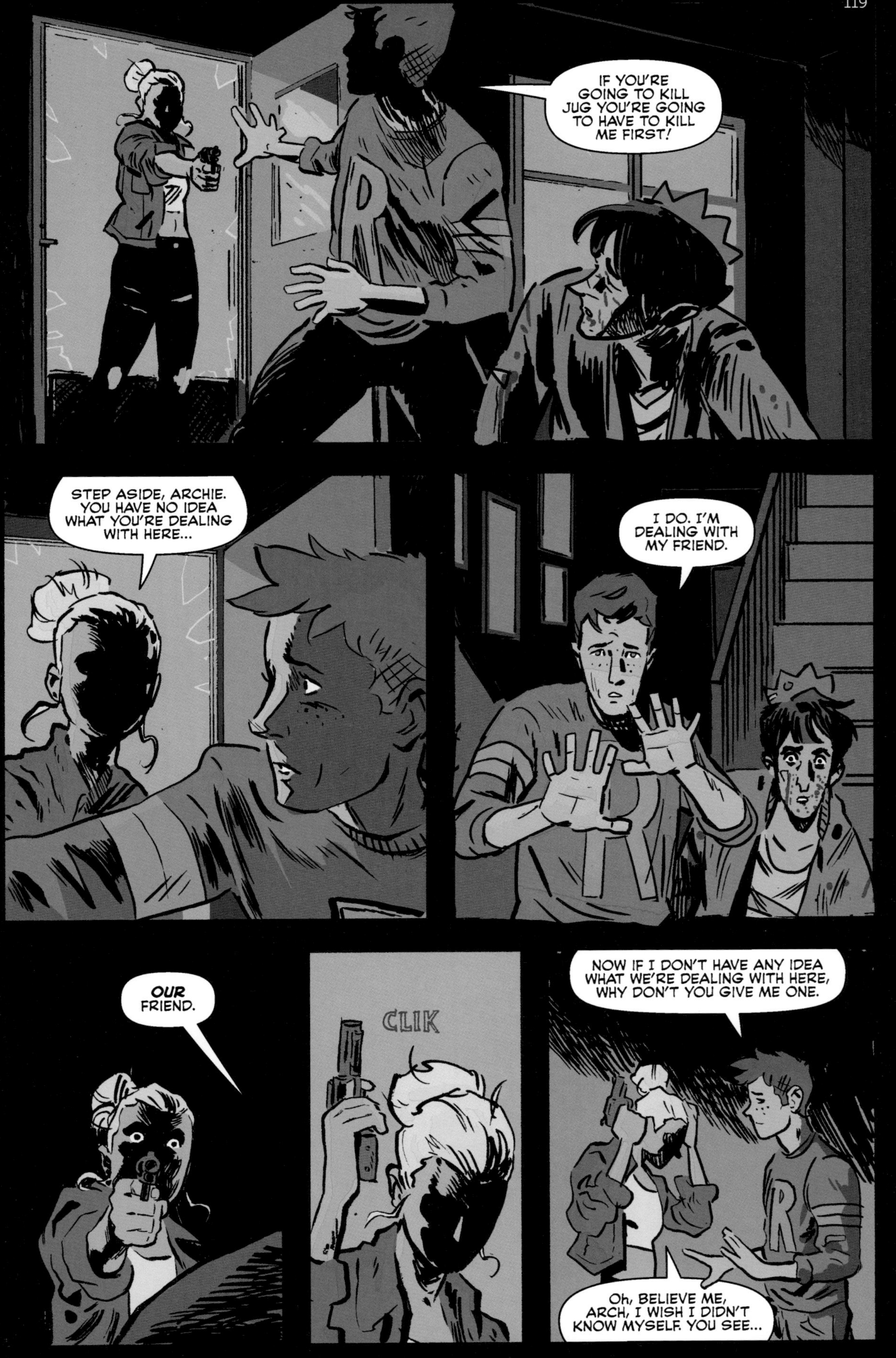
IF YOU'RE GOING TO KILL JUG YOU'RE GOING TO HAVE TO KILL ME FIRST!
STEP ASIDE, ARCHIE. YOU HAVE NO IDEA WHAT YOU'RE DEALING WITH HERE...
I DO. I'M DEALING WITH MY FRIEND.
OUR FRIEND.
CLIK
NOW IF I DON'T HAVE ANY IDEA WHAT WE'RE DEALING WITH HERE, WHY DON'T YOU GIVE ME ONE.
Oh, BELIEVE ME, ARCH, I WISH I DIDN'T KNOW MYSELF. YOU SEE...

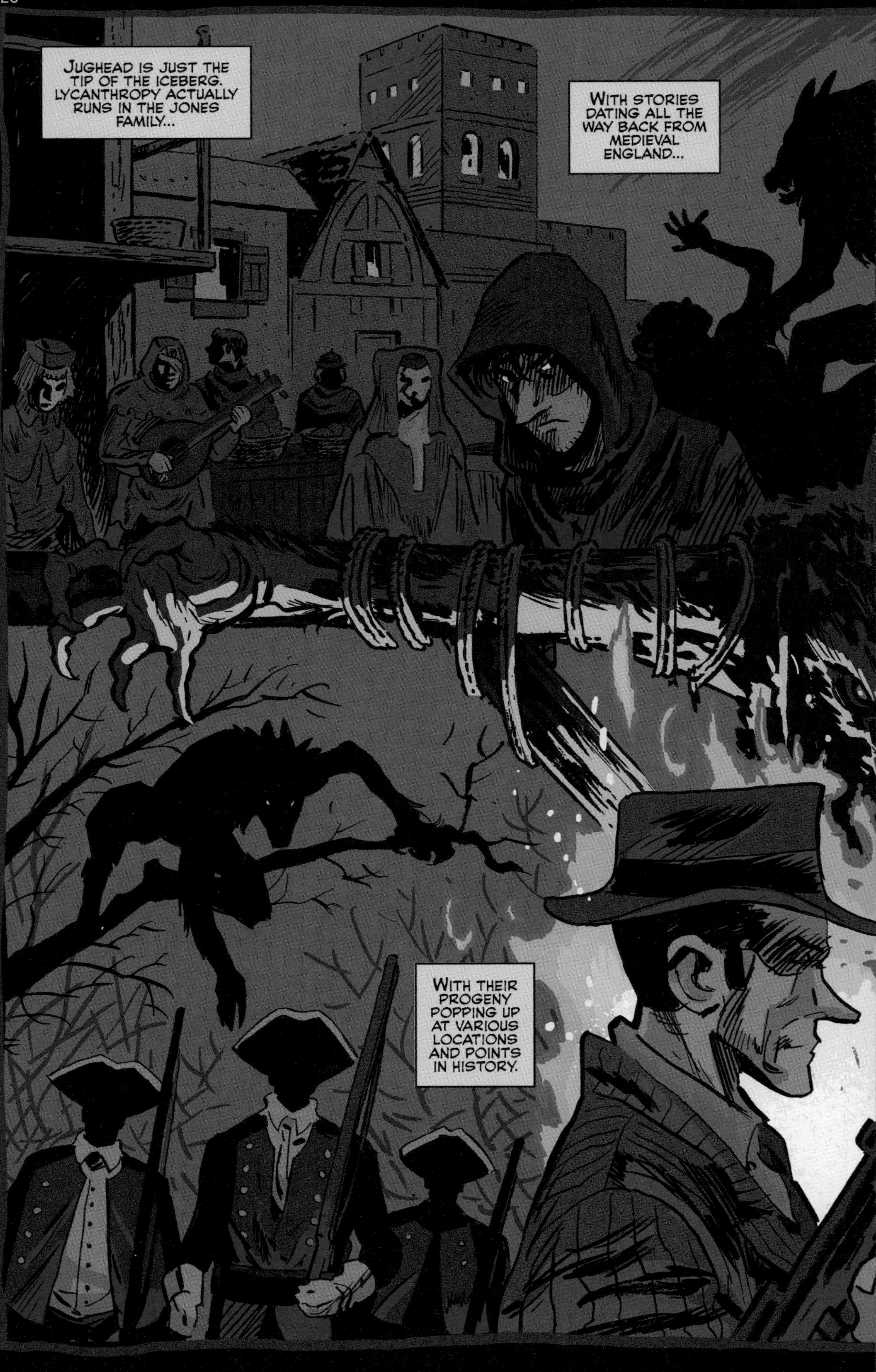
JUGHEAD IS JUST THE TIP OF THE ICEBERG. LYCANTHROPY ACTUALLY RUNS IN THE JONES FAMILY...
WITH STORIES DATING ALL THE WAY BACK FROM MEDIEVAL ENGLAND...
WITH THEIR PROGENY POPPING UP AT VARIOUS LOCATIONS AND POINTS IN HISTORY.

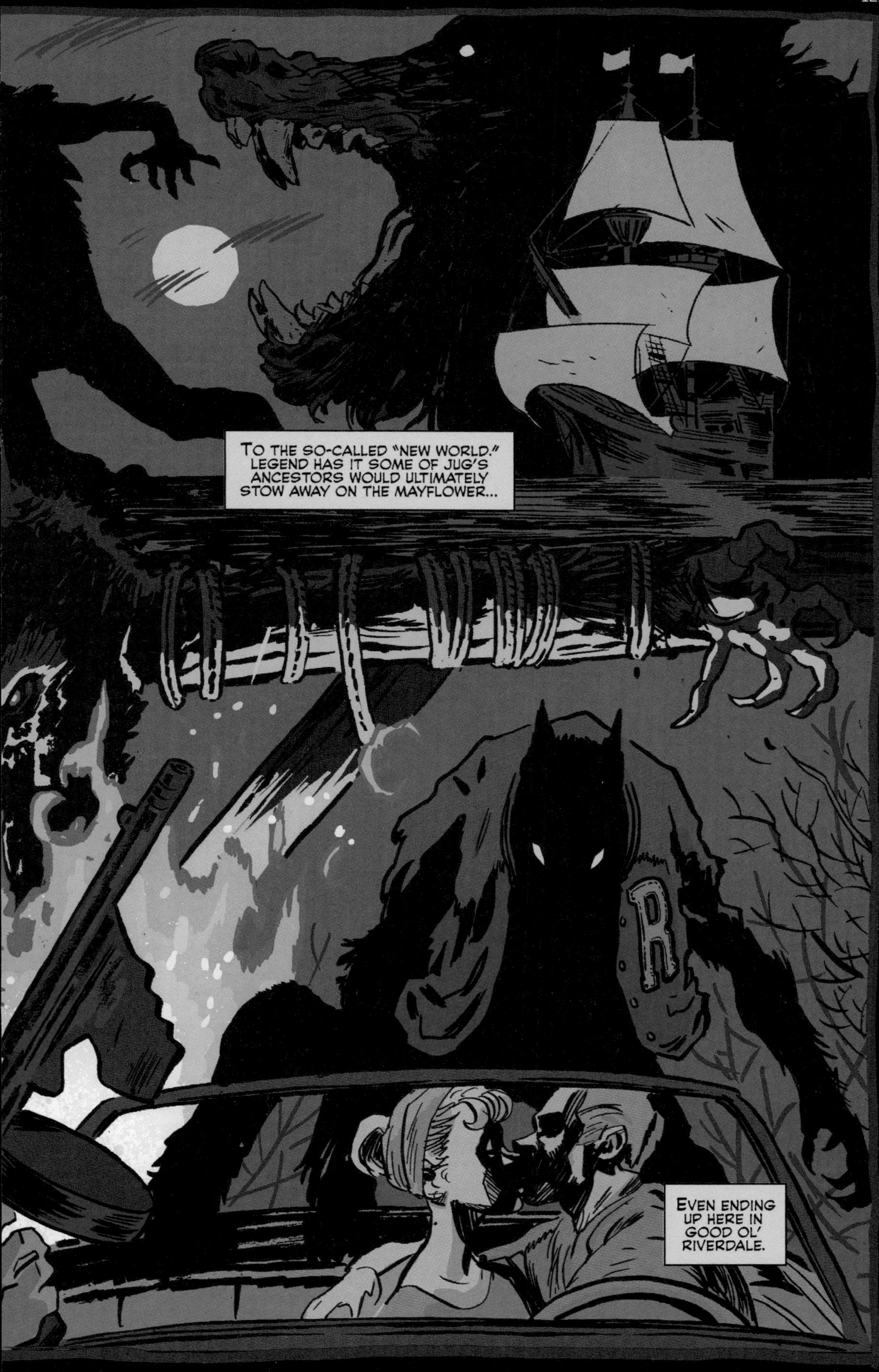
TO THE SO-CALLED "NEW WORLD." LEGEND HAS IT SOME OF JUG'S ANCESTORS WOULD ULTIMATELY STOW AWAY ON THE MAYFLOWER...
EVEN ENDING UP HERE IN GOOD OL' RIVERDALE.

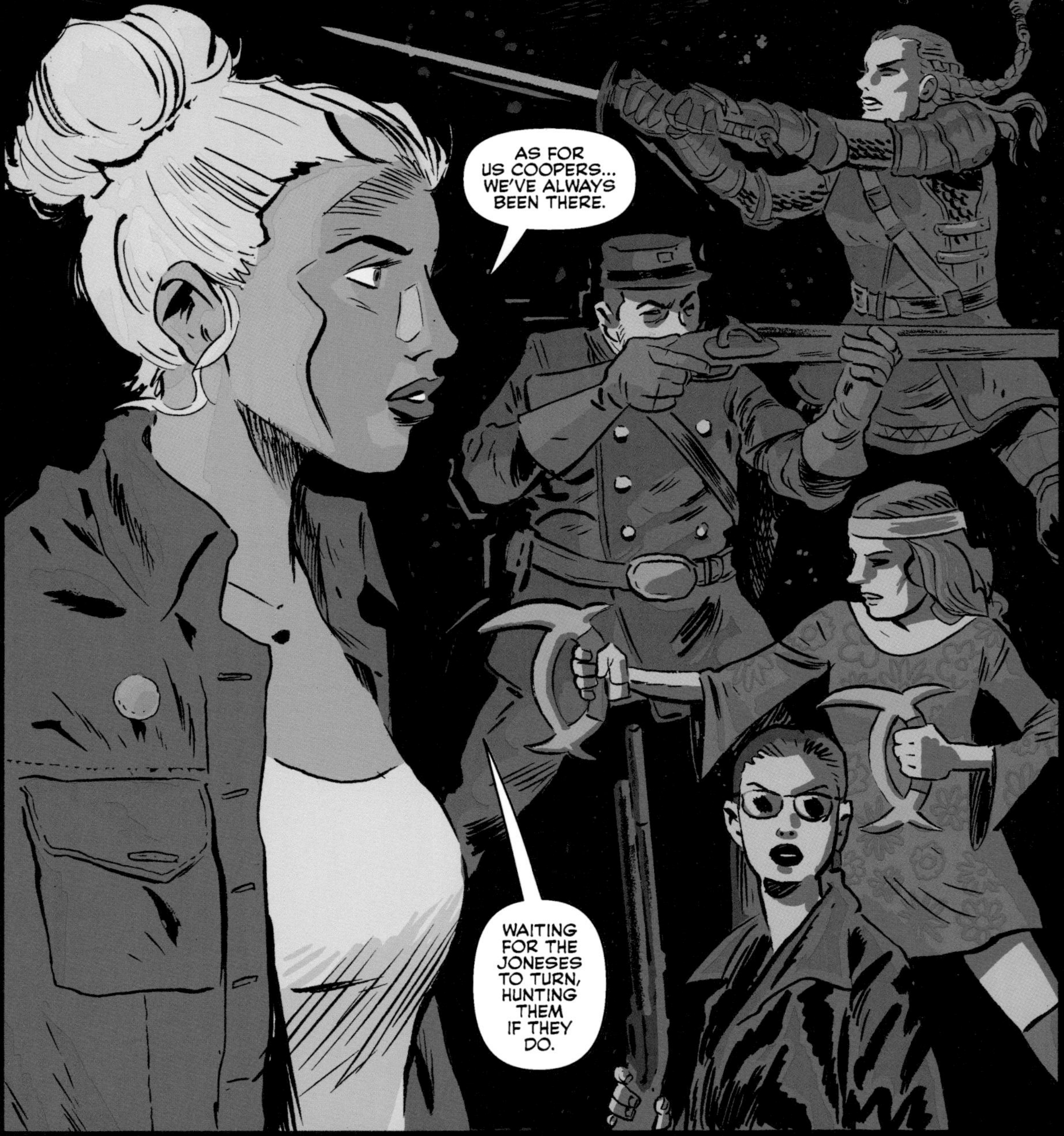
AS FOR US COOPERS... WE'VE ALWAYS BEEN THERE.
WAITING FOR THE JONESES TO TURN, HUNTING THEM IF THEY DO.

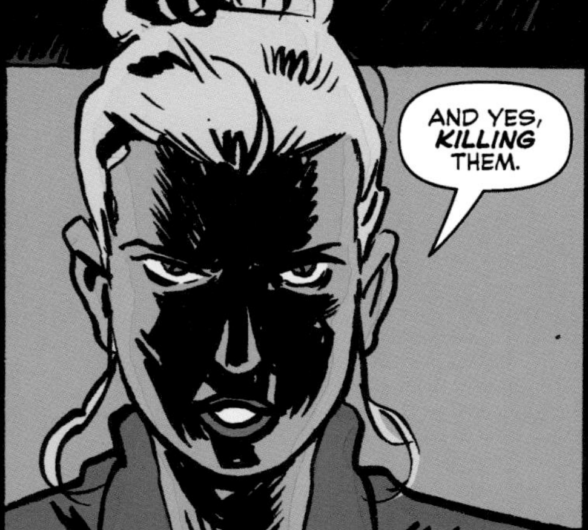
AND YES, ***KILLING*** THEM.

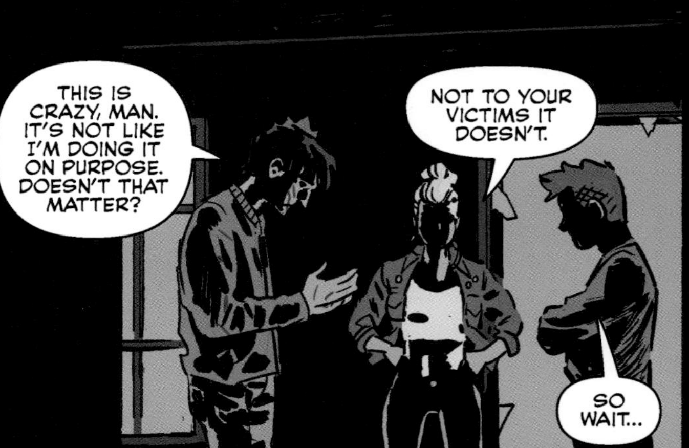
THIS IS CRAZY, MAN. IT'S NOT LIKE I'M DOING IT ON PURPOSE. DOESN'T THAT MATTER?
NOT TO YOUR VICTIMS IT DOESN'T.
SO WAIT...

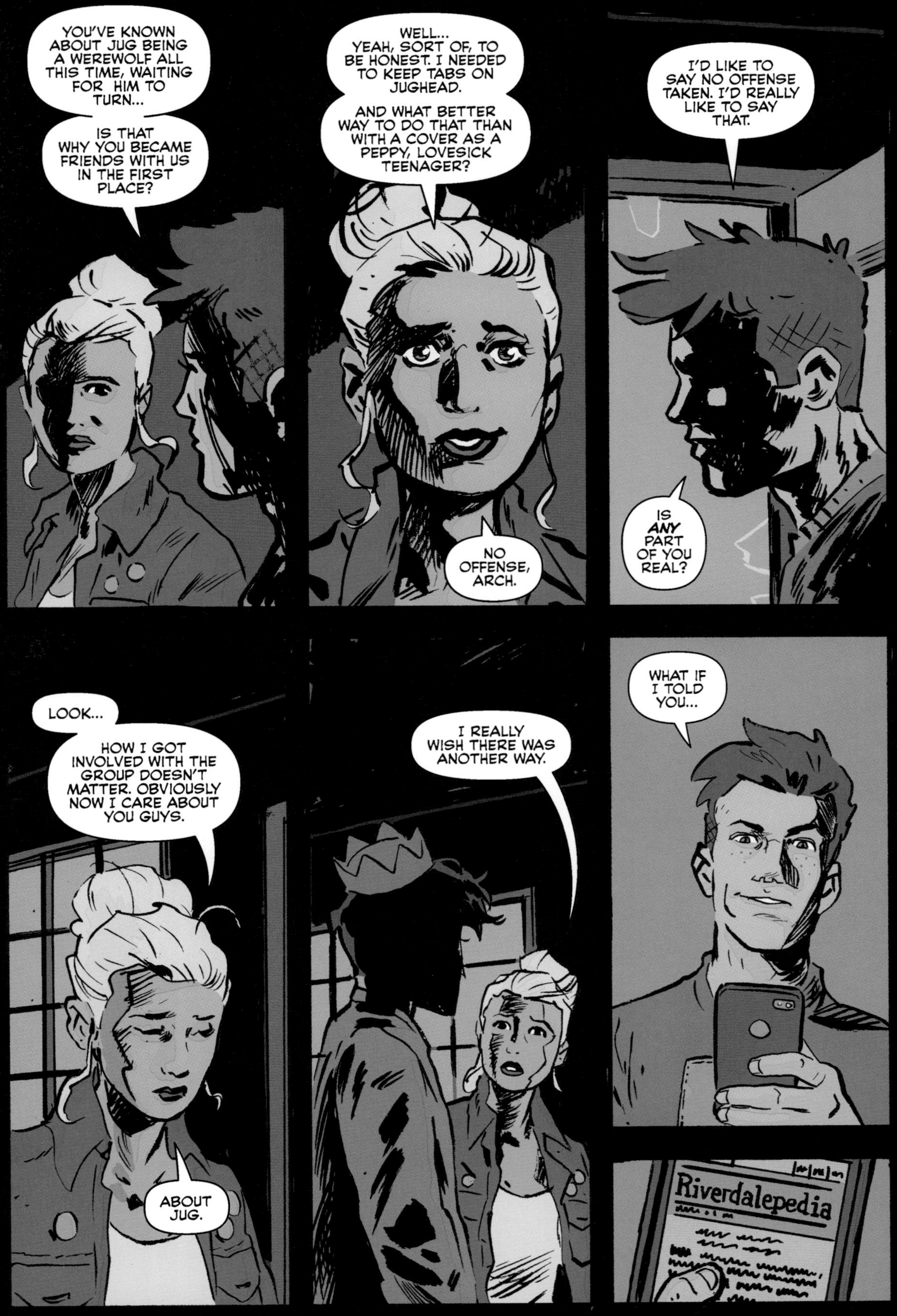
YOU'VE KNOWN ABOUT JUG BEING A WEREWOLF ALL THIS TIME, WAITING FOR HIM TO TURN...
IS THAT WHY YOU BECAME FRIENDS WITH US IN THE FIRST PLACE?
WELL... YEAH, SORT OF, TO BE HONEST. I NEEDED TO KEEP TABS ON JUGHEAD.
AND WHAT BETTER WAY TO DO THAT THAN WITH A COVER AS A PEPPY, LOVESICK TEENAGER?
NO OFFENSE, ARCH.
I'D LIKE TO SAY NO OFFENSE TAKEN. I'D REALLY LIKE TO SAY THAT.
IS **ANY** PART OF YOU REAL?
LOOK...
HOW I GOT INVOLVED WITH THE GROUP DOESN'T MATTER. OBVIOUSLY NOW I CARE ABOUT YOU GUYS.
ABOUT JUG.
I REALLY WISH THERE WAS ANOTHER WAY.
WHAT IF I TOLD YOU...
Riverdalepedia

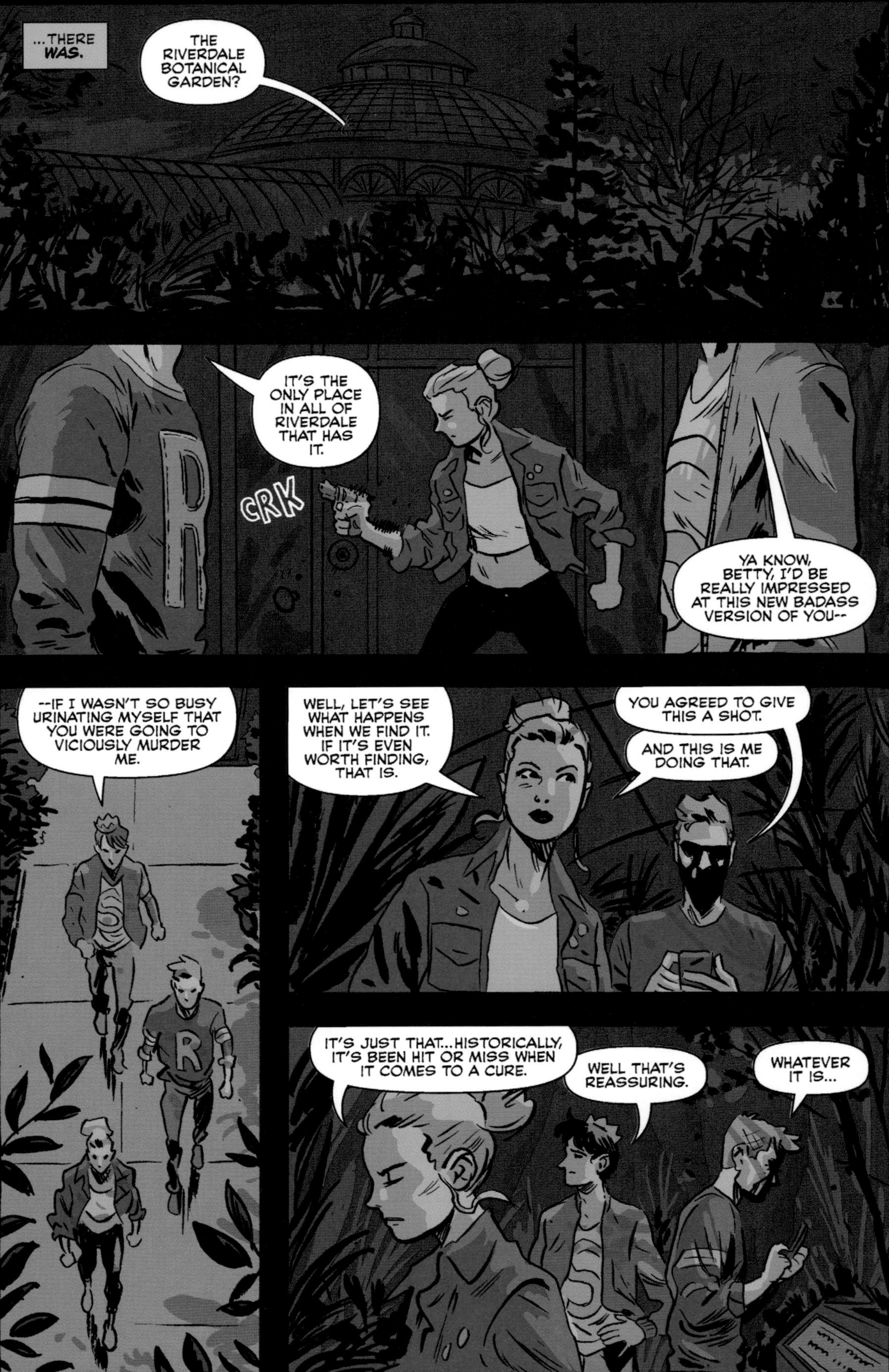

...THERE WAS.
THE RIVERDALE BOTANICAL GARDEN?
IT'S THE ONLY PLACE IN ALL OF RIVERDALE THAT HAS IT.
CRK
YA KNOW, BETTY, I'D BE REALLY IMPRESSED AT THIS NEW BADASS VERSION OF YOU--
--IF I WASN'T SO BUSY URINATING MYSELF THAT YOU WERE GOING TO VICIOUSLY MURDER ME.
WELL, LET'S SEE WHAT HAPPENS WHEN WE FIND IT. IF IT'S EVEN WORTH FINDING, THAT IS.
YOU AGREED TO GIVE THIS A SHOT.
AND THIS IS ME DOING THAT.
IT'S JUST THAT...HISTORICALLY, IT'S BEEN HIT OR MISS WHEN IT COMES TO A CURE.
WELL THAT'S REASSURING.
WHATEVER IT IS...

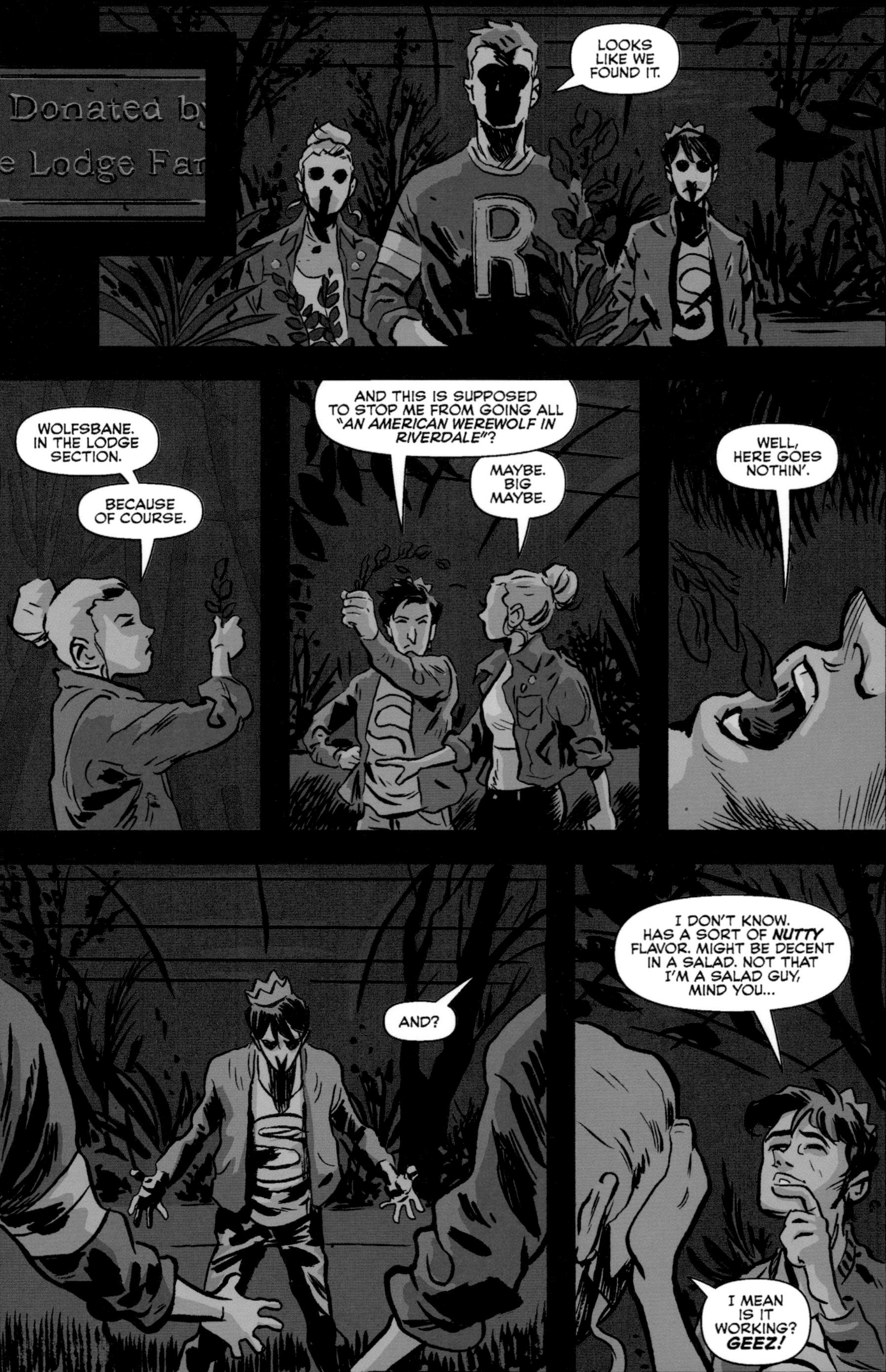
Donated by
e Lodge Far
LOOKS LIKE WE FOUND IT.
WOLFSBANE. IN THE LODGE SECTION.
BECAUSE OF COURSE.
AND THIS IS SUPPOSED TO STOP ME FROM GOING ALL *"AN AMERICAN WEREWOLF IN RIVERDALE"*?
MAYBE. BIG MAYBE.
WELL, HERE GOES NOTHIN'.
AND?
I DON'T KNOW. HAS A SORT OF ***NUTTY*** FLAVOR. MIGHT BE DECENT IN A SALAD. NOT THAT I'M A SALAD GUY, MIND YOU...
I MEAN IS IT WORKING? ***GEEZ!***

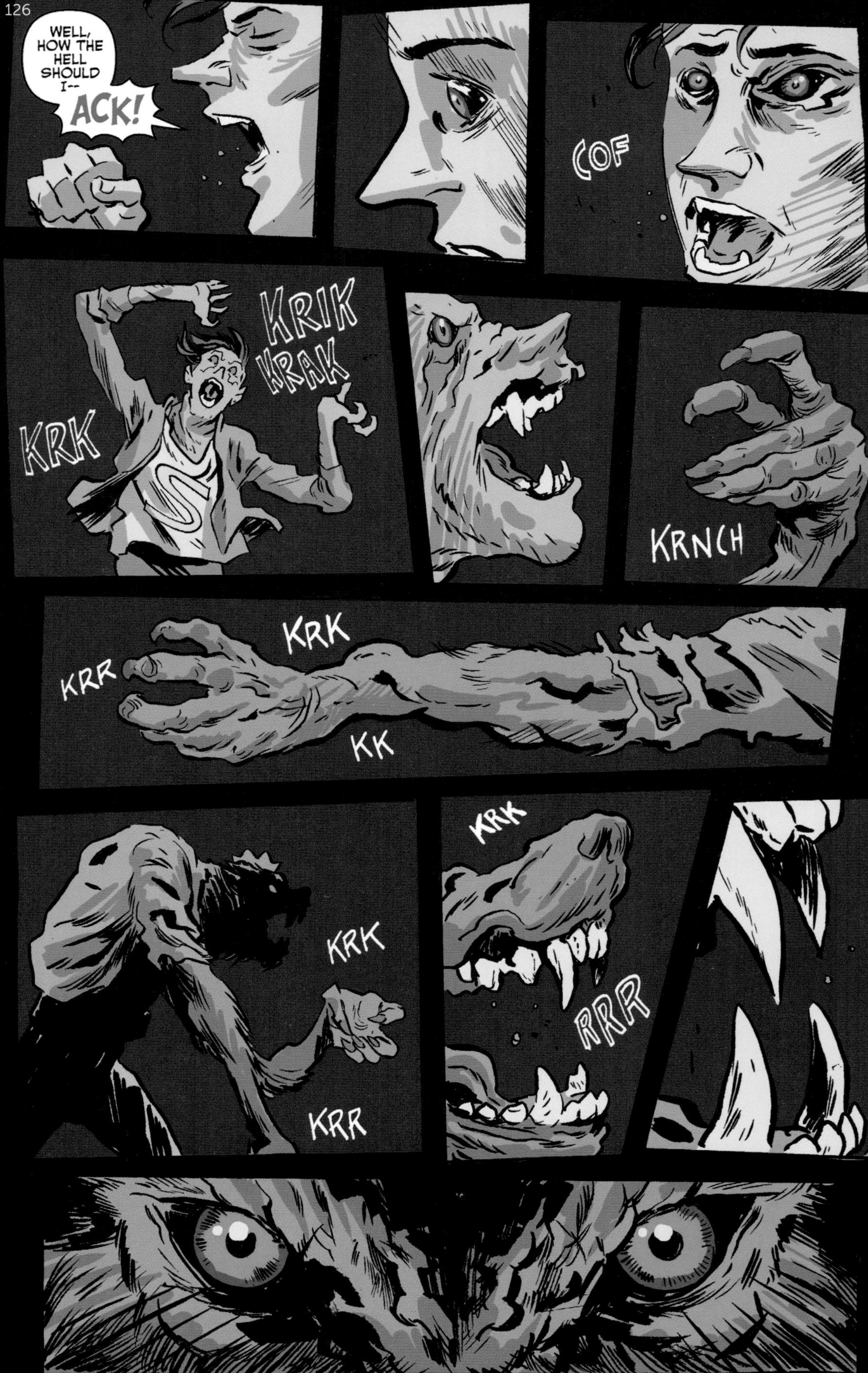
WELL, HOW THE HELL SHOULD I--
ACK!
COF
KRIK
KRAK
KRK
KRNCH
KRK
KRR
KK
KRK
KRR
KRK
RRR

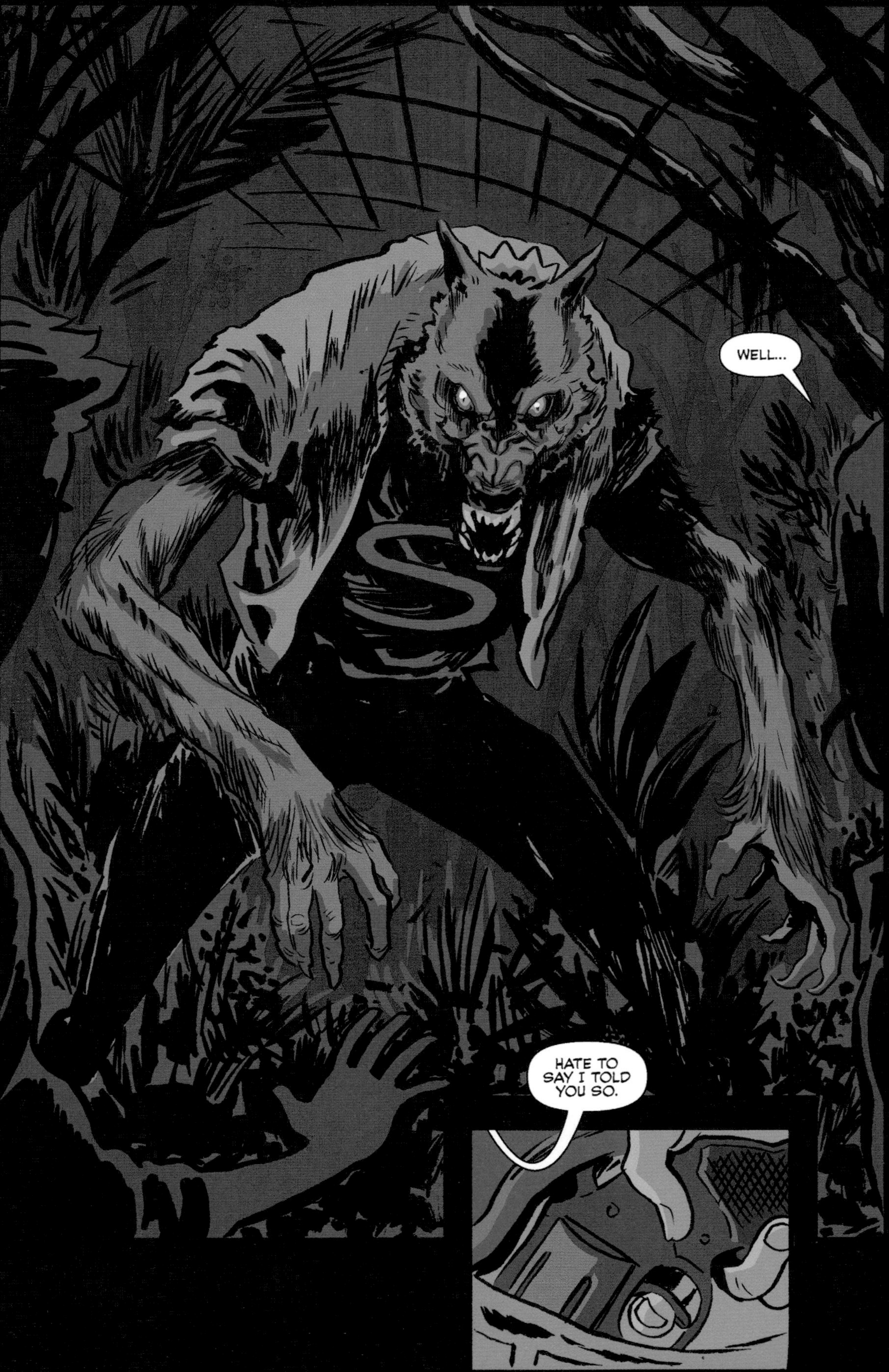
WELL...
HATE TO SAY I TOLD YOU SO.

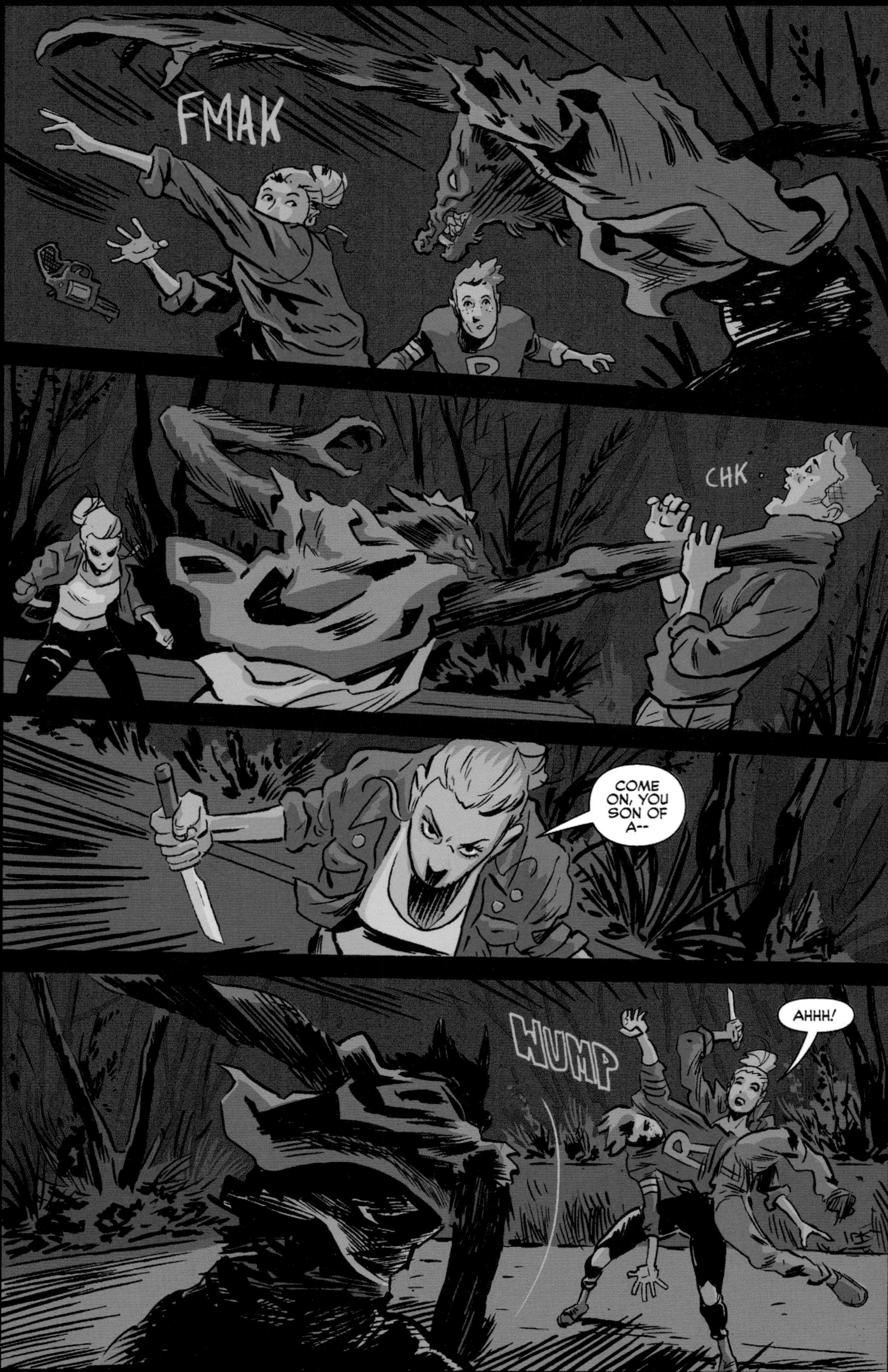
FMAK
CHK
COME ON, YOU SON OF A--
WUMP
AHHH!

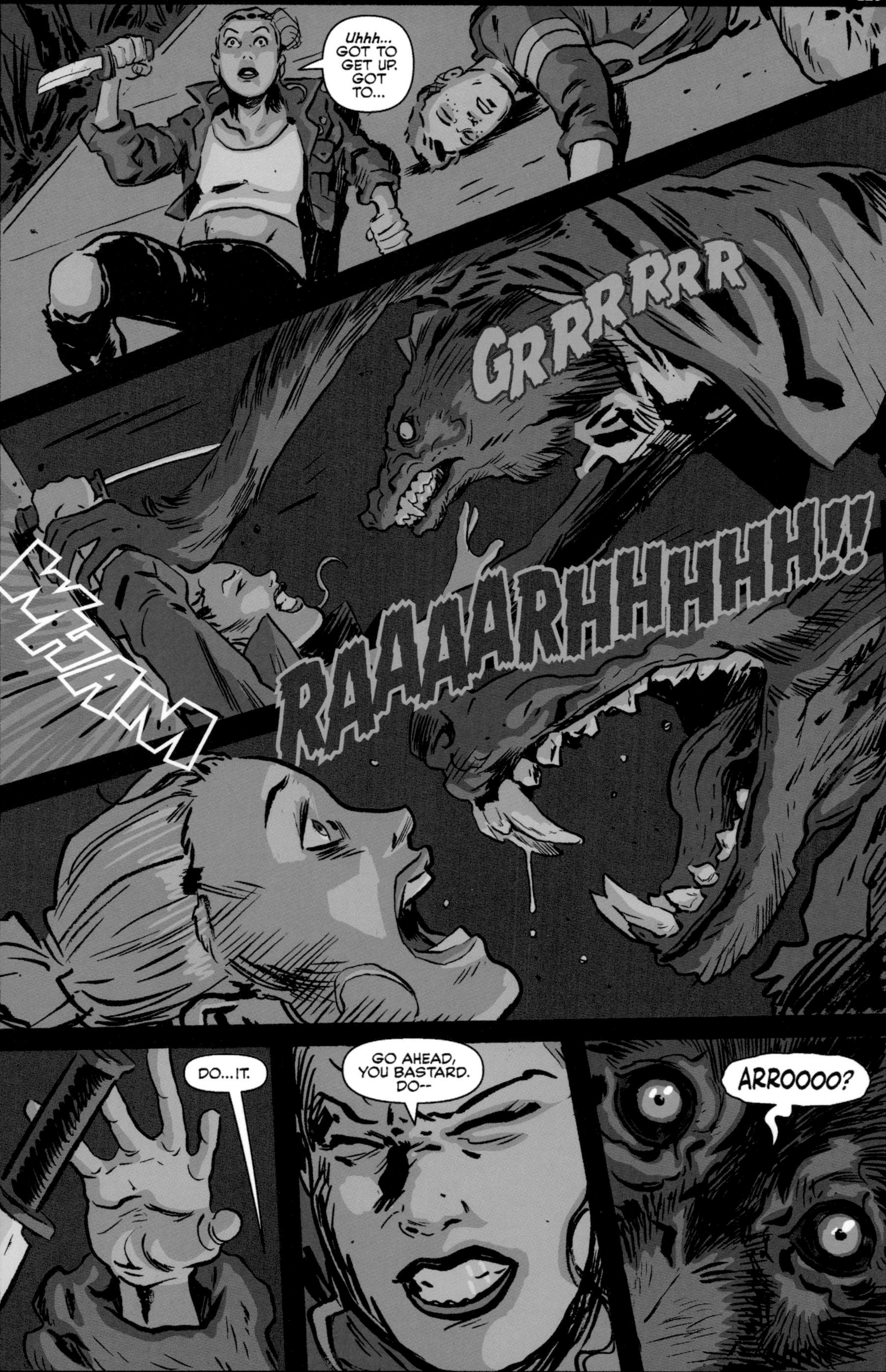
Uhhh... GOT TO GET UP. GOT TO...
GRRRRRR
WHAM
RAAAARHHHHHH!!
DO...IT.
GO AHEAD, YOU BASTARD. DO--
ARROOOO?

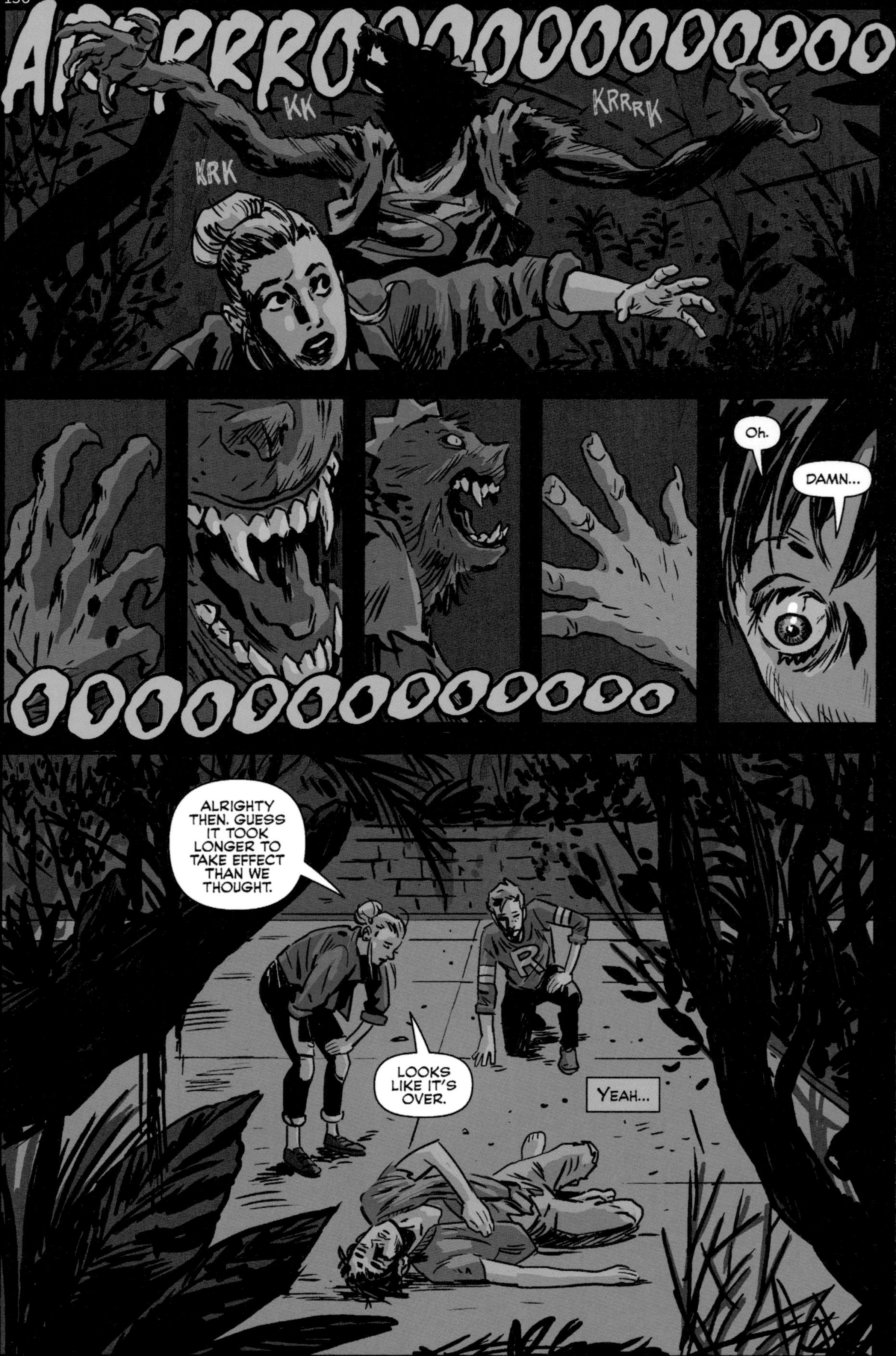
KK
KRRRK
KRK
Oh.
DAMN...
ALRIGHTY THEN. GUESS IT TOOK LONGER TO TAKE EFFECT THAN WE THOUGHT.
LOOKS LIKE IT'S OVER.
YEAH...

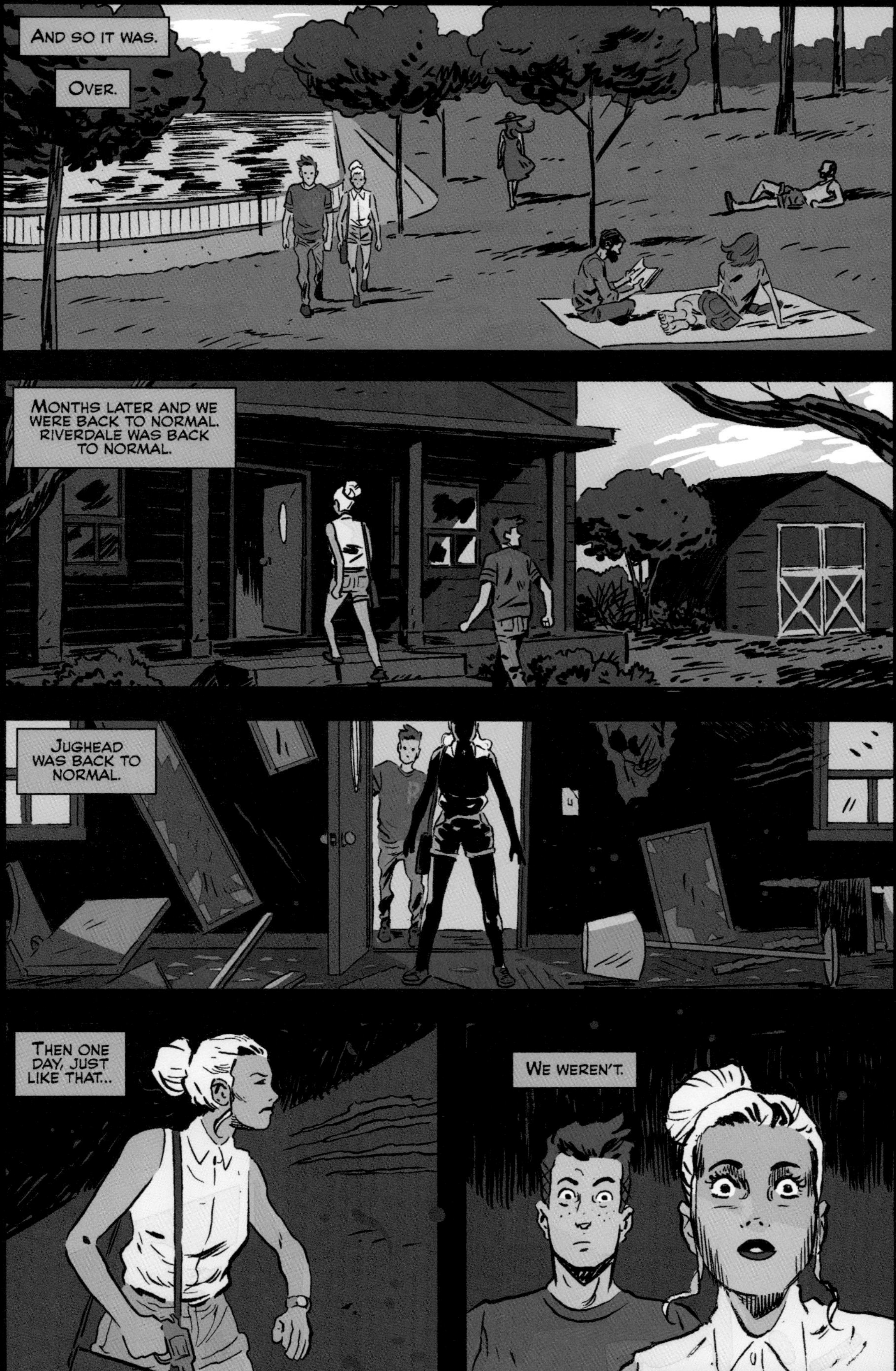

AND SO IT WAS.
OVER.
MONTHS LATER AND WE WERE BACK TO NORMAL. RIVERDALE WAS BACK TO NORMAL.
JUGHEAD WAS BACK TO NORMAL.
THEN ONE DAY, JUST LIKE THAT...
WE WEREN'T.

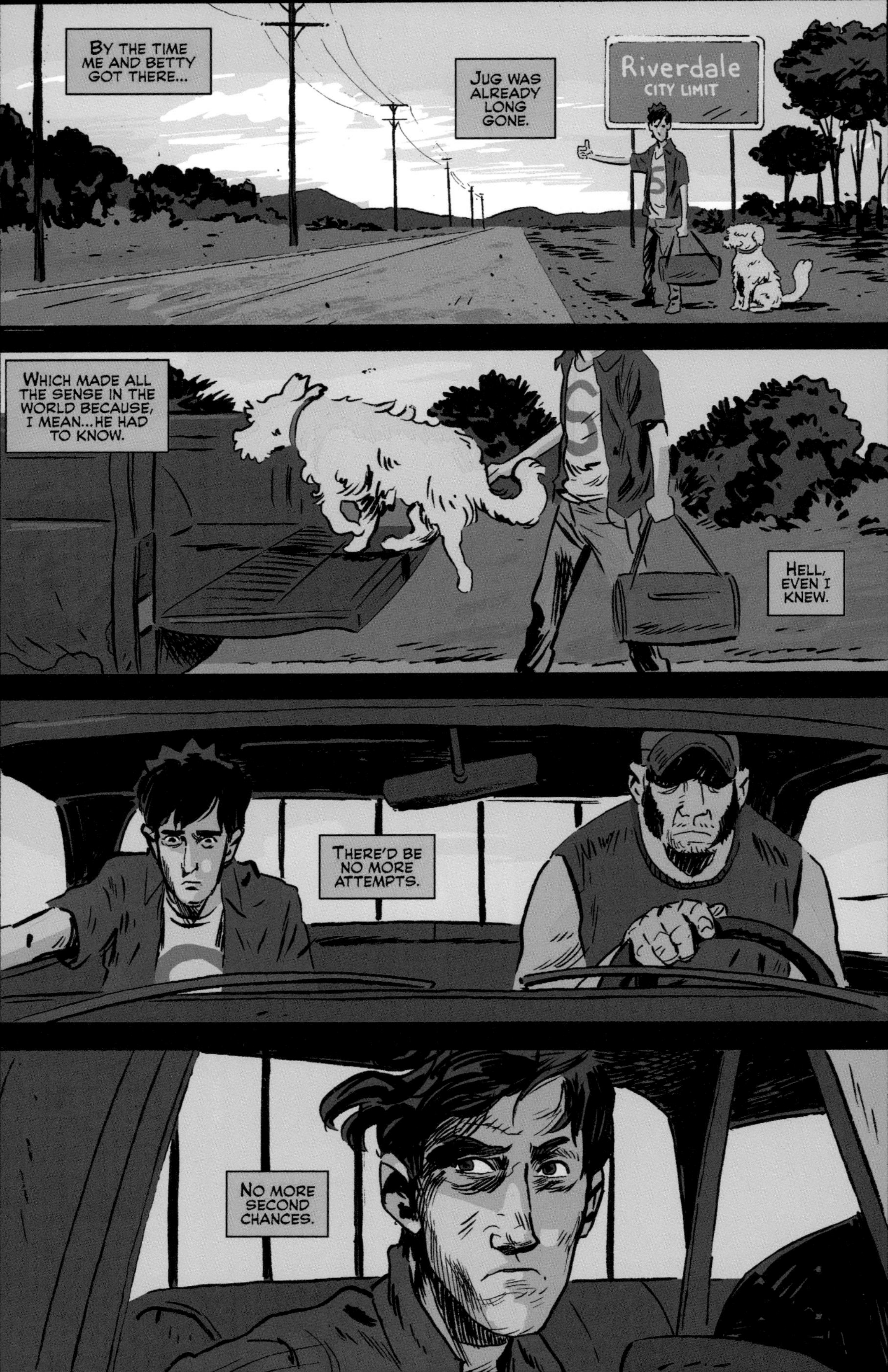
By the time me and Betty got there...
Jug was already long gone.
Riverdale
City Limit
Which made all the sense in the world because, I mean...he had to know.
Hell, even I knew.
There'd be no more attempts.
No more second chances.

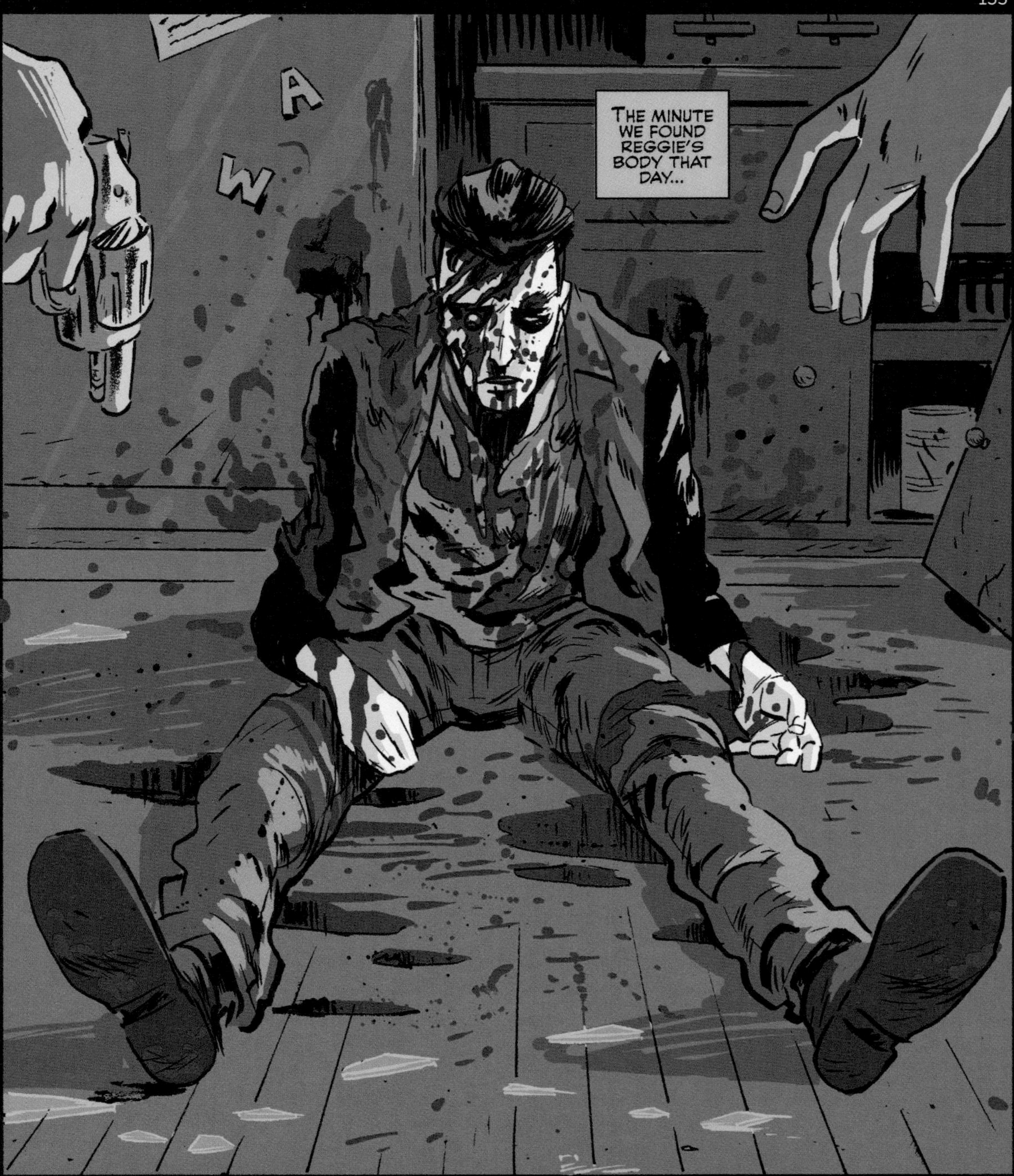
The minute we found Reggie's body that day...

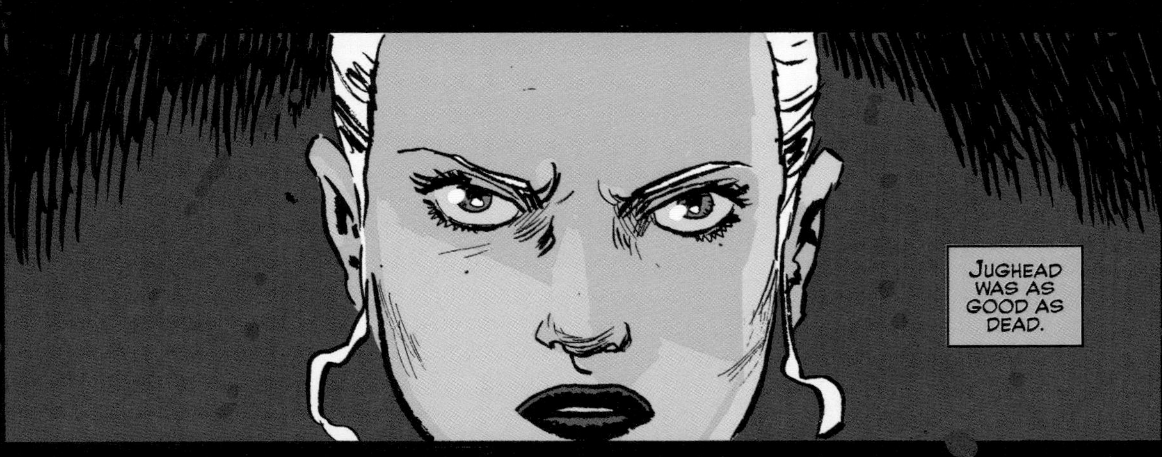
Jughead was as good as dead.

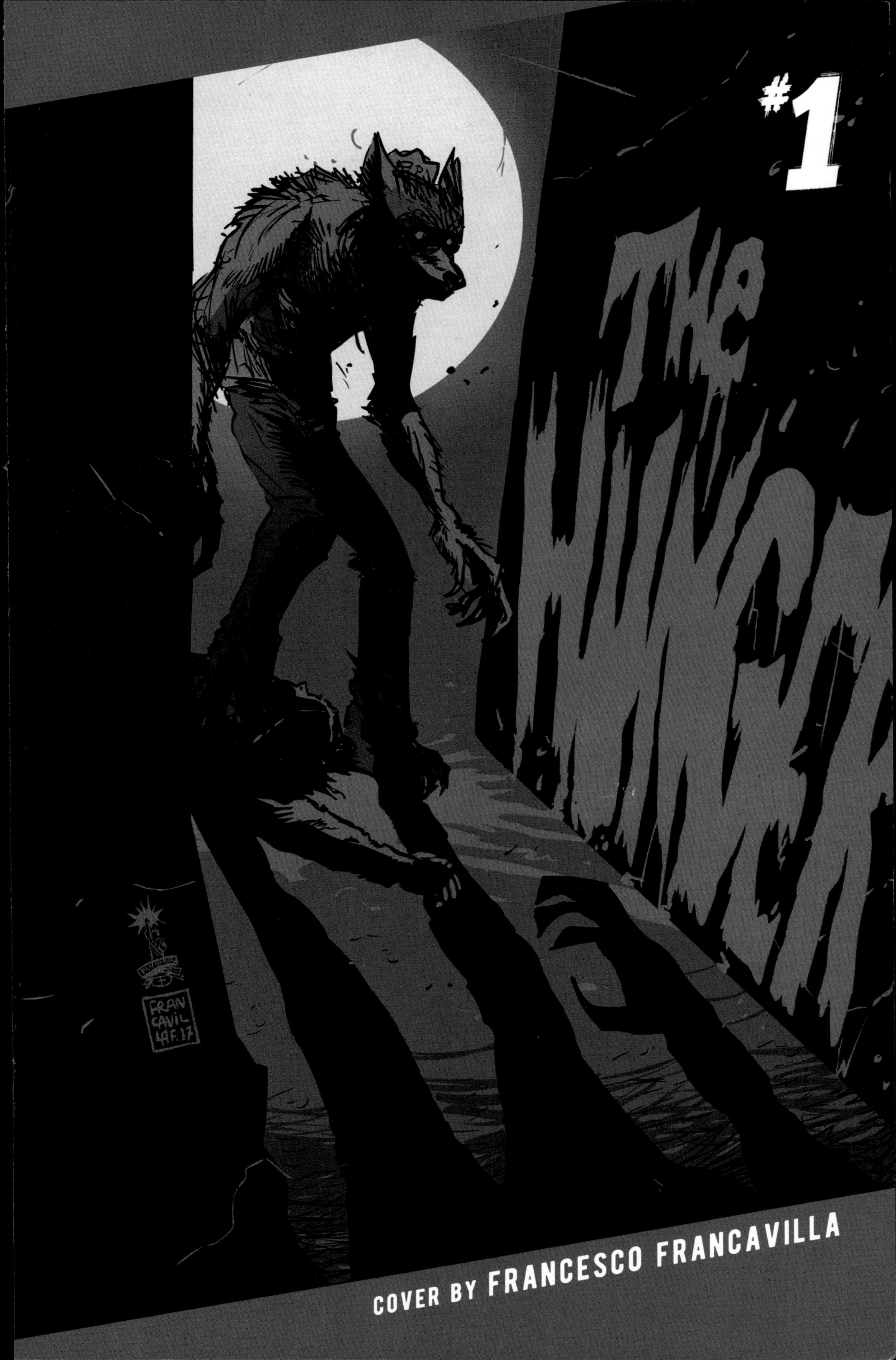
#1
THE

COVER BY FRANCESCO FRANCAVILLA

COVER GALLERY

JUGHEAD: THE HUNGER

1: Michael Walsh

2: Francesco Francavilla

3: Robert Hack

1

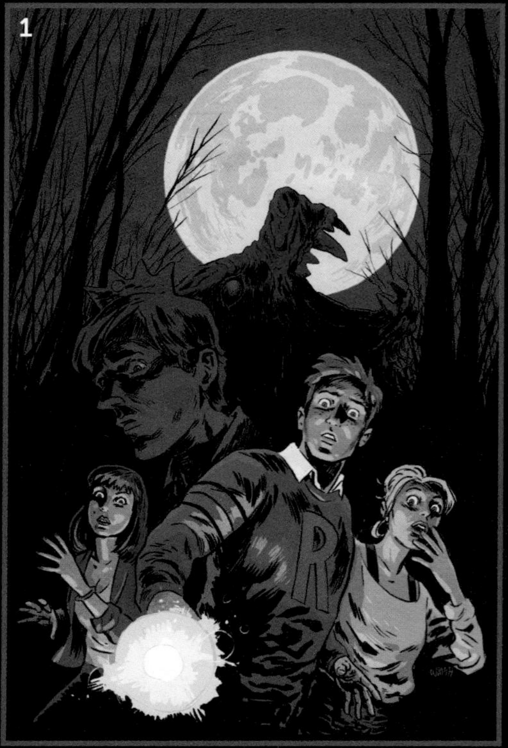

2

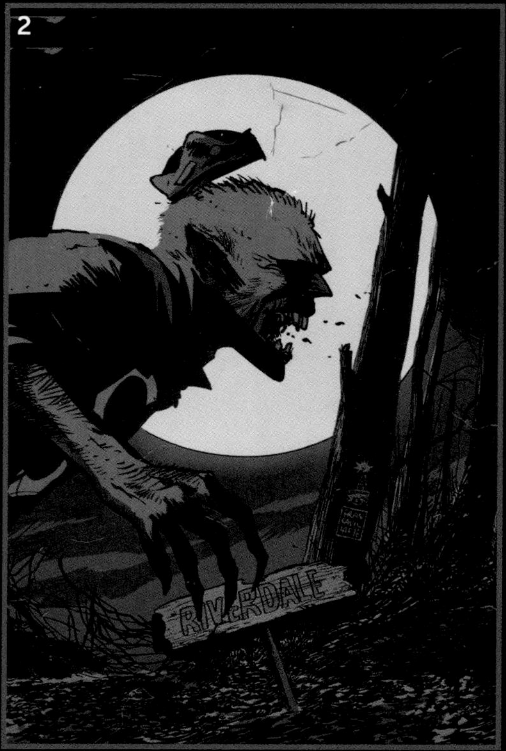

3

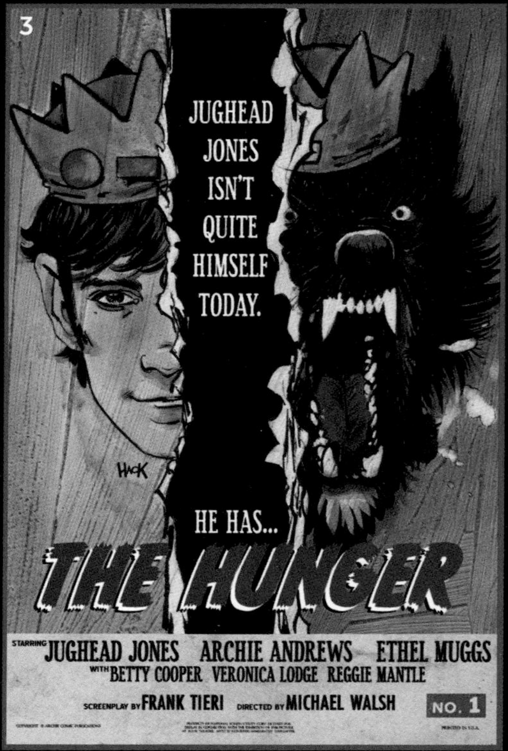
JUGHEAD JONES ISN'T QUITE HIMSELF TODAY.
HACK
HE HAS...
THE HUNGER
STARRING JUGHEAD JONES ARCHIE ANDREWS ETHEL MUGGS
WITH BETTY COOPER VERONICA LODGE REGGIE MANTLE
SCREENPLAY BY FRANK TIERI DIRECTED BY MICHAEL WALSH
NO. 1